God's Hope for Your Home

A Biblical Guide for Building a Godly Family

Lance D. Sparks

Copyright © 2011 by Lance D. Sparks

God's Hope for Your Home
A Biblical Guide for Building a Godly Family
by Lance D. Sparks

Printed in the United States of America

ISBN 9781619044029

All rights reserved solely by the author. The author guarantees all contents are original and do not infringe upon the legal rights of any other person or work. No part of this book may be reproduced in any form without the permission of the author. The views expressed in this book are not necessarily those of the publisher.

Unless otherwise indicated, Bible quotations are taken from The NEW AMERICAN STANDARD BIBLE®. Copyright © 1960, 1962, 1963, 1971, 1972, 1973, 1975, 1977, 1995 by The Lockman Foundation. Used by permission; The New King James Version (NKJV). Copyright © 1979, 1980, 1982 by Thomas Nelson, Inc. Used by permission; The Holy Bible, King James Version (KJV). Copyright © 1972 by Thomas Nelson Inc. Used by permission; and The HOLY BIBLE, NEW INTERNATIONAL VERSION (NIV). Copyright © 1973, 1978, 1984 by International Bible Society. Used by permission of Zondervan.

www.xulonpress.com

To my wife Laurie, who for over twenty-five years has been my faithful companion, best friend, and a godly influence to our children. All through the years she truly has made our house a home that is filled with the Lord, His love and life. I can hardly wait to come home to her each day.

Acknowledgements

I would like to offer a special thanks to:

My Dad and Mom, Ken and Nadine, for modeling to me through the years the biblical mandates set forth in God's Holy Word. Their unwavering commitment to the Truth is second to none and they have passed that legacy down to their children and grandchildren. There truly is "no greater joy than this, to hear of my children walking in the truth" (3 John 4).

Paula Miller, who took audio messages I preached from the pulpit and created a readable format. She was steadfast in her efforts, even while moving to Indonesia in the middle of the project. For that I am grateful.

Peggy Casler, who truly labored night and day to make sure all of our deadlines were kept. She effectively represents servanthood to all of us at Christ Community Church. It was she who got this project off the ground so families would be blessed.

Foreword by
John MacArthur

Let's face it. It is much harder to be consistent in obeying the simplest practical instructions of Scripture than it is to master the Bible's most complex academic doctrines. Explaining the hypostatic union, the nuances of trinitarian theology, and the complexities of supralapsarianism vs. infralapsarism is a fairly easy task compared to the difficulty of faithfully obeying relatively uncomplicated commandments like, "Honor your father and your mother" (Exodus 20:12); "Fathers, do not exasperate your children" (Colossians 3:21); and "Wives, be subject to your own husbands" (Ephesians 5:22).

In other words (to paraphrase something Mark Twain famously said), our biggest struggle is not with the things we *don't* understand in the Bible; the real trouble for us starts when it comes to applying some of the most basic—and clearest—teachings of Scripture.

Nowhere is that more obvious than right at home—in the context of our own families. Any pastor will tell you that the vast majority of pastoral counseling sessions deal with family matters. The overwhelming mass of sin issues that lead to church discipline stem from dysfunction in the family. The most painful, destructive moral failures that Christians fall into are rooted in the failure of family relationships. Nowhere are the pain and devastation of sin's consequences more strongly felt or more catastrophically destructive than in the family.

Remarkably, however, the Bible's instructions for the family are few and uncomplicated. There is no elaborate catalog of parental advice, no programmed approach to parenting, no detailed tutorial for the care and feeding of infants, and no complex child psychology for parents to master. Just a few very simple direct commandments, many assorted life-principles that certainly can be applied in the context of the family, and an invaluable catalogue of wise advice about life from the book of Proverbs—containing wisdom that applies to both parents and children.

We are expected, indeed, we are *commanded* (Deuteronomy 6:6-9), to do the hard work of applying these biblical principles to all areas of life, teaching them to our children, and making Scripture the central focus of everything we think, say, and do. In fact, there is enough in those few verses of Deuteronomy 6 to keep the faithful, conscientious parent occupied fulltime. Keeping the Word of God at the center of the family circle is not something than can be done part time like a hobby, nor is it an easy goal.

Lance Sparks has given families a practical and helpful head start with *God's Hope for Your Home*. I'm grateful for his clear, readable, engaging exposition of so many biblical principles that have direct application to family life. Whether you are a new parent or a seasoned grandparent, I know you will find this book supremely helpful. I'm delighted to see it in print. I hope it will motivate and encourage Christian families for generations to come.

John MacArthur

Contents

Preface		xiii
Chapter 1	External Forces	15
Chapter 2	Internal Pressures	29
Chapter 3	Building a Foundation (Part 1)	39
Chapter 4	Building a Foundation (Part 2)	47
Chapter 5	God's Exam for Engagement	57
Chapter 6	God's Meaning for Marriage	69
Chapter 7	God's Value on Vows	79
Chapter 8	God's Counsel for Couples: Spiritual Maturity	89
Chapter 9	God's Counsel for Couples: Acknowledging God	101
Chapter 10	God's Counsel for Couples: Personal Integrity	111
Chapter 11	God's Counsel for Couples: Meeting Needs	121
Chapter 12	God's Counsel for Couples: Sacrifice	133
Chapter 13	God's Counsel for Couples: Forgiveness	143
Chapter 14	God's Counsel for Couples: Spiritual Warfare	155
Chapter 15	God's Counsel for Couples: Money Matters	167
Chapter 16	God's Counsel for Couples: Communication	179
Chapter 17	God's Counsel for Couples: Dangers of Compromise	189

Chapter 18	God's Hallmarks for Husbands	199
Chapter 19	God's Wisdom for Wives	209
Chapter 20	God's Priority for Parents: Obedience and Discipline (Part 1)	221
Chapter 21	God's Priority for Parents: Obedience and Discipline (Part 2)	233
Chapter 22	God's Priority for Parents: Obedience and Discipline (Part 3)	245
Chapter 23	God's Charge to Children	259
Chapter 24	God's Instructions for In-Laws	269
Chapter 25	God's Fundamentals for Your Family	283

Preface

For many years I had a desire to produce a book that could be used as a guide to help families grow in their relationship with the Lord and with one another. Having been married for twenty-five years to my beautiful bride and having the wonderful privilege of raising eight children, six of whom still live at home, I wanted to share with you some of what the Lord has been teaching me. While this book in no way contains all you need to know about marriage, nor will it answer all your questions about parenting, it does promise to be unlike most other books written on the subject. *God's Hope for Your Home* is significantly more that the typical thematic or family anecdotes that make up the majority of books written on the family. It is specifically geared to help you understand that the only hope for your home is God. He has given us His Word which provides for us all the required information we need to honor His name and to make our home a place that lifts His name on high.

Having watched our families being attacked by the Adversary, controlled by culture, and corrupted by compromise, I believe it is imperative that we begin to implement God's fundamentals for every family and build our foundation on His principles.

I want to invite you to journey with me from the moment you decide to get married, until you become a grandparent and watch your children implement the biblical principles you have passed down to them. It is my prayer that you will remember the words of the Psalmist, "Unless the Lord builds the house, they labor in vain who build it" (Psalm 127:1).

How blessed is everyone who fears the Lord,
Who walks in His ways.
When you shall eat of the fruit of your hands,
You will be happy and it will be well with you.
Your wife shall be like a fruitful vine
Within your house,
Your children like olive plants
Around your table.
Behold, for thus shall the man be blessed
Who fears the Lord. (Psalm 128:1-4)

If this is your prayer, you are about to embark on an incredible journey that will last the rest of your life.

1

External Forces

The modern American family faces many pressures. Often fragile marriages or parent-child relationships are held together by little more than band-aids, paper clips, or rubber bands. Such make-shift repairs only work temporarily: too many tears peel the band-aids away; too much tension bends the clips; too much pressure snaps the bands. The Word of God offers more than temporary fixes for these human struggles. There is hope for everyone's home life no matter how serious the problems or how deep the conflicts may seem. This volume *God's Hope for Your Home* will explore the biblical essentials for maintaining healthy family relationships and living with a godly hope.

In Middle America, our home lives are often similar. We live together in our houses with a spouse, kids, and perhaps some cats or dogs. We have routines too, daily and weekly ones that keep us busy. However, in these relationships and routines, do our attitudes and actions honor the Lord and glorify His name? The average American family faces many conflicts, so the question is, *how can family members solve their relationship problems?* Although God's Word offers no quick fixes, it does offer principles from which we can derive guidance for the difficult dilemmas a family will often face.

Attacked by the Adversary

The first step in resolving family conflict is identifying the problem. We must recognize the adversary—Satan himself. Marriage is God's unique design, but Satan wants to destroy marriage. Our spouse is not our enemy. Nor are our children who rebel against authority. Nor is the dog that wets on the floor. Satan is. He attacks every home, constantly and relentlessly. His assaults aim at the weak links in our lives including emotional, physical, or financial difficulties, because he doesn't want our families to succeed.

A healthy Christian family is the greatest testimony of the work of Jesus Christ in the world. If Christian couples divorce and their family relationships breakdown, if they fail their testimony is silenced. Satan knows that. So he seeks to destroy families. He knows that non-Christians who are looking for hope won't come to us if we Christians don't offer any hope or effective role models; if our families are as dysfunctional as theirs. On the flip side, if we have healthy family relationships where moms and dads work through the difficulties and handle the hardships with dignity and faith, then others will be drawn to that lifestyle and ask, "How do you do that? How does that harmony develop in your house when it's not in mine?" When our families thrive, our success offers more opportunity to explain to others the power of God and His Word.

To understand God's design for families, it's important to start at the beginning. The opening chapters of Genesis describe how God created the first man. Once Adam married Eve, the attack from the adversary came. Genesis 3:1 reads,

> Now the serpent was more crafty than any beast of the field which the Lord God had made. And he said to the woman, "Indeed, has God said, 'You shall not eat from any tree of the garden'?"

Thus, this first question in the Bible expresses doubts about God—did God really say you can't commit that act? Notice Eve's response:

> The woman said to the serpent, "From the fruit of the trees of the garden we may eat; but from the fruit of the tree which is in the middle of the garden, God has said, 'You shall not eat from it or touch it, or you will die.'" (Genesis 3:2-3)

In Eve's response, she modifies the message. While the Bible states clearly that God has given us freely all things to enjoy (Romans 8:32), Eve left that detail out. Then Eve added a bit: "God has said, 'You shall not eat from it or touch it'" (Genesis 3:3).

Yet Eve could touch it; she just couldn't eat from it. Like Eve, if we don't understand God's message, then Satan will tempt and deceive us. The Bible warns readers not to add or take away from God's truthful Word. Eve didn't understand God's instructions clearly.

Similarly, Satan attacks us just as he did Adam and Eve. Satan came to Eve disguised in the form of a serpent—very crafty, very deceptive. He didn't look like a devil or reveal his true ugliness. The Apostle Paul says, "No wonder, for even Satan disguises himself as an angel of light. Therefore it is not surprising if his servants also disguise themselves as servants of righteousness, whose end will be according to their deeds" (2 Corinthians 11:14-15).

Paul points out that there are many people who disguise themselves as servants of righteousness. They may offer advice or counsel that sounds good to someone in crisis. However, all suggestions must be evaluated by asking, "What does the Bible actually say?" In Matthew's description of Christ's temptation, Jesus countered each of Satan's arguments with scriptural answers (see Matthew 4).

So in Eden, Satan capitalizes on Eve's confusion and deceives her: "The serpent said to the woman, 'You surely will not die!'" (Genesis 3:4). He's essentially saying, *"Eve, come on, do you really think you'll die? God won't kill you for eating a bit of fruit."*

In a parallel way, Satan tempts us. He convinces us that we will not suffer any ill consequences for our deeds. When facing conflicts with our husbands or wives, we often look for an easy escape. Many are tempted by the illusion of the "greener grass" of another relationship.

Marriage failures first begin with ideas: a wife might tell herself, *"I could leave my husband to find a man who'll treat me better."*

Or a man might think, *"I'd like to get to know that attractive woman at work. She's a lot more exciting than my wife."*

Satan cleverly encourages deception. Individuals rationalize bad behaviors and attitudes, and then deceive themselves. *"After all,"* a husband says, *"what's the harm in a few little secrets?"* That's how Satan pursues Eve when he says, "'For God knows that in the day you eat from it your eyes will be opened, and you will be like God, knowing good and evil'" (Genesis 3:5). He promises the woman godlike power which appeals to her pride. Every one wants to be a deity with authority and autonomy. Consequently, Eve believed what Satan said and not what God said—that if you eat of the tree of the knowledge of good and evil, that day you will die (see Genesis 2:17). God always explains the cost of sin. We must understand the penalties for disobedience so that consequences don't take us by surprise.

Satan's other strategy is to convince us that our misbehavior isn't so bad. We excuse irresponsible behavior and then find ourselves in a tremendously difficult predicament. That's when we realize that Satan lied! Adam and Eve fell for the deception and disobeyed God by rebelling against His commands. Genesis 3:16 records the cost of their sin: "To the woman He said, 'I will greatly multiply your pain in childbirth, in pain you shall bring forth children; Yet your desire will be for your husband....'" This phrase doesn't mean a woman will love and desire her husband; it means she will want to control him. The Hebrew word used in the passage as "desire" appears one other time in the *Pentateuch*, where God tells Cain, "'[S]in is crouching at the door; and its desire is for you, but you must master it'" (Genesis 4:7). So the woman seeks control over her husband. Conversely, the man shall "rule over you" (Genesis 3:16b). The word "rule" *mashal*, meaning with great authority. Thus the battle of the sexes is introduced in Genesis 3. The woman exerts her power. The man says, "No way" and wields his *mashal*, his great authority. Conflict ensues. Satan's hope is to divide couples and to demolish the marriage and the family.

As we learn these truths, Satan increases his attacks to distract us from repenting and growing. Resisting his evil requires strength. In Ephesians, Paul offers guidelines and exhortation for families including husbands, wives, children, and parents:

> Finally, be strong in the Lord and in the strength of His might. Put on the full armor of God, so that you will be able to stand firm against the schemes of the devil. For our struggle is not against flesh and blood, but against the rulers, against the powers, against the world forces of this darkness, against the spiritual forces of wickedness in the heavenly places. Therefore, take up the full armor of God, so that you will be able to resist in the evil day, and having done everything, to stand firm. (Ephesians 6:10-13)

Prayer must form the fabric interweaving our armor to prepare us for spiritual battle. Our ultimate conflict is not with family members but with Satan. When a couple marries, they say, "We will live on love; love conquers all." However, after six months some couples discover love conquers very little. For Christian and non-Christian couples, the pressures of life bring unresolved conflicts. Soon resentment and frustration overcome those romantic feelings. Recognizing evil forces at work is the first step to protecting family relationships. The next step is following God's plan for families.

Manipulated by the Media

The second pressure working against successful family relationships comes from the media's distorted perspectives. Music, television programs, and films often portray destructive behaviors and lifestyles. In Ephesians 5:11-12, the Apostle Paul reminds us, "Do not participate in the unfruitful deeds of darkness, but instead even expose them; for it is disgraceful even to speak of the things which are done by them in secret." Those "unfruitful deeds of darkness" like sexual promiscuity, pornography, or substance abuse, are regularly discussed and at times extolled in music, movies, and television. From exploitive talk shows and reality shows to R-rated movies and MTV, those secret deeds are rendered openly.

Even well-meaning Christians can be manipulated by deceptive media portrayals. For example, in a thirty-minute sitcom the character's problems are easily resolved. Further, in that two-hour movie, a global disaster of epic proportions can be averted through technology and a quick-thinking hero. Every problem has a solution; it all comes out okay. We can be conditioned to think there are quick fixes for our real life marriage problems, too.

Perhaps if we *dot the i's and cross the t's* correctly, then we'll find happiness. Unfortunately real life is not so simple. A marriage is a work in progress. Couples must willingly work at their relationships day after day. A family is like a building project that requires a strong foundation. If we builders take shortcuts, the home will crumble.

For families in crisis, God does provide help. Often, though, serious problems cannot be solved overnight. In the program *Leave It to Beaver* (1957-1963), June and Ward Cleaver faithfully resolved their conflicts by the show's end. No matter how great the conflict between Beaver and his brother Wally, the family found a solution before the last commercial break. Even in the 1990s show *Home Improvement*, where the bungling tool-man Tim accidentally blew up objects every episode, he always escaped serious injury. Finding solutions to real conflicts, however, requires commitment to God and to each other. God says, "I want you to trust Me; I want you to believe in Me." Spiritual commitment strengthens the commitment between a husband and wife. Be willing to believe God's promises.

From 2000-2002, MTV featured a program called *Jack Ass,* a prank show popular among American teens. Each episode featured a stunt man who performed outrageous antics, everything from sitting in a portable bathroom as it tipped over to wearing a fire-resistant suit hung with steaks while lying prone on a barbecue pit. Young viewers were so taken with the program that they often tried the stunts themselves. Junior high age boys suffered severe burns or other injuries trying to imitate antics from the shows. Despite the copy-cat injuries and the baseness of the entertainment, MTV spokeswoman Jeannie Kedas defended the network: "It's 'incredibly upsetting' when young people hurt themselves but MTV is not responsible."[1]

Mounting controversy about viewer injuries prompted MTV to cancel the television series after two seasons. However, studios have released three *Jack Ass* feature films over the last ten years. Media spokespersons regularly assert that television shows and films only reflect cultural values and do not influence them. However, the *Jack Ass* series illustrated that television can affect young minds. It's no wonder the name of the show is *Jack Ass*. It inspired ridiculous and dangerous behaviors. Yet teenagers are not the only ones under the power of programming.

Hours of television viewing shape everyone's thinking. What if we spent an hour reading the Bible for every hour spent watching TV? The result might be surprising. Four hours a night doing anything will change lives. Four hours spent reading God's Word could bring soul transformation.

Controlled by Culture

The third pressure on families comes from social influence. Culture often determines standards of behavior. As society changes Christians change, too. Yet Jesus Christ never changes. His character is from everlasting to everlasting. In 1 John, the writer explains culture's power and our responsibility to resist it:

> Do not love the world nor the things that are in the world. If anyone loves the world, the love of the Father is not in him. For all that is in the world, the lust of the flesh and the lust of the eyes and the boastful pride of life, is not from the Father, but is from the world. The world is passing away, and also its lusts; but the one who does the will of God abides forever. (1 John 2:15-17)

Declining social standards have corrupted our family values. The 2000 Census statistics revealed that only 23.5 percent of U.S. households represented traditional families—married couples with their children:[2] "Between 1990 and 2000, the number of cohabitating couples increased by 72 percent. They now make up 5.5 percent of the total population."[3] In the same period, single father households increased 62 percent, and single mother homes grew by 25 percent."[4] Further 2010 Census statistics reveal that over 50 percent of single respondents live with partners in unmarried relationships and only 45 percent of US teenagers live in traditional family situations.[5]

Culture influences our views about marriage, too. Couples often live together before the wedding thinking they will learn about one another first, and then decide whether marriage is for them. The number of couples cohabiting has increased dramatically over the last two decades: "By age 30, three-quarters of women in the U.S. have been married and about half have cohabited outside of marriage," according to a 2002 report by the Centers for Disease Control and Prevention.[6] However statistics also show that couples who do live together before marriage are more likely to divorce.[7] Cohabitation is contrary to God's design. On television and in movies, cohabitation and premarital sex are portrayed as acceptable social behaviors. In contrast, the Bible is very clear about sexual standards: "For this is the will of God, your sanctification; that is, that you abstain from sexual immorality" (1 Thessalonians 4:3). God's plan is for single individuals to remain sexually pure until they marry.

Social views regarding other types of relationships have changed as well. Acceptance of gay marriage is increasing, especially among young people. Media presentations featuring homosexual couples have increased dramatically in the last two decades. Putting these types of relationships in the public eye is a way of convincing the public that such behaviors are okay because individuals should be free to live out their desires as they choose. Yet God's Word asserts that marriage is reserved for men and women to live as husband and wife.

Another major stress in modern relationships is the increase in blended families. Barbara Kantrowitz in her *Newsweek* article "Step by Step" said,

> The original plot goes something like this…first comes love, then comes marriage, then comes Mary with the baby carriage. But now there is a sequel.

> John and Mary break up; John moves in with Sally and her two boys. Mary takes the baby Paul. A year later, Mary meets Jack who is divorced with three children. They get married. Paul, barely two years old, now has a mother, a father, a stepmother, a stepfather, five stepbrothers and stepsisters as well as four sets of grandparents, biological and step. And countless aunts and uncles. And guess what? Mary's pregnant again.[8]

Furthermore, dual-income families have become a major part of our culture. In the show *Father Knows Best* (1954-1960), the mother stayed home to care for her three lovely children, Bud, Kitty, and Princess. Today, close to two-thirds of all women work outside the home in the American workforce. As a result great numbers of children spend time in daycare. In fact, the number of daycare centers has increased dramatically in recent years to accommodate working mothers' needs. For mothers of preschoolers, fifty-nine percent have outside jobs.[9]

Such social change reflects the influence of our evolving cultural values. As a society, many individuals have decided to postpone having children for ten or fifteen years, so they can pursue careers and financial independence. Some remain single or childless to obtain various material benefits: acquire a high performance car, take nice vacations, or buy a second home. Children can be viewed as burdens. However, the Bible says children should be seen as gifts and rewards from God (Psalm 127:3).

In order to be happy, our culture says that we need two nice cars, plus a big house in an upscale neighborhood. It never hurts to wear designer clothes either. That way we appear successful in every area. These materialistic values control human desires. The Adversary uses advertising, along with our own greed and pride, to drive our decisions about lifestyles.

It is not necessarily wrong for a wife and mother to work outside her home. That decision rests with each individual family. Ultimately, the Lord must guide each couple's choices. The problem comes when a husband or wife neglects the family in order to maintain a certain standard of living. It's never God's will for Christians to disregard their family members just to pursue a career goal.

Crushed by Conflict

The fourth way the enemy attacks families is through conflict, specifically unresolved conflict. Such clashes are described in Proverbs 18:19: "A brother offended is harder to be won than a strong city, and contentions are like the bars of a citadel." Arguments build barriers if quarrels go unsettled. Living in a state of unresolved conflict is like being imprisoned. Pride also plays a role: "Through insolence [pride] comes nothing but strife" (Proverbs 13:10).

The roots of such strife can be traced to Genesis 3 where the husband says, "My wife can't control me; I am the authority figure of the home." Then the wife says, "No, I have to control you, so you won't control me." Rods of contention arise because of our selfishness and pride: "There are six things which the Lord hates, Yes, seven which are an abomination to Him: Haughty eyes, a lying tongue, and hands that shed innocent blood, . . ." (Proverbs 6:16-17). The very first one is "haughty eyes," or a prideful look.

Often marriage relationships suffer because of arrogance. Each one selfishly seeks his own way: "Hatred stirs up strife, But love covers all transgressions" (Proverbs 10:12). It's a contrast between hatred and love. When arguments intensify, the husband or wife is expressing hatred rather than love. Proverbs 15:17 reminds us, "Better is a dish of vegetables where love is than a fattened ox served with hatred." The more anger an individual expresses, the greater the chance that an argument will be destructive. When an argument escalates, "A fool's lips bring strife, and his mouth calls for blows" (Proverbs 18:6). Pride, arrogance, hatred, and unresolved contention can eventually lead to verbal and physical abuse against a spouse or a child.

However, there's an antidote: "The beginning of strife is like letting out water, so abandon the quarrel before it breaks out" (Proverbs 17:14). This proverb presents a basic principle for conflict resolution. Before the disagreement escalates into an uncontrollable flood of emotions, "abandon the quarrel." Don't nurse strong negative emotions. Proverbs 20:3 says, "Keeping away from strife is an honor for a man, but any fool will quarrel." It's honorable to end a disagreement. Walking away from the fight is winning. When a husband knows he's right but chooses to walk away from the argument, he achieves the greater victory. It's not necessary to prove a point.

Divided by Divorce

Many homes are divided by divorce. Almost one out of every four adults in the nation has experienced at least one divorce. Among those adults who divorce and remarry, the probability of a second divorce is higher. Some studies show that more than 60 percent of all divorced adults who remarry will divorce again. Hollywood and Madison Avenue have defended and celebrated divorce. When a celebrity couple divorces, articles often report how amicably the couple separated. Romantic comedies portray breakups as merely temporary setbacks. Recently divorced celebrities visit talk shows to discuss the benefits of their newly found independence. Audiences applaud the stars' intentions to finally focus only on themselves. Unfortunately, the average young woman who is victimized by divorce is not able to celebrate by taking a European vacation or buying a new wardrobe. She will not only face emotional pain but financial setbacks as well.

The glossy media portrayals of divorce must not influence our thinking. The anguish and destruction of broken relationships cannot be dismissed as irrelevant. Jesus openly discussed the divorce issue with the Pharisees. They asked, "Is it lawful for a man to divorce his wife for any reason at all?" Jesus stressed that in the marriage bond, "the two shall become one flesh." Then he told them, "What therefore God has joined together, let no man separate" (Matthew 19:3, 5-6). Unwilling to let the matter rest, the Pharisees countered:

> Why then did Moses command to give her a certificate of divorce and send her away? He [Jesus] said to them, "Because of your hardness of heart Moses permitted you to divorce your wives; but from the beginning it has not been this way." (Matthew 19:7-8)

It's important to notice God's provision for divorce—the hardness of the human heart. The reason for divorce in the community of Israel was because people had become cold to God's ways. When we let selfish motives determine our behavior, it comes down to what is "best for me." However, marriage is not built on having our own needs met. Marriage is built on a commitment, on vows spoken before God.

A heart that's unwilling to submit to what God's Word says is a heart that is becoming unfeeling and unresponsive: "How blessed is the man who fears always, but he who hardens his heart will fall into calamity" (Proverbs 28:14). Furthermore, Solomon says, "A man who hardens his neck after much reproof will suddenly be broken beyond remedy" (Proverbs 29:1). Beyond remedy—those are strong words. God tells us not to harden our hearts against His commands. In Hebrews 3:12-13, the Lord gives a similar warning: "Take care, brethren, that there not be in any one of you an evil, unbelieving heart that falls away from the living God. But encourage one another day after day, as long as it is *still* called "Today," so that none of you will be hardened by the deceitfulness of sin."

Our hearts become hardened because Satan convinces us that the sin we're going to commit is okay. Therefore, our hearts turn from righteousness. Our actions and attitudes communicate that we don't believe God. One of the signs of a hardened heart is a lack of forgiveness and compassion.

Christ rebuked the Pharisees in Mark 3 because they showed no compassion toward a man with a withered hand. When Christ healed him on the Sabbath, He pointed out their lack of compassion. Further, in Mark 16:14, Christ spoke to His disciples about their hard hearts because they refused to believe in His resurrection: "Afterward He appeared to the eleven themselves as they were reclining at the table; and He reproached them for their unbelief and hardness of heart, because they had not believed those who had seen Him after He had risen." When God says something and we don't respond, our consciences grow unfeeling and indifferent. For many couples, divorce occurs because they are serving themselves rather than God.

On the other hand, there are biblical grounds for divorce in Scripture. Sometimes a spouse is abandoned or betrayed. Against their desire and will, divorce finds them. Individuals who have suffered a divorce should never be labeled or stereotyped, ignored or ostracized.

The good news is that the Bible has great power: "'Is not My word like fire?' declares the Lord, 'and like a hammer which shatters a rock?'" (Jeremiah 23:29). The fire and force of God's Word can break down and renew the hardest heart. It can change us!

In the next three chapters, we'll explore more scriptural truths that can help Christians nurture strong relationships that will ultimately honor God.

Lord, as we contemplate the power of Scripture, help us to exhort each other in the Word; know the Word; have a receptive heart toward the Word; avoid an evil heart of unbelief; and listen to what You say. Amen.

2

Internal Pressures

Some of the greatest pressures on the American family come from external forces: the influence of Satan's attacks, the social pressures of media and culture, and the consequences of unresolved conflict. In addition, each individual is hindered by his own human pride and arrogance: "When pride comes, then comes disgrace, but with humility comes wisdom. The integrity of the upright guides them, but the unfaithful are destroyed by their duplicity" (Proverbs 11:2-3 NIV).

Pride and arrogance can lead to rebellion. Matthew 19 warns Christians about the hardness of the human heart. Men and women can become calloused to God's way of living. The writer of Hebrews warns about the deceitfulness of sin. Somehow, we think we can become better through our own efforts. We say, "I'm going to take control of my life. I'll solve these problems my own way." Instead of submitting to God's plan and design, we rebel against it. Every time we say "no" to God, our hearts become unreceptive to God's influence. If we continue in such rebellion, we will reap unhappy consequences.

To adequately confront these human tendencies, it's important to identify some internal factors that threaten family relationships: unrealistic demands, lack of forgiveness, abandonment, sinful compromise, and the desire for revenge. To deal with these pressures, it's vital to understand how developing a commitment to God's wisdom can provide solutions.

Devastated by Demands

First, our family relationships are being devastated by unrealistic demands. For example, husbands may demand that their wives act and look a certain way—thin, seductive, or fashionable perhaps. The wives, in return, expect their husbands to meet certain expectations, to workout, make big money, or give up golf. Often couples fail to accept one another for who they are. As a result, each makes suggestions, then requests, then pleas in the hope that the spouse will change. In a counseling session, a wife once said, "You know, my husband wants me to look a certain way, but I just can't compete with the *Playboy* images he stares at constantly. I'll never look like that." On the other hand, wives may think, *"Oh, why can't my mate act like that nice man at work or look like that handsome film star?"*

The problem is that our efforts to perfect our spouses will never succeed. If a wife or husband changes the way we desire (perhaps they lose weight or give up NFL football), we still may not love them fully. We will always find something about them that we don't like because we can never have the perfect mate. This dilemma has existed from the beginning of time. In Genesis, we learn that Adam found the ideal woman. She was created sinless, but her innocence did not last long because neither Adam nor Eve could be satisfied. In a similar way because we all have sinned, we'll never be perfect.

Media influence also affects our way of thinking. When an advertiser wants to sell a car, the company uses a beautiful woman as the spokesperson. The truth is, sex appeal sells. In addition, perfect images are a mainstay even for television news. There are no ugly newscasters. Instead they all have perfect hair, nice white smiles, and designer clothes. Three-hundred-pound reporters are never featured on television news for a reason. Such an image does not meet the "perfect" standard.

Often, therefore, these images unconsciously shape our perceptions and desires. A husband thinks that life would be better if his wife could only be more attractive or more generous. Instead of praying for her and bringing her various needs before the Lord, husbands criticize and find fault. However, Proverbs 5:18 reminds a man to rejoice in the wife of his youth. So a husband should rejoice with the wife God gave him and be excited about only her. In 1 Peter 3:7, there is a similar principle: "You husbands in the same way, live with your wives in an understanding way."

A husband must come to understand his wife's personality and character and honor her as his most prized partner. If husbands obeyed only this scriptural command, their married lives would be better overnight. Peter says a man's prayers can be hindered if he fails to obey God's commands. A man must honor his wife, in obedience, so that his prayers are not hindered (see 1 Peter 3:8). In essence God is saying, "Follow my instructions; then we can talk."

When our relationships are devastated by unrealistic demands, what should we do? We should pray rather than insist that our husbands do this or our wives do that. The reason we demand is that we believe that *we* can orchestrate change in our mates. But only God can change them. God can shatter a hard heart, tear down prideful spirit, and revolutionize a spouse's way of thinking. Keep on praying like the widow in Luke 18, who appealed continually to a judge for legal protection. From this parable, Christ said that men ought always to pray and not to faint (Luke 18:1-8). If we persist in praying, we won't lose heart. Like that determined widow, we must faithfully, persistently pray, asking God to make an unjust situation just. For the Lord says, "I tell you that He will bring about justice for them quickly. However, when the Son of Man comes, will He find faith on the earth?" (Luke 18:8).

We need to be the kind of people, the kind of husbands or wives who say, "I believe in God. I believe in His Word. I'm committing my life to Him and asking, 'Lord, you change my husband. Or you change my wife. Or you change my children. Lord, you work in their hearts. You do it.'"

Failure to Forgive

Second, our home relationships are being damaged by attitudes of unforgiveness, bitterness, jealousy, and rivalry. Yet the Bible says, "Let all bitterness and wrath and anger and clamor and slander be put away from you, along with all malice. Be kind to one another, tender-hearted, forgiving each other, just as God in Christ also has forgiven you" (Ephesians 4:31-32). In this passage, we're encouraged to put bitterness away and adopt an attitude of kindness and forgiveness.

Sadly, some couples never master the art of forgiveness. Instead, bitterness runs so deeply that no pardon is ever extended to the erring spouse. The biblical antidote for such bitterness is found in Colossians 3:12-14:

> So, as those who have been chosen of God, holy and beloved, put on a heart of compassion, kindness, humility, gentleness and patience; bearing with one another, and forgiving each other, whoever has a complaint against anyone; just as the Lord forgave you, so also should you. Beyond all these things, put on love, which is the perfect bond of unity.

God wants us to put on the golden chain of all the virtues. Christ is our example. People who possess an unforgiving spirit have not clearly understood the forgiveness of Christ in their lives and have not grasped the significance of Calvary. If God has forgiven us of our sins, the least we can do is to forgive our spouses, no matter what the sin. With all the adultery, with all the affairs, with all the cheating, with all the lying that takes place in marriage relationships, there needs to be a lot of forgiveness or nothing is going to change for those hurting couples. For the Lord's sake, we must consider these principles: "He who covers a transgression seeks love, but he who repeats a matter separates intimate friends" (Proverbs 17:9).

Love covers all transgressions. The bottom line is that we need to have love that covers a multitude of transgressions. We must willingly give ourselves sacrificially to our spouses, despite all their sins, imperfections and failures. Christ gave Himself to us by demonstrating His love toward us, even while we were at our worst, not at our best. We could never clean our act up enough to be our best or to be good enough for Him. So He came to us when we were still vile sinners.

Proverbs 19:11 says, "A man's discretion makes him slow to anger, and it is his glory to overlook a transgression." The problem is that we don't want to overlook a transgression; instead, we want to keep a record of it. Then we can bring that issue up next time a similar failure happens. I do that with my wife sometimes. (God forgive me.) I bring up her mistakes and doing so just tears my wife apart emotionally. Perhaps that's sometimes why I do it. I want the upper hand. Then God takes a spiritual knife and jabs it into me, and says, "You idiot. What are doing? That's not honoring your wife. That's not loving your wife." Beware the urge to gain the upper hand at the expense of your precious partner.

To confront the bad attitudes in our homes, we must consider Proverbs 20:9, "Who can say, 'I have cleansed my heart, I am pure from my sin?'" The answer is that nobody can. We're often so arrogant, boastful, and prideful that we think we're better than our spouses. A wife can think she has her act together, but her poor husband doesn't. The results of that thinking are a bitter attitude and unforgiving spirit. However, God says, "Wait a minute. Who are you to do withhold forgiveness? If I have forgiven your sin, the least you can do is forgive this one's sin."

Arrogance can destroy a marriage, especially when a husband or wife maintains that he or she is never wrong. Everybody likes to be right. Yet to help our marriages, we must admit our mistakes, acknowledge the fact that we have sinned, and humbly seek forgiveness from the one we've offended. When we do, then we will see how God breaks down the barriers erected from our anger, bitterness, and jealousy. Watch how God can bring healing when we forgive.

Abandoned by Actions

Third, our homes have been injured by acts of abandonment. That is, we are no longer trustworthy. The actions of untrustworthiness weaken the stability of our families. Many people have been physically abandoned because their spouses have deserted them. In other cases, the couple still lives together, but one has emotionally or mentally forsaken the other. A wife may put her affection, attention, and devotion someplace else; toward her children, friends, or her career. Then the two coexist within the walls of their house, but there's no marriage relationship to speak of.

Such abandonment is devastating. Some people actually physically abandon their mates and children by having extra-marital affairs. Yet we have more books on marriage, more seminars on marriage, and more preachers preaching on marriage than ever before. The situations get worse and worse because nobody's listening to sound advice. If they are listening, they're not doing anything about the problem. Satan can put blinders over our eyes so that we fail to see the truth:

> Drink water from your own cistern
> And fresh water from your own well.
> Should your springs be dispersed abroad,
> Streams of water in the streets?
> Let them be yours alone
> And not for strangers with you.
> Let your fountain be blessed,
> And rejoice in the wife of your youth.
> As the loving hind and graceful doe,
> Let her breasts satisfy you at all times;
> Be exhilarated always with her love.
> For why should you, my son, be exhilarated with an adulteress
> And embrace the bosom of a foreigner?
> For the ways of a man are before the eyes of the Lord,
> And He watches all his paths.
> His own iniquities will capture the wicked,
> And he will be held with the cords of his sin.
> He will die for lack of instruction,
> And in the greatness of his folly he will go astray.
> (Proverbs 5:15-23)

This passage warns that it is dangerous to leave one's family to pursue the adulteress or the adulterer. Seeking such pleasure destroys those whom we should love and protect. Solomon asks, "Who can find a trustworthy man?" (Proverbs 20:6b). We must commit to being trustworthy men and women who won't abandon our families, but instead remain true to the end. Such commitment bears a rich reward.

Corrupted by Compromise

Fourth, our homes are corrupted by compromise. So subtly—so easily—we disregard moral standards. John warns, "Little children, guard yourselves from idols" (1 John 5:21), and Paul reminds us to "flee from idolatry" (see 1 Corinthians 10:14). For us, idolatry is not bowing down before a foreign object in worship as though it were a god. We insist that we would never commit such an act. Yet if we covet our neighbor's wife, house, or other possession, we are idolaters. The Bible says, "For this you know with certainty, that no immoral or impure person or covetous man, who is an idolater, has an inheritance in the kingdom of Christ and God" (Ephesians 5:5).

Our affections are being swayed from the one true God of the universe and toward that pleasure which will satisfy our lusts. Paul states, "Whose god is their belly" or "Whose god is their appetite," which literally means *whose god is their lust* (Philippians 3:19). Idolatry causes us to set our affections elsewhere, on cheap imitations that can never truly satisfy.

Compromise tempts Christians to weaken their stand on the moral virtues of Scripture. We must beware of such a compromising spirit, of wanting more education or knowledge. The man Lot, in the Genesis account, looked longingly at the city of Sodom. Because he loved the Sodom lifestyle, he lost everything. As he heard the noise of the parties, the clank of the chariot parades, he wondered if Sodom society would be exciting and joyful. Unfortunately, the people of Sodom proved to be wicked, and the longer Lot stayed, the more he compromised. Eventually, he accepted a prominent place at the City gate; by then he was firmly entrenched in the society. Lot thought, *"This situation seems great. Not only am I living here, I'm leading. The people know and respect me."* However, God passed judgment on the city for its wickedness. One day, God's angel had to grab Lot by the hand to lead him and his wife and his children out of the city limits (see Genesis 18-19). His compromise cost him a great deal. He lost his home and his family. We must not follow his example.

Lot was not the only one. Genesis includes many instances when God's people made compromises that had disastrous consequences. The list is extensive:

- Abraham lies about his wife's identity (Genesis 12).
- Abraham compromises his purity by having sex with Hagar (Genesis 16).
- Abraham lies about his wife again (Genesis 20).
- Jacob deceives his father to gain Esau's inheritance (Genesis 27).
- Laban deceives Jacob by offering Leah, not Rachel, as a bride (Genesis 29).
- Rachel uses trickery to steal her father's property (Genesis 31).

To avoid the injuries of evil compromises, we must stand on the truth. Live as Daniel lived, never compromising. Live as Joseph lived, fleeing evil. Knowing that God is with us, we must follow positive examples.

Ravaged by Revenge

Last, our relationships can be wrecked by revenge. Solomon warns, "Do not say, 'I will repay evil'; Wait for the Lord, and He will save you" (Proverbs 20:22). We seek to injure the one who offended us. We think to ourselves, *"Never again will my wife embarrass me in public."* So we husbands look for ways to squelch our mates. Or perhaps we think, *"I'm going to make sure I keep him in line, so I will hold his past failures over his head for as long as he lives."*

What did Christ say about such attitudes? He reminds us, "'Vengeance is Mine, I will repay,' says the Lord" (Romans 12:19b). Repay evil with good (see Romans 12:21). In obedience to God, we must look for ways to forgive, love, and serve those who abuse us. That's what Jesus did. He gave His life away for those who hated Him in order that He might redeem them.

Many spousal relationships suffer from desires for revenge. Whenever we put our rights first, righteousness always suffers. Yet God provides a better way:

> Therefore if there is any encouragement in Christ, if there is any consolation of love, if there is any fellowship of the Spirit, if any affection and compassion, make my joy complete by being of the same mind, maintaining the same love, united in spirit, intent on one purpose. Do nothing from selfishness or empty conceit, but with humility of mind regard one another as more important than yourselves. (Philippians 2:1-3)

Those godly actions will revolutionize our damaged relationships. We must regard one another as more important than ourselves. What instruction!

Is there hope? Definitely! There's lots of hope. God gives five basic ingredients for building strong families: Fear the Christ. Our homes don't need reformation; they need redemption. We don't need to be reformed; we need to be redeemed. It begins with knowing Jesus Christ as Lord and Savior. "Fear God, and give Him glory... worship Him," said the angel in Revelation 14:7. That's the eternal gospel: "But there is forgiveness with You, that You may be feared" (Psalm 130:4).

Listen, the unbelieving world doesn't care what God says. The non-Christians have no "fear of God before their eyes" (Romans 3:18). But for the believer, the fear of God is instilled in his life, so he understands that if he sins against Almighty God, then there is a consequence. God says that whatever a man sows that shall he also reap (see Galatians 6:7). Knowledge comes from Jesus Christ Himself, who orchestrated and designed the family unit: "The fear of the Lord is the beginning of knowledge" (Proverbs 1:7). He will give knowledge, which is the root to all spiritual understanding:

> Who is the man who fears the Lord?
> He will instruct him in the way he should choose.
> His soul will abide in prosperity,
> And his descendants will inherit the land.
> The secret of the Lord is for those who fear Him,

And He will make them know His covenant. (Psalm 25:12-14)

The very depth of God, the knowledge of God, the intimate parts of God are made known to those who fear Him.

Lord, help us to fear You and revere You as the Christ. Please show us what we need to do. Explain to us very clearly what needs to happen to improve in our family relationships. Amen.

3

Building a Foundation
(Part 1)

Our hope is in the Lord. Often the Psalmist reminds his audience that through God's Word, we receive hope. This hope is sure because God's Word is true: "How blessed is he whose help is the God of Jacob, whose hope is in the Lord his God" (Psalm 146:5). This truth is reinforced in the New Testament as well when Paul writes, "For whatever was written in earlier times was written for our instruction, so that through perseverance and the encouragement of the Scriptures we might have hope" (Romans 15:4).

What is this hope for our home life and family relationships? The Psalmist says that unless the Lord builds the house, they labor in vain who build it (Psalm 127:1). Unless the Lord is building His precepts into our homes and our lives, everything we do will be empty, futile, and worthless because the construction effort will be through mere human power and not done through the energy of the Holy Spirit. God wants to build our homes; we must allow Him to do the work. Strong buildings need firm foundations, and the Bible provides the principles necessary for fostering healthy, loving family interaction.

First of all, we need to understand five foundational elements—those basic principles that will make our homes what God wants them to be. If we implement these principles in obedience, God will do a marvelous work in teaching us how to live with love and grace. The Bible says the Lord declares, "Those who honor me, I will honor" (1 Samuel 2:30 NIV).

Foundation One: Fear the Christ

The first principle is that we must understand what it means to fear the Lord. Psalm 112:1 declares, "Blessed is the man who fears the Lord" (NIV). Further, Proverbs 23:17 reminds us to "live in the fear of the Lord always." The concept is echoed throughout Scripture. The point is that we don't need reformation but transformation. That is the essence of the gospel: Fear God, give Him glory and worship Him (see Revelation 14:7). Thus, a family begins the upward journey of Christ-likeness when its members learn to revere God, for the man who fears God finds blessing and righteousness. Submission to God's commands is vital for our spiritual survival. To fear the Christ means surrendering to the Lord: "You who fear the Lord, trust in the Lord" (Psalm 115:11). God calls us to be holy: "Be ye holy as I am holy" (1 Peter 1:16 KJV). The first step to such holiness is submitting to the Lord's direction.

Foundation Two: Follow God's Commands

The second principle is that we must follow His commands. To be wise is to understand the Lord's will for us. King Saul is a prime example of a man who knew God but failed to follow His instructions. When Saul went to war with the Amalekites, he captured the livestock and spared the Amalekite king, Agag, which violated God's directives to destroy the enemy and take nothing away. Afterward, Samuel confronted Saul about his disobedience:

> Behold, to obey is better than sacrifice,
> And to heed than the fat of rams.
> For rebellion is as the sin of divination,
> And insubordination is as iniquity and idolatry.
> Because you have rejected the word of the Lord,
> He has also rejected you from being king. (1 Samuel 15:22b-23)

Our challenge is not to disregard God's commands, but to embrace them as we are empowered by the Holy Spirit.

The Apostle Paul specifically says that the will of God for believers is that they avoid drunkenness which is self-indulgent, and instead to be filled with the Spirit of God (Ephesians 5:17-18). Paul says that wisdom comes from understanding the will of the Lord. In fact, God's will for every Christian family is that each one be filled with the Holy Spirit. Such obedience will bring harmony in our relationships enabling us to sing to one another in "psalms and hymns and spiritual songs" (Colossians 3:16).

How can we be controlled by the Spirit of God in such a powerful and tangible way? In Colossians 3:16, Paul asserts that when believers let the word of Christ dwell in them richly, it is the same as letting God's Spirit control their lives. God speaks through His Spirit, and uses the Bible to infiltrate a person's life and dominate every part. We must allow ourselves to be controlled by the Spirit of God. We can be thankful and submissive to others when God controls our mind-set and desires. The answer to the curse described in Genesis 3 is presented in both Ephesians 5 and Colossians 3: we must allow the word of Christ to dwell in us richly—that is to let biblical concepts influence our outlook, attitudes, and behaviors. Any two spirit-filled people can live together in agreement when God directs each person's attitude.

Foundation Three: Fortify Convictions

The third principle is that we must fortify our convictions. That is, we need to have firmly-held beliefs that are extolled and lived out in our behaviors and decisions. Convictions derive from a certainty founded on the Word of God. In the Old Testament account, Joshua gathered the families and leaders together to address the nation of Israel. Joshua's speech, as recorded in Joshua 23, presents the basis for blessing and the consequences of compromise, outlining the five basic convictions that Christian families must have.

First, there must be a remembrance of God's ways. Joshua tells Israel that they should remember everything that God has done, for if at any time they forget what He has done, they will stray from the Lord and His plans for them. Amazingly, God had provided military victories, imparted supernatural provisions, and performed miracles—like making the sun stand still. Similarly, if we remember God aided us in the past, we can be assured that He is going to help us in times to come. Recalling God's previous blessings can build a family's faith and trust in God for the future:

> For He established a testimony in Jacob
> And appointed a law in Israel,
> Which He commanded our fathers
> That they should teach them to their children,
> That the generation to come might know,
>   even the children yet to be born,
> That they may arise and tell them to their children,
> That they should put their confidence in God
> And not forget the works of God,
> But keep his commandments. (Psalm 78:5-7)

As Christians, we can trust God's plan because God never changes. Since God has proved Himself faithful in the past, we can trust Him with the future.

Second, there must be obedience to God's Word. Joshua tells Israel that they need to obey the Word of the Lord: "Only be strong and very courageous; be careful to do according to all the law which Moses My servant commanded you; do not turn from it to the right or to the left, so that you may have success wherever you go" (Joshua 1:7). Likewise, our Christian families must choose obedience to the Word and its commands. We must obey in order to find success spiritually.

Third, there must be a severance from the world. The Christian must be in the world—live in society—but not be controlled by it. Joshua knew that if the Israelites didn't sever their ties with their surrounding cultures, they might soon be bowing to foreign gods. Jesus told His disciples, "Remember Lot's wife'" (Luke 17:32). Lot's wife grew so enamored with life in Sodom, its culture and pleasure, that she had to be dragged away by an angel. When she disregarded the warning of God and gazed back toward the city, she died. The lure of Sodom's delights was so strong that she could not escape it. Even when she left Sodom physically, her mind and heart remained captive. In a similar way, we can be enticed by the promise of riches, physical fulfillment, or other pursuits that culture extols. Yet to survive spiritually, we must pursue God's truth rather than physical pleasures or shallow social demands.

Fourth, there must be an allegiance in my walk. Joshua advises that Israel cling to the Lord their God (Joshua 23:8). Cleave to him. Hold tightly to him. As Christians, we should be so aligned with God that nothing can distract us from Him: "I meditate on You in the night watches....My soul clings to You" (Psalm 63:6, 8).

Fifth, there must be diligence in my worship: Joshua reminded his people to diligently love the Lord their God (Joshua 23:11). Similarly, our lives should be consumed with God, to honor Him and reverently worship Him. Like Joshua's audience, we must desire to love and serve God, with all our heart and all our soul (see Joshua 22:5). If we fail in our efforts, if these five aspects (remembrance, obedience, separation, allegiance, and diligent worship) are not part of the convictions of our families, then we, like the nation of Israel in Joshua's day, will face negative consequences.

The consequences of compromise produce three types of failure: defeat, disaster, and disgrace. Joshua spelled out these dangers for the Israelites. He explained that if they disobeyed then they could, "know with certainty that the Lord your God will not continue to drive these nations out from before you; they shall be a snare and a trap to you, and a whip on your sides and thorns in your eyes, until you perish from off this good land which the Lord your God has given to you" (Joshua 23:13). In that passage, Joshua's warning is clear. The Israelites' enemies would defeat them and would not be driven out. In the same way for our families to succeed spiritually, we must not allow the enemy to make inroads that overwhelm us through sin and discouragement. For defeat brings distress to the family and ultimately disgrace. Each Christian family should aim to be a testimony of the love of God to those who do not know Him.

Disaster and disgrace follow defeat. God promised Israel land and blessings, but Joshua warned the nation that they would face disaster if they failed to obey. And so it was. The book of Judges reports, "The people served the Lord all the days of Joshua, and all the days of the elders who survived Joshua, who had seen all of the great work of the Lord which He had done for Israel" (Judges 2:7). However, once Joshua died, the new generation strayed from the truth: "And there arose another generation after them who did not know the Lord, nor yet the work which He had done for Israel" (Judges 2:10). The disobedience of this second generation described in Judges illustrates the importance of remembrance. Therefore, the very first conviction our families must have is a remembrance of God's ways. There arose, after Joshua, a generation of Israelites who knew nothing of the work of God. They knew nothing of the past, about what God had done. They knew nothing about the incredible fall of the walls of Jericho or how God caused the sun to stand still or how they were able to defeat many enemies in the Promised Land.

Without a remembrance of God's ways, discouragement, sin, and discontent can lead us away from God. For that ignorant generation of Israelites, events did not end well:

> Then the sons of Israel did evil in the sight of the Lord and served the Baals, and they forsook the Lord, the God of their fathers, who had brought them out of the land of Egypt, and followed other gods from *among* the gods of the peoples who were around them, and bowed themselves down to them; thus they provoked the Lord to anger. So they forsook the Lord and served Baal and Ashtaroth. (Judges 2:11-13)

As a result of their idolatry and disobedience, the Lord sent judgment upon them. Their lands were plundered by enemies who captured and enslaved the once free people, "so that they were severely distressed" (Judges 2:15).

Their sin brought trouble just as Joshua had warned. For even when God raised up a righteous judge to lead the people, their rebellion and disregard for God's instructions remained. Yet, the Lord spared the people, not because of their obedience or disobedience but because of the Israelite judge who led in obedience to God (see Judges 2:16-18). "But it came about when the judge died, that they would turn back and act more corruptly than their fathers, in following other gods to serve them and bow down to them; they did not abandon their practices or their stubborn ways" (Judges 2:19). In other words, the people never really broke their ties with the culture around them. They would not obey the commands of the Lord or remember His ways. They were not allegiant to their God. As a result, "the anger of the Lord burned against Israel, and He said, 'Because this nation has transgressed My covenant which I commanded their fathers and has not listened to My voice, I also will no longer drive out before them any of the nations which Joshua left when he died'" (Judges 2:20-21).

It is a sad story. Yet it is even more tragic that a similar story is lived out over and over again in the lives of families all across America. There are families who go to church week after week, who put their sons and daughters in children's programs, who involve themselves in Bible studies, yet their homes are filled with distress because they have been defeated by the enemy and their homes have become a public disgrace. They seem "good" or "obedient" on the outside, but their attitudes and behaviors at home produce anger, selfishness and destruction. Consequently, they are unable to magnify the name of the Lord their God, and people no longer see God guiding them and blessing their lives.

On the opposite side, there are other families who have seen the mighty hand of God working in and through them. They have said, "Lord, we know that we're not perfect. We know that we fail, but we want to do what's right. We want to obey the commands in the Bible. We want to serve You. We want to worship You and honor You with our hearts and our lives."

The good news is that distressed families do not have to remain in a state of suffering. One step in the right direction, yielding to God's course can bring restoration and blessing. This chapter has discussed three principles of spiritual growth—fearing Christ, obeying God's commands, and building convictions. In the following chapter, we will explore the two remaining foundational elements to build strong families—establishing a family covenant and fulfilling commitments.

Oh Lord, give us strength and show us mercy. Help us become what You want us to be. Show us what great things can happen when we commit our lives to the Lord, Jesus Christ. Amen.

4

Building a Foundation
(Part 2)

Are daily pressures, temptations, and failures defeating your family? Has your home life become a disgrace because God is no longer honored there? Family members can often improve their difficult circumstances and conflicts when they decide to follow the precepts that God has given in the Bible: "For the Lord will not abandon His people on account of His great name, because the Lord has been pleased to make you a people for Himself. . . . Only fear the Lord and serve Him in truth with all your heart; for consider what great things He has done for you" (1 Samuel 12:22, 24).

Chapter Three presented three foundational principles necessary for spiritual growth:

- Fear the Christ,
- Follow God's Commands, and
- Fortify Family Convictions.

The remaining principles are discussed in this chapter. In order to produce spiritual growth in our families, we need to develop behavioral guidelines that follow the admonition that Joshua gave the children of Israel (as described in Joshua 23). Without a set of firm beliefs that guide our attitudes and behaviors, our families face ultimate defeat. Yet the good news is that we can begin transformation today by praying, "Lord, I want to follow You and serve You."

Foundation Four: Formulate a Covenant
God-ward

The fourth foundational principle is that we need to create a family covenant, one to which we can hold our family members accountable. If we were asked the following questions, most of us would not have an answer: What does your family believe? Why do they believe it? What does your family stand for? Many families have never thought through their beliefs and conviction. The solution to this dilemma is to create a covenant and Joshua explains how to do it:

> Now, therefore, fear the Lord and serve Him in sincerity and truth; and put away the gods which your fathers served beyond the river and in Egypt, and serve the Lord. If it is disagreeable in your sight to serve the Lord, choose for yourselves today whom you will serve: whether the gods which your fathers served which were beyond the River, or the gods of the Amorites in whose land you are living; but as for me and my house, we will serve the Lord. (Joshua 24:14-15)

Joshua had a family covenant. He said, "This is what my family is going to do." When Joshua presented his challenge, the people agreed saying, "We also will serve the Lord, for He is our God" (Joshua 24:18b). Yet in the book of Judges over and over again it is reported, "Every man did that which was right in his own eyes" (Judges 17:6 KJV).

A family covenant represents a deep commitment to obey God no matter what happens. Such an agreement says that family members are going to hold one other accountable to *what* they believe and remember *why* they believe. The covenant that my family has formed is both God-ward and man-ward. God must come first, of course.

1. The Sparks Family Covenant says, fear God. We start with the first foundational principle: *Fear the Lord* (see Chapter 3). The most important point a father ought to teach his children is not how to balance a checkbook; it's not how to drive a car; it's not how to hit a baseball. It is to teach a fear and reverence for the Lord. If parents do not teach children to honor God, then those children may, like the disobedient Israelites, do that "which is right in their own eyes." Having a proper concept of God is vital: "The fear of the Lord leads to life, so that one may sleep satisfied, untouched by evil" (Proverbs 19:23). In order to build confidence in our children, we must teach them to fear God:

> In the fear of the Lord there is strong confidence,
> And his children will have refuge.
> The fear of the Lord is a fountain of life,
> That one may avoid the snares of death. (Proverbs 14:26-27)

We protect our children when we teach them to honor God.

*2. The next point in our Family Covenant is to **adore God with all one's heart**.* A family needs to adore their God. They need to worship God more than anything. Mark 12 records the last question asked of Jesus while He was on earth. It is the greatest of all questions that Jesus answered. "One of the scribes came and heard them arguing, and recognizing that He [Jesus] had answered them well, asked Him, 'What commandment is the foremost of all?'" (Mark 12:28). Then, Jesus answered,

> "The foremost is, 'Hear, O Israel! The Lord our God is one Lord; and you shall love the Lord your God with all your heart, and with all your soul, and with all your mind, and with all your strength.' The second is this, 'You shall love your neighbor as yourself.' There is no other commandment greater than these." (Mark 12:29-31)

That's it. The Christian life is all about loving Jesus with all one's heart, mind, soul, and strength. Mark records that after Jesus' response, "no one ventured to ask Him any more questions" (12:34). Quite simply, if we don't want to adore Jesus Christ, there are no other questions to ask.

*3. Our Family Covenant says we are to **magnify** God.* "O magnify the Lord with me, And let us exalt His name together" (Psalm 34:3). Let the Lord be magnified: "Let them shout for joy and rejoice, who favor my vindication; And let them say continually, 'The Lord be magnified, Who delights in the prosperity of His servant'" (Psalm 35:27). Our homes need to be places where every conversation magnifies God and where everything that happens in the home magnifies God. Every decision that we make should center on one question: Will God be honored in this activity?

*4. Our Family Covenant urges us is to **imitate** God.* Our behaviors should mimic Christ. Paul says, "Be imitators of me, just as I also am of Christ" (1 Corinthians 11:1). Parents must teach their children from the gospels and talk about Christ and how He managed conflict, how He conversed with His enemies, how He faced difficulty, and how He responded to His men calmly but firmly when they were unbelieving. In that way, we teach children how to imitate Jesus.

*5. Our Family Covenant says to **learn** God.* "But grow in the grace and knowledge of our Lord and Savior Jesus Christ" (2 Peter 3:18 NIV). For the Christian, our life-long journey should be getting to know God because we want to learn more about Him every day." Jeremiah 9:23-24 declares, "Let not a wise man boast of his wisdom, and let not the mighty man boast of his might, let not a rich man boast of his riches; but let him who boasts boast of this, that he understands and knows Me, that I am the Lord who exercises lovingkindness, justice and righteousness on earth; for I delight in these things," declares the Lord" (NAS).

*6. Lastly, our Family Covenant says we **yield** to God.* "I beseech you therefore, brethren, by the mercies of God, that you present your bodies a living sacrifice, holy, acceptable to God" (Romans 12:1 NKJV). We must submit everything to God in a life of capitulation, where we are yielding to God and His instructions every day. Each person must be willing to put his or her life on the altar and say, "Lord, You take my hopes; You take my dreams; You take what I want, and You do whatever You want with it because it doesn't matter to me anymore. The only thing that matters is You."

We can never yield to God unless we've learned about Him— never submit unless we truly adore Him. A family who **f**ears God, **a**dores God, **m**agnifies God, **i**mitates God, **l**earns God, and **y**ields to God will be a **family** who glorifies His wonderful name.

Man-ward

In addition to a family covenant related to God, a family also should have a covenant guiding their behavior and how they will treat one another.

1. Family members must forgive one another: For if we fear and reverence God, then we'll forgive our family members. The Bible tells us that we are to be "tenderhearted, forgiving one another, even as God for Christ's sake hath forgiven you" (Ephesians 4:32 KJV). We know all of the weak points and failings of our dads and moms, our spouses and siblings, and all the bad traits in our kids. In order to live in harmony, we must have a forgiving spirit; otherwise, walls of bitterness will rise high. Be a forgiving person. God says that if we don't forgive our brothers, then He will not forgive us (Matthew 6:14-15).

2. Family members need to accept and admonish one another: Each one in the family is different. My wife and I have had eight children together, and not one of them is alike. They all have to be handled in different ways. Sometimes, my kids do things that I just don't like. Likewise, I'm sure I do things they don't like, but we have to accept one another. In Romans 12:3-8 it specifically describes the body of Christ and how we're all different, yet God made us so. How boring the world would be if we were all alike. God has taught me that I have to accept every one of my children just exactly as they are.

"We proclaim Him [Christ], admonishing every man and teaching every man with all wisdom, so that we may present every man complete in Christ" (Colossians 1:28). Then in Colossians 3:16, Paul says that if we let the word of Christ dwell in us richly, we will teach one another and admonish one another in psalms and hymns and spiritual songs. Not only should we accept others for the way they are, their unique personalities and quirks, but we must also be willing to admonish others when they sin. Some parents prefer to think their children make no mistakes. They offer only excuses for their son's misdeeds by saying, "That's just the way he is," or "It really wasn't his fault." A parent's failure to acknowledge his or her child's faults and offer proper admonition will result in problems for the child later on. Parents must stop wearing blinders and face the truth about their children. Mothers and fathers must accept their children for whom they are but also discipline them when they need correction.

*3. We must **minister** to one another:* "Do nothing from selfishness or empty conceit, but with humility of mind regard one another as more important than yourselves; do not merely look out for your own personal interests, but also for the interests of others. Have this attitude in yourselves which was also in Christ Jesus" (Philippians 2:3-5).

When we minister to one another, we learn selflessness and gain the ability to give ourselves away to help others and meet their needs.

*4. We must **intercede** for one another*: "Be devoted to one another in brotherly love; give preference to one another in honor;...rejoicing in hope, persevering in tribulation, devoted to prayer" (Romans 12:10, 12). Pray for one another. Children should learn to pray by themselves in their rooms at night before they go to bed. Parents must teach children to pray with them, for them, and for one another.

*5. We must **love** one another:* Families ought to memorize 1 Corinthians 13, the love chapter, then study it, and most importantly, obey it. Love keeps no record of wrongs. Yet many people do keep mental lists of offenses they are not willing or ready to forgive. If we truly love our husbands and our wives, then there's no need to remind them that they're not perfect. Our spouse's sin is no greater than our own. Godly families love one another.

*6. We must **yield** to one another*: "And be subject to one another in the fear of Christ" (Ephesians 5:21). A family covenant is always God-ward and then man-ward. So that's our personal family covenant from which we commit to hold one another accountable.

Foundation Five: Fulfill Commitments

The last foundational principle is to fulfill commitments. Caleb, who is mentioned in Joshua 14, exemplifies the essence of commitment in the Bible. Caleb's name is derived from the Hebrew word for "dog" because dogs are whole-heartedly devoted to their masters. So, in essence, his name means "whole heart," reflecting the Hebrew concept for "dog." Caleb traveled with Joshua to survey the Promised Land before the Israelites' years of wilderness wandering. Of the twelve spies who returned to report on the vastness of Canaan, Caleb was the first to remind the people that God had promised them the territory. While the other spies emphasized the threat of giants and other dangerous obstacles, Caleb insisted that the people should claim the land God had given them. He remained fearless and firm in his commitment.

Caleb is described repeatedly in Scripture as a man who fully followed the Lord (see Numbers 14, Numbers 32, Deuteronomy 1, and Joshua 14). In the scene described in Joshua 14, Caleb asks Joshua for his rightful inheritance:

> [A]nd now behold, I am eighty-five years old today. I am still as strong today as I was in the day that Moses sent me; as my strength was then, so my strength is now, for war and for going out and coming in. Now then, give me this hill country about which the Lord spoke on that day, for you heard on that day that Anakim *were* there, with great fortified cities; perhaps the Lord will be with me, and I shall drive them out as the Lord has spoken." So Joshua blessed him and gave Hebron to Caleb the son of Jephunneh, for an inheritance. Therefore, Hebron became the inheritance of Caleb the son of Jephunneh the Kenizzite until this day,

because he followed the Lord God of Israel fully. (Joshua 14: 10b-14)

Caleb fulfilled his commitment to the very end. First, because he was committed to God's promises. In Joshua chapter 14, five times Caleb used the expression "the Lord spoke." Because God promised the land, Caleb believed. When the nation of Israel said, "No" to entering Canaan, they wandered for forty years. Yet Caleb still believed he could take the land, that it belonged to him. He remained committed to God's promises.

Second, Caleb was convinced of God's presence. After returning from his spy expedition, he and Joshua told the Israelites, "[T]he Lord is with us; do not fear them" (Numbers 14:9). Later, in Joshua 14:10, Caleb was convinced that God remained with him. He was essentially telling his kinsman, "If God is for me, who can be against me?"

Lastly, he was confident of God's provision. He says, "[P]erhaps the Lord will be with me, and I shall drive them out as the Lord has spoken" (Joshua 14:12). Because he remained committed to God's promises, his loyalty never wavered. Because he was convinced of God's presence, his resolve never weakened. Because he was confident in God's provision, his love never waned. This man fulfilled his commitment to the end. In the book of Joshua, there is only one man who fully expelled the enemy from his land—Caleb, the man who fully followed the Lord his God. His life and actions epitomize commitment. Caleb settled Hebron, the very place where God spoke to Abraham face-to-face. Hebron symbolizes sweet intimacy and sweet communion.

When we fully follow the Lord our God with all our hearts, we will have intimacy and victory. If we fulfill our commitments to the end, God will go with us. We must not quit. Caleb refused to quit; thus he obtained God's provision for him. God blessed him.

By establishing a family covenant (that encourages children to both honor God and love each one in the family) and determining to fulfill our commitments, we can teach our children the best way to live.

Lord, we want intimacy with You. We want victory with You and for You, as Caleb achieved. Help us be committed to Your promises, convinced of Your presence, and confident in Your provision. Amen.

5

God's Exam for Engagement

To marry or not to marry—that is the question. Couples who contemplate marriage have many questions. They often wonder—is this person my true love? The truth is that before marriage, most individuals do not know much about love. Others may think they are in love when they really are not: "All things are lawful for me, but not all things are profitable....But the one who joins himself to the Lord is one spirit with Him" (1 Corinthians 6:12, 17).

Some people get married for all the wrong reasons. Couples might say, "Well, we're not sure a marriage will succeed, so let's just live together on a trial basis." In 1970, 523,000 couples lived together without being married. By 1998, US Census records indicate the number of cohabiting couples rose to 4.2 million.[1] Some singles may think they can determine whether or not the relationship is right for them through a pre-marriage living arrangement with the man or woman they love. Unfortunately, cohabitation is no measure of marital success since the National Survey of Families and Households reports that more than 50 percent of cohabiting couples will divorce within the first five to ten years of their marriage.[2]

These statistics reveal that living together doesn't really answer the questions that single people have about success in marriage. In fact, there is a great deal of uncertainty about love and marriage. Therefore, it's important for Christians to explore a multitude of relationship questions as they contemplate life either as a single or married person.

Should I marry or remain single?

Few people ever ask, "Has God designed me for marriage?" Sometimes individuals marry for the wrong reasons: they want to get away from their parents, they crave companionship, or they want security. None of these reasons is biblical. It's better to consider one's motives and contemplate the idea of actually remaining single.

In Matthew 19, Christ discussed the issue of remarriage: "Because of your hardness of heart Moses permitted you to divorce your wives; but from the beginning it has not been this way. And I say to you, whoever divorces his wife, except for immorality, and marries another woman commits adultery" (Matthew 19:8-9).

The disciples responded, "If the relationship of the man with his wife is like this, it is better not to marry" (Matthew 19:10). In other words, the men were saying, "I'm not sure we should even get married if we can't just leave a wife for any cause." They possessed this "all or nothing" attitude because in those days, if the wife burned the family's meal, the husband could get rid of her and seek another woman who was a better cook.

Yet Christ spoke against such frivolous divorce. So the disciples concluded that it might be better not to marry at all than be saddled by commitment. Then Christ replied,

> "Not all men can accept this statement, but only those to whom it has been given. For there are eunuchs who were born that way from their mother's womb; and there are eunuchs who were made eunuchs by men; and there are also eunuchs who made themselves eunuchs for the sake of the kingdom of heaven. He who is able to accept this, let him accept it." (Matthew 19:11-12)

Thus in Matthew 19, Jesus is addressing the issue of singleness. Eunuchs in Christ's day were men who had been castrated for service as slaves. However, that is not the total application of the word "eunuch." In both Hebrew and Greek the word "eunuch" came to mean an official officer of the court, someone who literally refrained from the duty of family in order to serve his government. Daniel was a eunuch. Yet Jews would never think of self-mutilation or castrating themselves. Instead, they would choose to refrain from family life in order to serve the government and became high officials in the court. That's an important concept to understand.

In light of that discussion with His disciples, Jesus describes three types of people who are single. The first group is comprised of those people who are single because they were born that way. The second are people who are single because of the circumstances of other men, and the third are people who are single because of personal choice or personal commitment. The Apostle Paul sheds additional light on this subject of singleness. Paul was a Pharisee, son of a Pharisee and a member of the Sanhedrin. Further, he was married at least for some period of his life. However, when he wrote to the Corinthians, he was not married: "I wish that all men were even as I myself am. However, each man has his own gift from God, one in this manner, and another in that. But I say to the unmarried and to the widows that it is good for them if they remain even as I. But if they do not have self-control, let them marry; for it is better to marry than to burn with passion" (1 Corinthians 7:7-9).

In this passage, Paul tells his audience that for some, remaining single is a good choice. Paul suggests that such singleness is a "gift of celibacy" (v 7). It is a concept also mentioned in the Matthew 19:12. There are some who are eunuchs at conception. That is, such individuals were born without any desire for marriage or any desire for family. They are very special people, who can have the potential to possess a unique relationship with the Lord.

The second group includes those who are single by some circumstance. There were some, as Christ said, who were made eunuchs by other men. In a modern context, there are some who are single by circumstances beyond their control. They are widowed, divorced, or have not found a suitable mate. Thus various circumstances have dictated their singleness. They might not want to be single, but they are.

The third category includes those whom Christ says are single because of their commitment to the Kingdom of Heaven and their personal choice:

> But I want you to be free from concern. One who is unmarried is concerned about the things of the Lord, how he may please the Lord; but one who is married is concerned about the things of the world, how he may please his wife, and his interests are divided. The woman who is unmarried, and the virgin, is concerned about the things of the Lord, that she may be holy both in body and spirit; but one who is married is concerned about the things of the world, how she may please her husband. This I say, for your own benefit; not to put a restraint upon you, but to promote what is appropriate and to secure undistracted devotion to the Lord. (1 Corinthians 7:32-35)

Therefore, some people, by virtue of choice, have said, "I want to serve the Lord. I'm going to be undistracted in my ministry, and I'm going to give my life in full commitment to Him." The man who is married has a commitment to his wife, and the wife has a commitment to her husband. They must provide for each other in relationship and partnership. However, the single individual has made a commitment, by personal choice, to serve the Lord.

Sometimes married Christians look at single people and say, "Well, they should get married." Yet it's not God's plan for every person to be married. We must understand that a lot of individuals get married for the wrong reasons. Some people get married for security, putting all their confidence in their spouses. Unfortunately, one's spouse is unable to provide ultimate safety. True security is in the Lord Jesus Christ. When we put our security in others, we become insecure because another human being cannot do for us what we hope or desire. A woman might marry for companionship and a sociable partner, but after the marriage, the husband stops talking. He sits in front of the television, reads the newspaper, and avoids conversation. However, God says that He's our companion. He is a friend who sticks closer than a brother (Proverbs 18:24).

There is a legitimate need for marriage; that need is a sexual one. Paul says that if one has strong sexual desires, he should find a marriage partner: "It's better to marry than to burn with passion" (1 Corinthians 7:9). Those who feel such fervor do not have the gift of celibacy. Furthermore, Psalm 84:11 says, "No good thing does He [the Lord] withhold from those who walk uprightly." When my first wife died, I was a young man with a small son. Knowing that I did not have the gift of celibacy, I asked the Lord to bring another woman into my life. I prayed, *"Lord, I'm committing my life to walking uprightly, to serving You, to honoring You. I want my whole life to be consumed with glorifying Your name. Please bring that right woman to me."* Not long after that, He brought me Laurie. God proved faithful in bringing me a good wife.

For those who do not possess the gift of celibacy, their sexual desires are not to be met outside the marriage union: "Yet the body is not for immorality, but for the Lord, and the Lord for the body. ... Flee immorality. Every other sin that a man commits is outside the body, but the immoral man sins against his own body" (1 Corinthians 6:13b, 18). So the first question a Christian must ask is, *"Should I remain single?"*

If divorced, am I free to marry again?

If there is a biblical consent for divorce, then there is a biblical opportunity for remarriage: "Yet if the unbelieving one leaves, let him leave; the brother or the sister is not under bondage in such cases, but God has called us to peace" (1 Corinthians 7:15). In this context, Paul is talking about the believer who is married to the unbeliever. If the unbeliever says, "I want nothing to do with your faith, your church, or you," and if the unbeliever departs, then Paul says to let him leave. The Christian is not under bondage in such cases, for God has called them to peace. A Christian is able to remarry once she has been divorced, providing there are biblical grounds for the divorce.

First, if there is immorality on the part of a partner, then the spouse may remarry. If a man obtains a divorce for the cause of his partner's immorality, Jesus states in Matthew 19:9 that the man is free to remarry.

Second, one may marry again if the unbelieving partner departs (1 Corinthians 7:15). If the unbeliever says, "Look, I'm out of here," the wife may release him. Christians may often be urged to pursue an errant spouse. However, the Bible says that if the unbeliever wants to leave, let him leave. That's a command.

Third, remarriage is permissible if one's partner dies (1 Corinthians 7:39). It is understood that a widow or widower is free to remarry.

Fourth, if one's former partner remarries, then the divorced spouse is free to remarry as well. If a husband divorces his wife for reasons other than biblical ones, (perhaps irreconcilable differences), and later that husband remarries, there is absolutely no chance for reconciliation. Therefore, the wife is free to marry again because her former husband has already entered another relationship. That husband, in a practical sense, has already committed immorality or adultery (see Matthew 19:9), so it follows that the former wife is free from her obligation to the ex-husband.

If a woman is divorced on biblical grounds and her partner remains unmarried, is she free to remarry? Paul says, "But to the married I give instructions, not I, but the Lord, that the wife should not leave her husband (but if she does leave, she must remain unmarried, or else be reconciled to her husband), and that the husband should not divorce his wife" (1 Corinthians 7:10-11). The Bible never suggests that the believer initiate a divorce. In fact, forgiveness plays a supreme part in marriages. Therefore, Paul says if a wife divorces her husband, or a husband leaves his wife, she or he should remain unmarried to allow for reconciliation. If they remain single, there's always a chance that they can reconcile.

If a partner has not committed immorality and is a believer but has left the marriage, then the spouse must wait for God to work. He or she should pray that somehow God will bring the husband and wife back in order that they might glorify the Lord. The individuals should pray for reconciliation. However, it is possible that the erring spouse may not repent and may reject the idea of reconciliation.

Still, Paul says very clearly that if a Christian divorces, he or she should remain unmarried, otherwise, there is absolutely no chance of reconciliation. Further, Matthew 19:9 says if we divorce for any reason other than immorality, then essentially we commit adultery when we remarry. In addition, we make the partner an adulterer. So Paul warns couples against such actions. Christian couples should remain open to the idea of reconciliation. When a marriage relationship unravels, the husband or wife often say, "We don't get along. Everything has fallen apart, and it's never going to come together again. So I'm out of here. Life has got to be better for me than this." In those cases, divorce often ensues.

However, it is important for couples to stay the course and not give up. Even when separated, women or men should pray for their husbands or wives. They should ask God to do a tremendous work. If they marry someone new thinking that they're going to resolve the issues by finding a better spouse, they often bring the same problems and a lot more emotional baggage into the next marriage.

The average divorced person marries someone else four months later. Instead of rushing into another relationship, it's important for individuals to take time to grow in their faith and Christian maturity. Such time and effort allows one to understand more of God's will for her life. It is a mistake to think that marrying someone different will solve all relationship conflicts. A second marriage may create even more complications. In fact, 60 to 70 percent of those divorced people who remarry will likely get divorced again.[3] That's why it's important to remain unmarried to allow time for growing spiritually and resolving conflicts.

Can I marry a divorced person?

If a person who has never been married desires to marry a divorced person, it is permissible: "Are you bound to a wife? Do not seek to be released. Are you released from a wife? Do not seek a wife. But if you marry, you have not sinned; and if a virgin marries, she has not sinned. Yet such will have trouble in this life, and I am trying to spare you" (1 Corinthians 7:27-28). There are three categories of single people described in this passage; the virgin, the widow, and the unmarried person or the divorced person. If a single person is contemplating marriage to a divorced person, he or she must consider several important factors. It is important to learn why the person is single again and what happened in the previous relationship that caused the marriage to end. Every divorced person has a story; it's important to learn if that story is true.

For example, in one church where I served as associate pastor, a man from the congregation had a severe heart attack. His condition was dire, and as he lay in the coronary care unit clinging to life, his family members assembled in the waiting room. At one point, his doctor arrived and asked for Mrs. _____ . Two ladies stood up and responded, "Yes?" The women looked at each other in surprise. Each insisted that she was the dying patient's wife, Mrs. _____. Both women had four children with them. So there each wife was in the waiting room thinking that her husband was going to die, and then she discovered that for 25 years the man she called her husband had been living a lie. He had been married to two different women and had been hiding one wife and family from the other. The two women and their eight children were shocked and devastated. The story illustrates the importance of truly knowing about the person one plans to marry, especially if he or she has been divorced.

When Paul praises the benefits of remaining single, he is trying to spare us from trouble. When two people who have a sin nature live together under the same roof, they are going to argue and bicker. Yet the good news is that the Spirit of God is able to do a mighty work in a couple's relationship. When husbands and wives put God first, God helps them become that husband or wife that He wants them to be.

Can I marry a non-Christian?

There is no fellowship in darkness. If we are children of the Light, we cannot marry those who are children of the darkness and expect things to turn out right. "Do not be bound together with unbelievers; for what partnership have righteousness and lawlessness, or what fellowship has light with darkness?" (2 Corinthians 6:14). Some individuals insist that the context of this scriptural passage is that of a business partnership. However, the same principle is reinforced in 1 Corinthians 7:39: "A wife is bound as long as her husband lives; but if her husband is dead, she is free to be married to whom she wishes, only in the Lord." Thus, the woman can marry whomever she wishes as long as the person is a believer.

There are times when a believing Christian marries an unbeliever then later the person comes to accept Jesus as their personal Savior. However, such situations are the exception not the rule. Because God is a good God, He sometimes overrules our sins for His divine purposes. Yet Scripture is clear, we sin against God by marrying an unbeliever.

Even if Christians merely date non-Christians, the relationship can pose problems. If the couple develops emotional attachments, then breaking up later over issues of faith will be difficult. In these situations, a Christian might think, *"If I pray hard enough, if I live the right kind of life, I know this person I'm dating will come to believe in Christ."* The danger is that we are capable of rationalizing anything in the hopes of getting what we want. However, rationalizing cannot take the place of the truth of God's Word. We cannot violate God's Word and then expect God to bless our marriages: "Do not be deceived, God is not mocked; for whatever a man sows, this he will also reap" (Galatians 6:7).

Remember, "missionary dating" is always a risk. For example, I dated a girl in high school who was slender, athletic, and gorgeous. Being an athlete myself, I figured a relationship with her could really work well. So I took her out, shared the plan of salvation with her, and to my delight, she gave her life to Christ. The problem was, though, that she didn't sincerely become a Christian in order to seek forgiveness for her sin. She just wanted to keep dating me. In the same way, I compromised by candy-coating the truth of the Gospel. I left out important details about faith in Christ to make my message more palatable to her. My parents were skeptical of the relationship and developed a "wait and see" attitude.

When she showed little interest in church, I dragged her there anyway. As our relationship progressed, I realized that the faith in Christ that was important to me was not a faith that was important to her. The relationship did not last, obviously, but it demonstrated to me how easy it is to be drawn into relationships that are not healthy. Emotional attachments can be deceiving and troublesome.

Should I have children?

Every couple must ask, "Do we want to have children?" Children are a blessing from the Lord:

> Behold, children are a gift of the Lord,
> The fruit of the womb is a reward.
> Like arrows in the hand of a warrior,
> So are the children of one's youth.
> How blessed is the man whose quiver is full of them;
> They will not be ashamed
> When they speak with their enemies in the gate.
> (Psalm 127:3-5)

In my case, I always thought I wanted only two children. However, my wife Laurie had other ideas. So together we now have eight children; many more than I planned, but each one is a unique blessing to us.

The Bible is very clear about having children: "Be fruitful and multiply" (Genesis 1:28 KJV). This aspect of marriage (that of procreating, populating the earth, having children) is an important concept described in Jeremiah: "Take wives and become the fathers of sons and daughters, and take wives for your sons and give your daughters to husbands, that they may bear sons and daughters; and multiply there and do not decrease" (Jeremiah 29:6). Each couple must consider having children and think about how many children they should have.

God designed marriage as the best place to bear and nurture children. Babies are not supposed to be born in relationships outside of the wedding bond, but to be born within the nurturing realm of marriage with a mother and father. Christians can have a positive influence on society through their children, by raising a Godly generation that, like a flaming arrow that flies into the night, will shine like a light and stand for righteousness. As children grow in biblical wisdom and godly knowledge, they will make an impact for Jesus Christ.

Can I handle the responsibility of marriage?

In marriage, husbands and wives share a great deal of responsibility for finances, emotional support, care and nurture of children, and the everyday aspects of keeping a home. "But if anyone does not provide for his own, and especially for those of his household, he has denied the faith and is worse than an unbeliever" (1 Timothy 5:8). In this passage, Paul urges his audience to provide for the needs of their households, to be responsible husbands and wives. A husband must be sure he can provide for the financial wellbeing of his wife and children. There must be a partnership between wives and husbands to complete chores and support one another. The husband should not let himself be consumed by sports or other hobbies that keep him from his family. Likewise, wives must not put friends or other pursuits before her spouse and children.

Have I sought counsel from my parents?

The Bible states clearly that parents can offer wisdom and guidance to children, even adult children. "My son, observe the commandment of your father and do not forsake the teaching of your mother; bind them continually on your heart" (Proverbs 6:20-21a). An astute child will go to his parents and ask, "Is this a wise move for me?" Parents know much about their children, and they can offer insight about the kind of person their son or daughter ought to marry.

Is this relationship God's will for my life?

The will of God is for us to abstain from sex before marriage. "For this is the will of God, your sanctification: that you should abstain from sexual immorality" (1 Thessalonians 4:3 NKJV). There are many issues to consider as Christians contemplate that fundamental question, should I marry? It's important to review the questions outlined in this chapter, to seek biblical answers, and to ask for God's clear direction in making such important life decisions. "Delight yourself in the Lord; And He will give you the desires of your heart" (Psalm 37:4).

Lord, we want to follow Your moral will. Please direct our paths. Help us to meditate on Your law day and night so that it becomes our delight. Make Your desires our desires. Amen.

6

God's Meaning for Marriage

When most men and women wed, they know little if anything about marriage or what is required to have a fulfilling relationship. Books, movies, and real-life relationships modeled by parents, grandparents or others give couples some idea. Yet for all practical purposes, newlyweds don't have the foggiest notion about what their future together holds. The traditional vows state, "It is a union that is not to be entered into lightly or inadvisably, but reverently, discretely, soberly," and most importantly, "in the fear of God." When a couple speaks those vows, they are leaving their former lives as singles behind and cleaving to one another. Such commitment is a biblical concept described by the Apostle Paul:

> For this reason a man shall leave his father and mother and shall be joined to his wife, and the two shall become one flesh. This mystery is great; but I am speaking with reference to Christ and the church. Nevertheless, each individual among you also is to love his own wife even as himself, and the wife must see to it that she respects her husband. (Ephesians 5:31-33)

There's a funny story about a little boy who was attending his first wedding. After the service, he asked his cousin, "How many women can a man marry?"

The cousin responded, "Sixteen."

The boy asked, "Sixteen? How did you get sixteen?"

The cousin replied, "Oh that's easy. All you have to do is add it up, just like the pastor said, 'Four better, four worse, four richer, and four poorer.'"

Similarly, Christian couples in love have all kinds of grandiose (but perhaps misguided) ideas of married life. They fantasize about how their future will include the beautiful cottage complete with a picket fence, lovely lawn, new cars, obedient kids, cute pets, great jobs and involvement in the greatest church ever. During the engagement period, such dreams are held dear by many loving couples. However, reality does not often match that fantasy. As time passes, the lovers realize that the little rental cottage sans picket fence is dumpy, the lawn weedy, the car clunky, the kids annoying, the pets a problem, the hubby unemployed, and the church quite flawed.

Eventually, the husband or wife asks, "What happened? How did a future that looked so promising, go bad so fast?" The problem is that most people in love don't understand marriage. However, there are seven biblical elements of a marriage that, if understood, can change a couple's unrealistic expectations and can mitigate the disillusionment that many spouses face.

Marriage: A Pictorial Union

When God speaks of marriage, He describes a pictorial union. According to Paul's explanation in Ephesians 5:22-33, marriage is primarily a picture of Christ's relationship to the church. This principle is the most basic and foundational element of marriage, and if understood properly, will completely change the way we view our husbands or our wives. It is a foundational standard vital to a successful relationship. Paul makes the comparison between marriage and the church very clear:

> Wives, be subject to your own husbands, as to the Lord. For the husband is the head of the wife, as

> Christ also is the head of the church, He Himself being the Savior of the body. But as the church is subject to Christ, so also the wives ought to be to their husbands in everything. Husbands, love your wives, just as Christ also loved the church and gave Himself up for her, so that He might sanctify her, having cleansed her by the washing of water with the word, that He might present to Himself the church in all her glory, having no spot or wrinkle or any such thing; but that she should be holy and blameless. (Ephesians 5:22-27)

This passage from Ephesians 5 is familiar, yet its instruction is much neglected in Christian marriages. This concept in Ephesians provides a graphic demonstration to the world that God has an ongoing and unending relationship with the bride, whom He loves and for whom He died. That's the metaphor presented. Human relationships symbolize the divine relationship between Christ and the church. The husband and wife are one flesh. So the Spirit of God is one with Jesus Christ and His church. As a church is to respond to Christ, so the woman is to respond to her husband. As Christ loved the church, so husbands are to love their wives. These symbols automatically elevate marriage to a level beyond any other human institution, except the church. God says, "I have something to show the world, and I'm doing that in human marriage relationships." Thus, marriage is a picture.

If we could draw that picture, how would it look? What do our marriages portray to others? Do they portray Christ and His love for the church? Marriage is not about our happiness. Marriage is primarily a picture of Christ's love for the church. The questions that arise then are: Will Christ ever stop loving the church? Will Christ ever divorce the church? The answer is "no" to both questions, of course. So then, we must ask ourselves: *"Does my marriage picture Christ's love for the Church?"*

Many times when I counsel a young couple whose relationship is troubled—filled with conflict—a discouraged wife may say to me, "But you don't understand; I hate my husband." That's when

I reply, "That's good news because the Bible says we are to love our enemies" (Matthew 5:44). The Scriptures say that "while we were still sinners, Christ died for us" (Romans 5:8 NIV). While we were Christ's enemies, He demonstrated His love to us. This love principle is fundamental. Christian couples have a wonderful opportunity to demonstrate love despite the fact that they feel resentment and anger toward each other. Just as they were separated from God, because they were dead in their trespasses and sin, it was *His* initiative and *His* love that were demonstrated to them even when they were in a sinful state as His archenemy.

That perspective completely changes a person's view of marriage because it's not about happiness. One's marriage is about God, about Christ, and about His love for the church. So each of us should answer this one question at the end of every day: How did we demonstrate to the world Christ's love for the church? When we fall short, we can say, "You know, I didn't make it here. I had the opportunity, but I blew it." That's when we ask for forgiveness and try again. Our goal should be to view each day as an opportunity to exercise sacrifice. When we are in the midst of chaos and anarchy, we can seize the opportunity to demonstrate patience and sensitivity. We understand the picture that we must paint for others is of Jesus Christ and His love for the church.

Our happiness depends on our relationship to the living God, not our relationship to our spouses. Christ is essentially saying, "I've come to give you the abundant life. I've not come merely to give you life, but I've come to give you the greatest of all lives. Your life and its abundance depend upon your relationship to Me. It has nothing to do with your spouse. It has nothing to do with your circumstances. It has nothing to do with the jalopy you drive. It has nothing to do with the dumpy house you live in. It has everything to do with your relationship with Me" (based on John 10:10).

Problems often arise when we Christians allow temporal desires and cultural influences to dictate what happiness is. Couples develop false expectations about happiness in marriage. We come to believe that if we could just have the right spouse, the right car, the right house, and the right job, then we would find contentment. So naturally, when those situations do not meet expectations, individuals become depressed and downcast. Suddenly life is terrible and everything is falling apart. However, the truth is that our relationship with God is what's most important. If we understand that, we then understand that our marriages should picture Christ's love for the church. Therefore, when non-Christians look at us, they don't just see our marriages, but they see Christ reflected in our relationships.

Evangelicals today are having a difficult time living out the gospel because their own marriages are failing. According to statistics reported by The Barna Group, 28 percent of all born again, evangelical Christians in America are divorced.[1] Americans are looking for a model, a picture, that will show them Christ, yet our own Christian marriage relationships aren't succeeding. We preach that our God is the all-powerful Lord of the universe. We say our God can save us from sin and take a person's life from where it was—once an adulterer, once a murderer, once an effeminate person, once a thief—and transform it. Yet when we allow our marriages to fail, our hypocrisy is evident to all. Unbelievers then ask, "What kind of God do you serve? What kind of God doesn't care about your marriage?"

Christians must answer those questions. One of the most powerful testimonies we can have is a strong marriage. Therefore we must work at marriage and work to stay together. Satan targets our marriages to sow seeds of discontentment just as he tempted Adam and Eve in the Garden of Eden (Genesis 2-3). Satan knows exactly what the marriage institution is and he seeks to destroy it. A Christian marriage, like a magnifying glass facing the world, must display the brightness, beauty and bigness of God Almighty. "O magnify the Lord with me, and let us exalt His name together" (Psalm 34:3). That's marriage—a pictorial union.

Marriage: A Permanent Union

Marriage is a permanent union. The statement, "For this cause a man shall leave his father and mother and shall cleave to his wife. And they shall become one flesh" is the only statement about marriage that is stated four times in the Bible. First, it is explained in Genesis 2:24 before the fall of Adam and Eve. Then it is reiterated three times in the New Testament (see Matthew 19:5, Mark 10:7, 1

Corinthians 6:16). God repeats the concept to emphasize the importance of marriage.

The word "cleave" means "to be glued together." It refers to a strong bonding of two separate objects so that they become inseparable. God meant marriage to last a lifetime. Therefore, a partner is one who is not an additional add-on, but one who becomes indivisible with their spouse.

Many people marry with an escape plan in mind: *if this doesn't work out, I can always get a divorce*. However, for those who enter marriage with that attitude, divorce is much more likely to occur. For a couple to find success in marriage, the word "divorce" should never even be mentioned because once a husband or wife raises the possibility, it becomes an option. When troubles come and conflicts intensify, the divorce decision seems the easy way out. Such attitudes and actions have produced a non-committal society.

The vows a couple makes are vows to God. The Bible says, "It's better not to vow than to make a vow and not fulfill it" (Ecclesiastes 5:5 NIV). Couples must ask themselves, "Did I really mean those vows about 'for better and for worse' when I said them?" Marriage is a permanent union meant to last until death or until the Lord returns.

Marriage: A Predetermined Union

Marriage is a predetermined union. In His discourse on marriage, Christ said, "So they are no longer two, but one flesh. What therefore God has joined together, let no man separate" (Matthew 19:6). Notice in this passage that it is not the priest, the pastor, the bishop, nor the justice of the peace who joins couples together, but it is God. If God has joined us as husbands and wives, no man should seek to separate what God has put together. Marriage as a union was predetermined in the mind of God in eternity past. Genesis 2:22 records God's actions at creation: "The Lord God fashioned into a woman the rib which He had taken from the man, and He brought her to the man."

Now God, the divine miracle worker, fashioned one woman for Adam. Similarly, God gave us a wife or husband. So we must see that person as God's gift: "House and wealth are an inheritance from fathers, but a prudent wife is from the Lord" (Proverbs 19:14). So whether a marriage is between two believers, or between a believer and an unbeliever, or two unbelievers, or an arranged marriage, God has joined them together.

God is in control of everything: "The mind of man plans his way, but the Lord directs his steps" (Proverbs 16:9). We can make all the plans we want, but God directs our steps. "Man's steps are ordained by the Lord" (Proverbs 20:24). Reliance on God's sovereignty is absolutely essential if we are to grasp God's meaning for our individual marriages.

Marriage: A Purposeful Union

Marriage is a purposeful union. The Lord God said, "'It is not good for the man to be alone'" (Genesis 2:18 NIV). Since it's not good for the man to be alone, God created for him a suitable helper. God had a purpose in the union of Adam and Eve—to bring two people together. Isolation is not beneficial for human beings. "He who separates himself seeks his own desire, He quarrels against all sound wisdom" (Proverbs 18:1). The idea is that the person who chooses isolation is self-centered and also unwise. By creating the woman Eve for Adam, God provided a solution for man's isolation. This design offers an intimate companionship, friendship, and partnership, between one man and one woman so that they might be fruitful and multiply. Such a union brings protection for that man and for that woman.

Paul says that when you are together, make sure that you don't separate when it comes to sexual intimacy because if you do, Satan may bring conflict into your marriage:

> The wife does not have authority over her own body, but the husband does; and likewise also the husband does not have authority over his own body, but the wife does. Stop depriving one another, except by agreement for a time, so that you may devote yourselves to prayer, and come together again so that Satan will not tempt you because of your lack of self-control. (1 Corinthians 7:4-5)

The admonition is that the couple should only separate if both agree to commit themselves to prayer. In God's design, sexual intimacy protects a marriage relationship.

Marriage: A Precious Union

Marriage is a precious union. The two shall become one flesh. In God's eyes, we become the total possession of our spouses. One flesh is not just about sex; it's emotional, spiritual, and relational oneness. We become one with our spouses in mind, spirit, direction, and emotion. In addition, children become an incarnation of that oneness and love. In marriage, the mom and dad come first; the children are second. That understanding provides supreme security for children, for they need to know that their father and mother are so committed to each other that nothing will divide them. Such commitment provides stability for all family members and allows sons and daughters to grow and flourish.

Marriage: A Provisional Union

Marriage is a provisional union. Men are to honor their wives as the weaker vessel. "You husbands in the same way, live with your wives in an understanding way, as with someone weaker, since she is a woman; and show her honor as a fellow heir of the grace of life, so that your prayers may not be hindered" (1 Peter 3:7). Men are stronger than women physically; in addition, they are usually stronger emotionally. Thus the man is to give the wife what she needs because he becomes that stabilizing factor in the marriage: the strong one, the leader, the provider.

In Ephesians 5:23-33, Paul explains how the man is to provide for his family. He is to purify his wife. He is to cleanse her as Christ cleansed the church. Like Comet cleanser that makes objects bright, the husband sanctifies and sets the wife apart from past relationships. The wife also has responsibilities:

> An excellent wife, who can find?
> For her worth is far above jewels.
> The heart of her husband trusts in her,
> And he will have no lack of gain.

She does him good and not evil
All the days of her life. (Proverbs 31:10-12)

Thus, she provides and cares for her husband. As a virtuous woman, as the model wife, "She looks well to the ways of her household, and does not eat of the bread of idleness" (Proverbs 31:27). She does what is necessary because she also plays a part as provider within the marriage.

Marriage: A Pleasurable Union

Marriage is a pleasurable union. "Marriage is to be held in honor among all, and the marriage bed is to be undefiled" (Hebrews 13:4). God designed marriage to be good and to be enjoyable. Therefore, the husband's body is not his own, but his wife's. And the wife's body is not her own but the husband's (1 Corinthians 7:4). God wants married couples to experience the pleasure of oneness:

> Let your fountain be blessed,
> And rejoice in the wife of your youth.
> As a loving hind and graceful doe,
> Let her breasts satisfy you at all times;
> Be exhilarated always with her love.
> For why should you, my son, be exhilarated with an adulteress
> And embrace the bosom of a foreigner?
> For the ways of a man are before the eyes of the Lord,
> And He watches all his paths. (Proverbs 5:18-21)

God gives us a union that is designed to be pleasurable. Understanding the scriptural meaning of marriage (that it is a pictorial, permanent, predetermined, purposeful, precious, provisional, and pleasurable) will change our relationships. God will honor our efforts when we put the needs of our spouse before our own.

Lord, give us the perspective we need to understand Your design for our marriages. May we delight in You, Lord, and Your ways, honoring our spouses as You intended. Amen.

7

God's Value on Vows

Joe Aldrich asserts that marriage can bring disillusionment. Couples "soon learn that a marriage license is just a learner's permit and ask with agony, 'Is there truly life after marriage?'"[1] Marriage brings many uncertainties. A man or woman must learn not how *to find*, but how *to be* that "right partner" in the relationship. No one has all the answers in finding the perfect mate. We are to trust God daily for all things, including our husbands or wives. "Marriage is to be held in honor among all" (Hebrews 13:4).

One way couples can strengthen their relationships is to frequently review the sacred marriage vows they voiced on their wedding day. After a few years, they may not even remember what they actually said to their bride or groom during the ceremony. They just repeated the words that the pastor, judge, or justice of the peace gave them. Yet God places a very high premium on vows.

Before Laurie and I married, she considered the gravity of making a life-long commitment to me. She wrote down her concerns about the commitment that marriage required. Here is her prayer:

> Lord, marriage will be a big undertaking. Sometimes I feel overwhelmed. Sometimes I doubt that I can handle all that it entails. Marriage is a lifetime commitment; a lifetime that includes struggles, sorrow, and uncertainty. Thank you, Lord, for making me

> still so I can listen to You. Thank you for making me realize in these few quiet moments of anxiety, the depth of the commitment marriage brings. It is now, Lord, more than ever before, that I see I will need to draw on Your strength. You have given me a wonderful man. He loves You. He loves me. He desires a relationship that puts You first. Yes Lord, "I do" means forever. "I will" means we face life's uncertainties together: for richer or for poorer; in sickness and in health. Lord, Lance is the one You've given to me. In my periods of anxiety, Lord, You bring such comfort. I trust You to make me what You desire me to be.

Laurie's entreaty reveals the many doubts in her mind. She was leaving the known for the unknown. Yet she was trusting that God would make her into the woman He wanted her to be.

During our ceremony, these are the words I proclaimed to my bride:

> The Psalmist said, "No good thing would the Lord withhold from those who walk uprightly." Although my walk with God has not been perfect, He has blessed me with the most wonderful woman in the world. I believe that God in His sovereignty has chosen you for me. I will be eternally grateful. Those familiar words designed for days such as this, "for better, for worse, for richer, for poorer, in sickness and in health, until death do us part," are not really words to me but, in fact, a reality. I submit myself to you as Christ did the church by giving of myself to love, honor, and cherish you. This, my love, is what I promise each day and forever.

I meant those words then and continue to mean them now. My first wife died of cancer and suffered for more than fifteen months before she went to heaven. During that crisis, I realized that a marriage commitment was indeed "for better, for worse, for richer, for poorer, in sickness and in health." So when I married Laurie, I knew full well what those words meant. I could say the vow with authority. Having survived a tragedy, I knew about the reality and rewards of a marriage commitment.

The wedding ceremony must be considered more than a celebration or a necessary ritual. On the day a couple marries, they are making a serious vow—a vow to God. Even if the guy and gal hightail off to Las Vegas and marry in one of those wedding chapels, it's still official. Some representative there in the City of Las Vegas holding governmental authority unites the man and woman in "holy" matrimony. That governmental officer is in God's ultimate authority. "For there is no authority except from God, and those which exist are established by God" (Romans 13:1b). Therefore, the one performing a wedding ceremony is God's representative, and it follows that the vows are under God's authority as well.

The vow is also made to the spouse. The Bible has much to say about such commitments. "If a man makes a vow to the Lord, or takes an oath to bind himself with a binding obligation, he shall not violate his word; he shall do according to all that proceeds out of his mouth" (Numbers 30:2). If one makes a vow; she is obligated to fulfill that vow. Further, we are reminded in Ecclesiastes 5:4-5 about the importance of such promises. "When you make a vow to God, do not be late in paying it; for He takes no delight in fools. Pay what you vow! It is better that you should not vow than that you should vow and not pay." Sometimes promises are made in times of distress:

> I shall come into Your house with burnt offerings;
> I shall pay You my vows,
> Which my lips uttered
> And my mouth spoke when I was in distress. (Psalm 66:13-14)

At a crisis point, a person might say, "Oh God, just get me out of this financial difficulty, and I'll give lots more money to the church for the rest of my life." It's like the soldier's fox-hole prayer: "Lord, just get me out of here alive, and I'll give my life to You." Then when the emergency is over, the person disregards his promise.

The writer of Proverbs says that it's wrong to make a rash vow, to consecrate something to God and then afterward, renege or forget that promise. "It is a trap for a man to say rashly, 'It is holy!' And after the vows to make inquiry" (Proverbs 20:25). It's like the young man who said, "Oh, I love you with all of my heart. I will do whatever it takes to be with you. I will swim the greatest ocean, cross the highest mountain, run the driest desert, and if it doesn't rain tonight, I'll be over to see you." We must answer for our broken promises. Vows must be kept because God places a high value on them.

Every year on our anniversary, my wife and I review our vows, just to make sure we're doing what we said we were going to do. Renewing vows is a good habit for husbands and wives. In addition, there are five basic principles that exemplify God's value on vows and remind us of the importance of our pledge in marriage.

A Vow Certifies Integrity

Vows can certify one's integrity. Jesus Christ discussed the importance of vows. "Again, you have heard that the ancients were told, 'You shall not make false vows, but you shall fulfill your vows to the Lord'" (Matthew 5:33). In this situation, Christ is attacking the Rabbinical teaching by which the Jewish people were living. In Matthew 5:37, Christ addresses the verbal integrity of the Jewish nation: "But let your statement be, 'Yes, yes' or 'No, no'; anything beyond these is evil" (Matthew 5:37).

Just before this statement, Christ addressed the issue of divorce and remarriage. Perhaps the two subjects are linked because the Jews were divorcing their wives for any cause. They would rewrite the law to obtain a divorce if their wives displeased them. So right on the heels of that topic, Jesus addresses the importance of verbal integrity. It's not by accident that the vows discussion follows the divorce and remarriage passage. The Jewish people had become frivolous about their wedding vows. Christ says, "But I say to you, make no oath at all, either by heaven, for it is the throne of God" (Matthew 5:34). They believed that they could swear by anything and then renege on that pledge because they had not made a vow "to the Lord." For example, they might say, "I swear on the city of Jerusalem," or "I swear by the temple."

People would say, "Oh, if you're going to swear by the temple of Jerusalem, it must be true." However, it was really just their way out, their way to disregard a vow. If they said, "I swear to you by the Name of the Lord," then they would be required to keep their promise. But if they swore by anything else, they could back out. The bottom line is that Christ wants us to be truthful at all times. Our word must be our bond. The person of God, the person of integrity, is one who speaks the truth from the heart and does not change his word (Psalm 15:4).

God wants truthfulness in the heart of His people because out of the heart, one speaks (Matthew 12:34). That's why James says, "But above all my brethren, do not swear either by heaven or by earth or with any oath; but your yes is to be yes and your no, no, so that you may not fall under judgment" (James 5:12). Since God is a God of truth, He demands that His people speak and live truth. The clearest indicator of our spiritual condition is our speech.

When a man is committed to Christ, he becomes a new creation. So if he broke his word before he was a believer, then as a believer, he ought to keep his word because he's now following the law of God. Marriage partners must be sure they can trust each other. If a husband or wife gives a reason for doubt, then all of a sudden, the marriage bond weakens. When we keep our word, we certify our integrity. We must put a stronghold on that which is true and let everybody know, "This is my word. You can count me."

A Vow Clarifies Responsibility

When a person makes his vows, he is clarifying to all (even himself), his clear responsibility. "For this reason a man shall leave his father and his mother, and be joined to his wife; and they shall become one flesh" (Genesis 2:24). When the man decides to leave home to start his own family, he's also making a decision to lead. In so doing, he is saying, "I understand my responsibility as the husband." Likewise, the woman says, "I understand my responsibility as the wife. I am making a vow to God to fulfill my responsibility and my duty."

Some may give excuses saying, "When I married, I didn't know what my responsibility or duty was." In some instances, men who get married assume they're going to continue golfing, fishing, or bowling with their buddies. They think that their wives must understand that a husband cannot possibly forsake his social life with the guys. For a few months, a wife may indulge such attitudes and behaviors. But when children enter the family and pressure for their care increases, the wife will say, "Time out. I'm tired of taking care of the children by myself. It's your turn." The man may cling to his desire to go with his buddies for a golf day or Monday night football. However, by doing so, he is avoiding his primary responsibility.

In a vow, one is clarifying his responsibility to all by saying, "I am forming a new relationship and leaving those other relationships behind." That's one reason why married men and women do not keep seeing old girlfriends or boyfriends once they are married. The spouse must become the best friend, the confidante, the prayer partner, and the guidance counselor. One leaves old relationships to enter into a primary relationship with the wife or husband.

In Colossians, Paul says, "Wives, be subject to your husbands, as is fitting in the Lord. Husbands, love your wives and do not be embittered against them" (3:18-19). Husbands must love their wives because that decision to marry is a decision to lead, a decision to love, and a decision to learn.

A husband must learn what makes his wife tick, what upsets her and what makes her the way she is. Husbands lead by loving. He must say to himself, *"I love my wife so much that I'm going to learn all there is about her because she is my prize possession."* The mandate for the man is to lovingly lead. The wisdom for the woman is to sincerely subject herself to his leadership.

In the Garden of Eden, Adam was unwilling to assume the responsibility of leadership. The serpent came and deceived Eve about God and His goodness. Adam did nothing. Adam said nothing. When Eve misquoted the command of God, Adam should have intervened to lead his wife. He should have said, "Oh, no honey. That's not what God said." However, Adam didn't take a stand. He allowed Eve to believe a lie. Therefore, his silence brought sin and death to mankind. God gave him a helper suitable. Similarly, God has given men today suitable helpers.

A Vow Confirms Loyalty

This concept of loyalty also derives from Genesis 2:24, "Therefore shall a man leave his father and his mother, and shall cleave unto his wife: and they shall be one flesh" (KJV). The bond formed in "one flesh" means that one is loyal to the husband or to the wife physically, emotionally, and spiritually. No woman in her right mind would marry a man who says, "I promise to be loyal to you on the weekends or until somebody else comes along." Instead, the woman wants a guy who says, "I promise to be loyal to you forever, no matter who comes along, no matter whether it's convenient or not."

Cleaving is costly, but its reward is intimacy. On my left finger, I wear a wedding band, symbolizing commitment to my wife. This ring, picturing an unending circle of love, tells everyone I'm taken. A wedding band is a reminder to all that we are loyal to one person forever. We must be willing to break with any force or person that would hinder that oneness.

When a bride walks down the aisle, her identity and loyalty change. She takes on a new name. For example, when my wife Laurie came down the aisle, she was an Aker through and through. However, once she married me, she became a Sparks with a whole new identity. Now she didn't feel different or look different at that moment. But by the very nature of the ceremony, she took on a new identity.

When a person becomes a Christian, they receive a new nature. They become a new creation, yet they may not feel any different. When I became a Christian, I felt no radical difference. Nothing seemed to outwardly change. However, before conversion, I was captivated by Satan. After accepting Christ, I became God's captive. If at any time in my relationship with the Lord, I return to my old master, I create a problem with my new Master. Marriage relationships work the same way. If at any time in a marital relationship, I decide to go back to my old friends to seek advice or gain wisdom, I will experience conflict with my new-found identity. Marriage is a picture of Christ's relationship to the church. A believer's loyalty to God is demonstrated in his or her loyalty to their spouse. That's why when husbands and wives understand marriage they understand that the vows confirm their loyalty.

A Vow Challenges Spirituality

In Ephesians 5:22-6:4, Paul gives instruction about the family and marriage. Then in 6:10 he begins a discussion about the wiles of the devil. Nothing will challenge our spirituality more than the conflicts faced in married life. When I was single, I had little problem walking with God. However, when I married, I faced new challenges because for the first time, I shared life with my wife. I slept with someone who knew me. My life was laid bare before my wife, so I faced new spiritual challenges. It was as if Satan was telling me, "You thought you were good. Let me tell you something. You're rotten. And I'm going to use your wife to show you how rotten you are. And later I'll use your kids to show you how horrible you are."

When our spirituality is challenged, we must make a commitment to discipline ourselves to godliness as never before. We must let the word of Christ dwell in us richly. Such a challenge is good. It keeps us humble and prayerful and hungry for God's Word. Here's the principle: the institution of marriage is failing because our devotion to the Master is faltering.

As spiritual leaders, we husbands and fathers must teach our family members about God's ordained plan for them. We must help them to understand that God is doing a great work, even though the circumstances look bad. God is working in our families, even though situations look like they're falling apart. Maintaining a balanced, positive attitude, trusting what God is going to do, and maintaining our fellowship with the Lord is vitally important.

Being spiritually strong is one of the greatest challenges of our lives. As men, we must be able to meet that challenge. We must face it through the power of Almighty God at work in us, and then we must watch what God does to make us stronger.

A Vow Communicates God's Sovereignty

When Jesus addressed His audience in Judea about marriage and divorce, He reminded the people that what God has joined together, no man should separate (Matthew 19:1-6). If God has joined a couple together, then their vows communicate God's sovereignty. God never changes His mind and says, "Oh, sorry. I gave you the wrong girl. Let Me take her back."

We must trust God's sovereign plan in marriage. In the Garden of Eden, God instructed Adam to name all the animals. Perhaps in that classification process, Adam said, "I name you, Mr. and Mrs. Gorilla, and you, Mr. and Mrs. Zebra. Oh, and you two are Mr. Bull and Mrs. Cow." Then eventually, Adam realized that everybody had a partner except him.

To meet Adam's need, God put him to sleep, took a rib from his side, and fashioned the woman—what a marvelous process. In God's process, He took something from Adam, but gave it back in the form of a woman, beautiful Eve. The act showed Adam once again his need for someone, a human mate.

It is no surprise that men and women have different personalities, aptitudes, and interests. In marriage these differences are often magnified. The husband and wife may be complete opposites. Yet the differences reflect one person's need for another because one fills in where the other one is empty. In the sovereign plan of God, Adam received what he needed to function as a complete man. That divine sovereignty continues for each generation, as God gives men and women suitable helpers specifically for them. God had a marvelous plan and wedding vows confirm it. Therefore, when husbands and wives uphold their vows, they are saying, "Thank you, God, for this divine plan. Thank You, God, for specifically choosing the man or woman I need to make my life complete."

Father, we thank You, Lord, for Your wonderful work in our relationships. Help us understand Your plan for our families. Give us strength to uphold our commitment to You and to our partners. Give us patience, endurance, and love to serve our wives and husbands and see them as the gift You meant them to be. Amen.

8

God's Counsel for Couples: Spiritual Maturity

To have a successful relationship, every couple must establish a firm foundation on which to build healthy attitudes, behaviors, and actions. These relationships must begin with love, not just romantic love, but the kind of love described in 1 Corinthians 13. This love is patient, kind, unselfish, and truthful (v 4). It "bears all things, believes all things, hopes all things, endures all things" (v 7).

In the popular wedding poem "The Art of Marriage," poet Wilfred A. Peterson asserts that a couple must have the "capacity to forgive and forget." He closes the poem with the observation that the art of marriage is "not only marrying the right person. It is being the right person" (lines 13-14). Peterson's statement raises an important question. How does a man or woman become the "right person," the kind of partner who obeys God?

An essential element in becoming that "right partner" is developing spiritual maturity. This maturity strengthens our commitment so that we can say, "Lord, I have done everything I possibly can to honor and glorify You in my marriage." In order to succeed, we must understand the spiritual foundation God has provided for creating a successful marriage relationship.

It Begins with a Divine Inheritance

"Blessed be the God and Father of our Lord Jesus Christ, who according to His great mercy has caused us to be born again to a living hope through the resurrection of Jesus Christ from the dead, to obtain an inheritance which is imperishable and undefiled and will not fade away, reserved in heaven for you" (1 Peter 1:3-4). A born again believer has an inheritance. They have received from God a blessing, a gift that cannot be destroyed, defiled, diminished, or displaced. If we receive an inheritance in our family whether it's of some monetary value or not, it will fade away. However, God's inheritance never fades away or diminishes; it's His gift to us.

In Acts 26, Paul speaks about his confrontation with Christ on the road to Damascus: "'for this purpose I have appeared to you, to appoint you a minister and a witness...to open their [the Gentile's] eyes so that they may turn from darkness to light and from the dominion of Satan to God, that they may receive forgiveness of sins and an inheritance among those who have been sanctified by faith in Me'" (vv 16, 18). Paul's ministry was to preach the Gospel so that people would find faith. That saving faith is part of a divine inheritance. This holy gift is imperishable and lasts forever. When we become Christians, we become one with Christ; therefore, we receive everything the Father gives to the Son. We are heirs of God and fellow heirs with Christ (Romans 8:17).

Our inheritance is a great blessing: "In Him also we have obtained an inheritance, having been predestined according to His purpose who works all things after the counsel of His will, to the end that we who were the first to hope in Christ would be to the praise of His glory" (Ephesians 1:10b-12).

Our inheritance is based on the fact that we are one with Christ: "giving thanks to the Father, who has qualified us to share in the inheritance of the saints in Light" (Colossians 1:12). Because God has gifted us with His inheritance, He makes us part of His family. We can't earn this inheritance. God has to do all the work.

We are "in Christ." That phrase is used 169 times in the New Testament to describe our relationship with the living God. Four principles explain what it means to be "in Christ." If we are going to be the right partners in our marriage relationships, we have to know for certain that Jesus Christ is Lord of our lives and that we are "in Christ."

One who is in Christ experiences a distinct transformation: In 2 Corinthians 5:17, Paul explains that being "in Christ" makes us "a new creation" where the old things pass away and all things become new. The new person is radically and fundamentally different than he or she was before coming to Christ. The Greek tense used in this passage emphasizes that not only are these converts different but also they remain different. They don't go back to the old way but remain transformed. A metamorphosis occurs. The classic illustration is, of course, Saul who became the Apostle Paul. He was once a violent aggressor, a blasphemer by his own testimony (see 1 Timothy 1:13). God transformed him so Paul had firsthand experience when he spoke to others about the process:

> Or do you not know that the unrighteous will not inherit the kingdom of God? Do not be deceived; neither fornicators, nor idolaters, nor adulterers, nor effeminate, nor homosexuals, nor thieves, nor the covetous, nor drunkards, nor revilers, nor swindlers, will inherit the kingdom of God. Such were some of you; but you were washed, but you were sanctified, but you were justified in the name of the Lord Jesus Christ and in the Spirit of our God. (1 Corinthians 6: 9-11)

A person who is in Christ is characterized by a distinct transformation. He comes alive: "so also in Christ all will be made alive" (1 Corinthians 15:22). At a funeral, there is a difference between the dead one in the casket and the people who walk by the casket. Similarly in the spiritual realm, there is a distinct difference between those in Christ and those not in Christ. Those not in Christ are dead in their trespasses and sin. They're spiritual zombies who need to be made alive spiritually.

When Christ gives us life, He quickens us and brings total change. For instance, the world is characterized by hate. The Christian is characterized by love and forgiveness. The unbeliever is characterized by his lust for more while the Christian is characterized by contentment. Paul says in 2 Corinthians 5:14, "For the love of Christ controls us." God gives us new motives; He has given us the ministry of reconciliation (2 Corinthians 5:19). Thus, we must ask ourselves these questions: *"Am I a changed man in Christ? Am I a changed woman in Christ? Has God done something in my life, for which He deserves all the glory?"*

Life in Christ is conducted in a different dimension: That spiritual dimension is outlined in Ephesians 2:6: "[God] raised us up with Him, and seated us with Him in the heavenly places in Christ Jesus." Therefore our conduct exemplifies that we live in a different world. We are aliens, strangers in a foreign land. Consider Abraham: "By faith he lived as an alien in the land of promise, as in a foreign land, dwelling in tents with Isaac and Jacob, fellow heirs of the same promise; for he was looking for the city which has foundations, whose architect and builder is God" (Hebrews 11:9-10).

Abraham and his descendants died before receiving these promises, yet "if they had been thinking of that country from which they went out, they would have had opportunity to return. But as it is, they desire a better country, that is, a heavenly one. Therefore God is not ashamed to be called their God; for He has prepared a city for them" (Hebrews 11:15-16).

Paul further explains that "our citizenship is in heaven" (Philippians 3:20). We have been rescued out of the domain of Satan into the domain of Christ and His kingdom. He has seated us in the heavenly places in Christ Jesus. That means we live in a completely different dimension. This earthly life is temporary and transitory as Paul explains:

> Set your mind on things above, not on things that are on the earth. For you have died and your life is hidden with Christ in God. When Christ, who is our life, is revealed, then you also will be revealed with Him in glory. Therefore consider the members of your earthly body as dead to immorality, impurity, passion, evil desire, and greed, which amounts to idolatry. (Colossians 3:2-5)

Our distinct transformation allows us to live in a different dimension as a new creation. Those earth dwellers who are not in Christ focus on the material world, and the tangible elements they can see and hold. However, those who live for God will one day rule and reign with Him forever.

Life in Christ is characterized by a sense of satisfaction: Because believers in Christ set their affections on eternal values, there is a deep satisfaction that unbelievers do not possess. "Blessed are those who hunger and thirst for righteousness, for they shall be satisfied" (Matthew 5:6). The earth dwellers are discontent. They see everything on a horizontal plane, but the believer focused on things above can live a contented life because his affections are set on eternal matters, not on transitory situations.

Discontentment comes into marriage when husbands or wives look horizontally instead of vertically. We must remember that Christians are already seated in the heavenly places with Christ. That's important to grasp. Christ said, "I am the bread of life. He who comes to Me shall never hunger, and he who believes in Me shall never thirst" (John 6:35 KJV). Christ will supply all of our needs. He will take care of us (See Psalm 33, Psalm 34, Psalm 25, and Psalm 125). That's God's promise.

> The Lord sustains all who fall
> And raises up all who are bowed down.
> The eyes of all look to You,
> And You give them their food in due time.
> You open your hand
> And satisfy the desire of every living thing.
> The Lord is righteous in all His ways
> And kind in all His deeds.
> The Lord is near to all who call upon Him,
> To all who call upon Him in truth.
> He will fulfill the desire of those who fear Him;
> He will also hear their cry and will save them.
> (Psalm 145:14-19)

Such awareness of God's provision frees us to minister to our spouses because the Lord will take care of all our needs. Shortly after Malcolm Muggeridge, the well-known British journalist, became a Christian, he delivered the sermon "Living Water" in Queens Cross Church in Aberdeen, May 26, 1968. In his talk, Muggeridge addressed this concept of eternal perspective:

> I may, I suppose, regard myself, or pass for being, a relatively successful man. People occasionally stare at me in the streets—that's fame. I can fairly easily earn enough to qualify for admission to the higher slopes of the *Inland Revenue*—that's success. Furnished with money and a little fame even the elderly, if they care to, may partake of trendy diversions—that's pleasure. It might happen once in awhile that something I said or wrote was sufficiently heeded for me to persuade myself that it represented a serious impact on our time—that's fulfillment. Yet I say to you, and I beg you to believe me, multiply these tiny triumphs by a million, add them all together, and they are nothing—less than nothing, a positive impediment—measured against one draught of the living water Christ offers to the spiritually thirsty, irrespective of who or what they are. What, I ask myself, does life hold, what is there in the works of time, in the past, now to come, which could possibly be put in the balance against the refreshment of drinking that water?[1]

Muggeridge's point is that a person's fame, success, or fulfillment pales in comparison to the Living Water, Christ Himself, who satisfies the deepest thirst of the soul.

Life in Christ brings affliction of the soul: Peter explains this dilemma. "Beloved, I urge you as aliens and strangers to abstain from fleshly lusts which wage war against the soul" (1 Peter 2:11). We're engaged in a battle to have our own way and to live the way we want. Yet, Peter says, "as aliens and strangers" such selfish desires must be ignored. The Christian will not become a popular person in the world. In fact, Christ says that all those who desire to live holy lives in Christ Jesus shall suffer persecution.

These four principles describe what it means to be "in Christ." Since we Christians have received a divine inheritance, we have the resources to be the right marriage partner. So we each must ask ourselves these questions: *"Do I have a relationship with the Living God? Have I been transformed? Do I live my life in a different dimension? Do I live with a satisfaction and contentment that only Jesus Christ can give? Do I struggle with the affliction that wages war against my soul because I'm living for the King of Kings and the Lord of Lords?"*

It Blossoms in a Disciplined Reverence

Whether at morning or night, the believer must set time aside to revere and worship God.

> It is good to give thanks to the Lord
> And to sing praises to Your name, O Most High;
> To declare Your lovingkindness in the morning
> And Your faithfulness by night. (Psalm 92:1-2)

To become the right marriage partner requires us to live disciplined lives where we spend time alone with God, admiring and worshipping Him. The Bible says that God seeks true worshippers. By nature, the creatures in Heaven worship Almighty God and God says that's the way He wants us to live on earth. In the morning and in the evening, we should express our loving-kindness to Him. A.W. Tozer said, "Retire from the world each day to some private spot, even if it be only the bedroom....Stay in the secret place until the surrounding noises begin to fade out of your heart and a sense of God's presence envelopes you."[2] It takes discipline to find the time for worship and Bible study, yet we must never be too busy for God. We must spend time with our heavenly Father, our Maker, our Creator.

It's Balanced by a Determined Obedience

Having a sense of divine inheritance and a disciplined reverence brings determined obedience. When people spend time with God, there's a certain beauty about their lives. It is characterized by a spiritual fragrance. Communion with God produces a spiritual blooming that others notice.

We can learn from other godly men and women who demonstrate this quality.

Christ chose men to be with Him. His disciples followed Him, watched what He did and listened to what He said. Eventually they pleaded, "Lord, teach us to pray." Though these men failed at first in the Garden of Gethsemane, they eventually grew in maturity. Their experiences described in Acts testify to their spiritual growth.

People who spend time with their God are different. So when we become the "right" marriage partners, our husbands and wives will want to follow us and commune with us. When a husband becomes the right partner, his wife will walk around saying, "I want to follow you today. I want you to teach me how you reflect God's fragrance." Success in marriage is not about *marrying* the right person, it's about *being* the right partner.

If God's our divine priority, then we should follow His precepts. We should not ask, "But what about him or what about her?" Christ tells us to follow Him. "He who has My commandments and keeps them is the one who loves Me; and he who loves Me will be loved by My Father, and I will love him and will disclose Myself to him" (John 14:21). When we listen to Christ's instruction, He will manifest Himself to us. Such spiritual maturity comes with discipline. Paul said, "I discipline my body and make it my slave, so that, after I have preached to others, I myself will not be disqualified" (1 Corinthians 9:27).

It's Beautified in a Desert Experience

The Christian life is beautified in a desert experience. John Newton described the process in a hymn:

> I asked the Lord that I may grow
> In faith and love and every grace;

Might more of His salvation know,
And seek more earnestly His face.

'Twas He who taught me thus to pray,
And He, I trust, has answered prayer!
But it has been in such a way,
As almost drove me to despair.

I hoped that in some favored hour,
At once He'd answer my request;
And by His love's consuming pow'r,
Subdue my sins and give me rest.

Instead of this He made me feel
The hidden evils of my heart;
And bathe the angry pow'rs of hell
Assault my soul in every part.

Yea more, with His hand He seemed
Intent to aggravate my woe;
Crossed all the fair designs I schemed,
Blasted my gourds, and laid me low.

Lord, why is this, I trembling cried,
Wilt thou pursue thy worm to death?
"Tis in this way," the Lord replied.
"I answered prayer for grace and faith.

These inward trials I employ,
From sin and pride, to set thee free;
And break thy schemes of earthly joy,
That thou may'st find thy all in Me."[3]

John Newton prayed that he would grow closer to God. However, God did something unexpected. He made the poet low; He aggravated his life, and God took him to an undesirable place. In order to develop the poet into a spiritual man, God led him to the desert.

Sometimes, marriage relationships enter a similar desert. Their life is dry, barren, and cracking under the heat and pressure of daily life. The husband and wife see no oasis on the horizon. Understand this, if we are going to be the right partner, our beauty will come because of desert experiences. A. W. Tozer said, "It is doubtful whether God can bless a man greatly until he has first of all hurt him deeply."[4] This blessing of God happens in the desert experience. The Psalmist said, "Before I was afflicted I went astray, but now I keep Your word" (Psalm 119:67). When we experience affliction and the barrenness of life, then God says, "I'm going to teach you about Me and about who I am. So throw yourself on Me, and I will sustain you, guard you, and protect you."

God told Israel,

> "'For I know the plans that I have for you,' declares the Lord, 'plans for welfare and not for calamity to give you a future and a hope. Then you will call upon Me and come and pray to Me, and I will listen to you. You will seek Me and find Me when you search for Me with all your heart.'" (Jeremiah 29:11-13)

When we experience a life full of adversity, the circumstances might look bleak, but God says that He will orchestrate His plan so that we will fall on our faces before Him. He is telling us, "I want you to seek Me, and when you seek Me, you'll find Me. I will be unlike anything you've ever known before." When building toward spiritual maturity, our marriages are beautified in the desert experience. That's why the Psalmist says in Psalm 90:15 these unbelievable words, "Make us glad for as many days as you have afflicted us, for as many years as we have seen trouble" (NIV).

It's Battled Against with a Diabolical Vengeance

During times of spiritual growth, we must battle against a diabolical vengeance. When we follow God and obey His Word, then we will face attacks on our lives and marriage relationships. To stand against diabolical vengeance, we must be prepared and armed for the attack. "Your adversary, the devil, prowls around like a roaring lion, seeking someone to devour" (1 Peter 5:8). As soldiers for Christ, we face many battles. If we're not armed properly, we could lose. Our offensive weapon is the Bible, the sword of the Spirit (see Ephesians 6:17). Our marriages will be exactly what we make of them.

Lord, arm us for the battle of life. Give us the strength and discipline we need to put You first. May Your Word and guidance perfect us, so that we may love our husbands and wives unselfishly. Through our obedience and commitment, bless our relationships so that our lives may glorify You. Amen.

9

God's Counsel for Couples: Acknowledging God

God is so concerned about our marriages that He guarantees us success and the survival of our relationships if we follow biblical principles.

> His divine power has granted to us everything pertaining to life and godliness, through the true knowledge of Him who called us by His own glory and excellence. For by these He has granted to us His precious and magnificent promises, so that by them you may become partakers of the divine nature, having escaped the corruption that is in the world by lust. (2 Peter 1:3-4)

Peter explains that God has given us all things that pertain to life and godliness. In fact, everything that centers on true living and that leads to godliness is in the Word of God. This godliness produces an "abundant life" (see John 10:10).

What are the biblical foundations necessary for a magnificent marriage? We can't find them in the ABC guidebooks for marriage offered in our local bookstores or the counseling videos available online. Only the Bible offers the wisdom required to form the strong foundations necessary for marital success. These spiritual building blocks teach us what God wants for our marriages.

The Way

The first foundational principle to godliness is that we must acknowledge God as the divine priority in our lives. Therefore, men and women must acknowledge God as supreme in their lives and marriage relationships. In Deuteronomy 6, we find insight into God's plan for marriage. Deuteronomy is literally called the "second law" providing a reiteration of God's laws and instructions as the people of Israel were about to enter Canaan, the Promised Land. Moses offered his last words to the nation; one last pep talk, one more bit of inspiration, and one last set of guidelines to make sure the Israelites knew exactly what to do as they started a new life.

Deuteronomy's repetition underscores the importance of God's instructions. In fact, the Ten Commandments appear again in Deuteronomy 5 (they appear first in Exodus 20) because Moses wants the people to understand God's laws. The nation of Israel was about to invade a pagan culture that had no understanding of a holy God. So the words he would give to the husbands, wives, and children would help them understand their responsibility in that pagan society. Similarly, for our families to be successful wherever we live, we must know the precepts of Deuteronomy 6. Like Israel, we also live in a pagan society and God expects our families to live righteously. God guarantees not only our survival in that society, but He also guarantees our success when we put Him first.

Deuteronomy is also a book of transition, chronicling Israel's shifting to a new generation. There had been forty years of wandering, when God had said that everybody over the age of twenty would die in the wilderness. When the succeeding generation arose, it marked the fulfillment of God's promise. The former rebellious generation had refused to listen to God forty years before, but the grown children could enter the land God had provided. Deuteronomy marks this generational shift and the movement from the temporary to the permanent.

Instead of wandering, the people would settle down. Instead of living in tents, they'd have houses. Instead of the manna wilderness diet, they'd eat milk and honey, and drink the wine of Canaan. They faced a new realm, and a new revelation. God *showed* the Israelites that He loved them, but He never *told* them that He loved them until this revelation in Deuteronomy 4:37: "Because He loved your fathers, therefore He chose their descendants after them. And He personally brought you from Egypt by His great power." From Genesis to Numbers, the text never speaks specifically of God's love for His people. Yet in Deuteronomy, His love for Israel is recounted several times:

> For you are a holy people to the Lord your God; the Lord your God has chosen you to be a people for His own possession out of all the peoples who are on the face of the earth. The Lord did not set His love on you nor choose you because you were more in number than any of the peoples, for you were fewest of all peoples, but because the Lord loved you and kept the oath which He swore to your forefathers, the Lord brought you out by a mighty hand and redeemed you from the house of slavery and from the hand of Pharaoh King of Egypt. (Deuteronomy 7:6-8)

Thus, in Moses' farewell address, he reminds them of God's love (See also Deuteronomy 10:15 and Deuteronomy 23:5). Moses was preparing the Israelites to live in a righteous and successful way. Moses knew to survive the turmoil and chaos of a pagan culture meant nurturing strong family relationships. So he explained their newfound responsibilities.

Acknowledge God by Listening Intently

Moses told the people how to have a long life:

> Now this is the commandment, the statutes and the judgments which the Lord your God has commanded me to teach you, that you might do them in the land where you are going over to possess it, so that you and your son and your grandson might fear

the Lord your God, to keep all His statutes and His commandments which I command you, all the days of your life, and that your days may be prolonged. (Deuteronomy 6:1-2)

We acknowledge God as the divine priority when we listen intently to Him. This concept is the cornerstone of the successful family and what makes a marriage magnificent. Moses said Israel must listen to God. "O Israel, you should listen and be careful to do it, that it may be well with you and that you may multiply greatly, just as the Lord, the God of your fathers, has promised you, in a land flowing with milk and honey. Hear, O Israel! The Lord is our God, the Lord is one! You shall love the Lord your God with all your heart and with all your soul and with all your might" (Deuteronomy 6:3-5). There's something life changing about anxiously waiting for God to speak. The blessed man listens intently:

> Now therefore, O sons, listen to me,
> For blessed are they who keep my ways.
> Heed instruction and be wise,
> And do not neglect it.
> Blessed is the man who listens to me,
> Watching daily at my gates,
> Waiting at my doorposts.
> For he who finds me finds life
> And obtains favor from the Lord.
> But he who sins against me injures himself;
> All those who hate me love death. (Proverbs 8:32-36)

The people were admonished to hear what God had to say (see also Psalm 81:8-11, Revelation 2-3, Isaiah 48:12-17). God says, if you listen and obey my commandments, you will be like the unending river (Isaiah 48:18a). When we struggle, and situations prove difficult, we must listen to God because He also promises us well-being and righteousness like the waves of the sea (Isaiah 48:18b).

Something as simple as listening to God can change everything in our marriage relationships. Could it be that there are problems in our marriages because we are unwilling to listen to God's promptings about our attitudes, values, and lifestyles? We must listen intently to God.

Acknowledge God Through Learning Intensely

We should learn intensely from God and be careful in our study. "Only be strong and very courageous; be careful to do according to all the law which Moses My servant commanded you; do not turn from it to the right or to the left, so that you may have success wherever you go" (Joshua 1:7). I have a library full of books offering advice about family and marriage, church growth, and programming. Yet, very few of these publications emphasize the importance of acknowledging God as the divine priority. If we put Him first, we can listen and learn. "Study to shew thyself approved unto God, a workman that needeth not to be ashamed, rightly dividing the word of truth" (2 Timothy 2:15 KJV).

Acknowledge God by Living Intentionally

When Moses told the Israelites, "O Israel, you should listen and be careful to do it," he was describing how to live intentionally for God. If we violate biblical principles, we are not living the way God designed. If we don't believe God, we won't practice and live a biblical lifestyle of obedience and sacrifice.

If we live intentionally for God, we will teach God diligently, we will talk of God decidedly, and we will think on God drastically.

> These words, which I am commanding you today, shall be on your heart. You shall teach them diligently to your sons and shall talk of them when you sit in your house and when you walk by the way and when you lie down and when you rise up. You shall bind them as a sign on your hand and they shall be as frontals on your forehead. You shall write them on the doorposts of your house and on your gates. (Deuteronomy 6:6-8)

Moses instructs us to teach these commands to our children because in the future they are going to ask why the family has kept certain statutes.

> When your son asks you in time to come, saying, "What do the testimonies and the statutes and the judgments mean which the Lord our God commanded you?" Then you shall say to your son, "We were slaves to Pharaoh in Egypt, and the Lord brought us from Egypt with a mighty hand. Moreover, the Lord showed great and distressing signs and wonders before our eyes against Egypt, Pharaoh and all his household; He brought us out from there in order to bring us in, to give us the land which He had sworn to our fathers." (Deuteronomy 6:20-23)

When was the last time our sons or daughters asked us anything about God? We must tell our children all the great things about Him. The best time to teach children is when *they* ask the questions. It's when they're in the car, at the dinner table, at the mall, or spinning in a ride at Disneyland. Those are times when children ask, "What happens if our car crashes?" Or "What will we do if this roller coaster spins off the rails to the ground below?" As parents, we respond, "Well, we'll go to heaven. Don't worry because we'll see Jesus."

It's important to talk about our eternal destiny. For example, once while eating with my family at McDonalds, my son asked me, "Hey Dad, how am I gonna' figure out God's will for my life? I mean, how did you and mom find God's will?" His questions gave me an opportunity to teach about discerning the will of God. Those are key times when children ask questions about spiritual issues. We need to capture those opportunities with our children and our spouses. The bottom line is, we must live intentionally for God.

Moses also told the Israelites that they must think about God drastically. Even in the twenty-first century, Jewish people wear phylacteries, little leather boxes that contain copies of the Law of Moses, on their heads or wrists. God says that this is what He wants us to do—to live life for Him in a drastic way. It doesn't mean we have to go around with Bibles glued to our foreheads. The point is that wherever we look, our gaze is cast through the grid of the Scriptures and whatever our hands reach for needs to be evaluated through that spiritual frame.

The Orthodox Jews have taken this instruction to the extreme and literally *wear* the Law of God. However, if God is our divine priority, then we must look at life through the eyes of God, to see what God sees. In a pagan culture where people don't know God, we must teach God diligently, talk of God decidedly, and think on God drastically. Such actions demonstrate that we are living for God intentionally and that's what it means to acknowledge God as the divine priority.

Acknowledge God by Loving Incessantly

We must love God incessantly. "Hear, O Israel! The Lord is our God, the Lord is one! You shall love the Lord your God with all your heart and with all your soul and with all your might" (Deuteronomy 6:4-5). The word "all" speaks of totality—not something partial or casual. It speaks of intensity, unquestionable fervency, and whole-heartedness. God demands whole-hearted devotion. Jesus spoke of people who honor Him with their lips, but their heart is far away from Him (see Matthew 15:8). Some individuals can speak the words of God, but they don't love Him with a sincere, burning passion. Each Christian must ask, *"Do I love God with all my heart, soul, mind, and strength? Are my passions centered on God alone?"*

Children know our attitudes about Bible study and church and prayer. They know what we love, and they are not fooled. When we consider how to love God and live for Him, we must keep in mind the acrostic for FAMILY:

>
> **F**ear God
> **A**dore God
> **M**agnify God
> **I**mitate God
> **L**earn God
> **Y**ield to God

Developing these concepts can build a strong family. A biblical family acknowledges God as their divine priority. They love insistently, live intentionally, learn intensely, and listen intently to God.

The Warning

Following the instructions of Deuteronomy 6, Moses issued a warning to the people not to forget God. The Israelites received many blessings in Canaan: "splendid cities which you did not build, and houses full of good things which you did not fill, and hewn cisterns which you did not dig, vineyards and olive trees which you did not plant, and you eat and are satisfied" (Deuteronomy 6:10b-11). These conditions were far better than those experienced in their wilderness wanderings. Moses warned them that once they had all this to be careful and "not forget the Lord who brought you from the land of Egypt, out of the house of slavery" (Deuteronomy 6:12). God brought the children of Israel out of Egyptian bondage, so how could they ever forget? Yet they did forget and the prophet Isaiah chronicled the rebellion of God's people:

> "Listen, O heavens, and hear, O earth;
> For the Lord speaks,
> 'Sons I have reared and brought up,
> But they have revolted against Me.'" (Isaiah 1:2)

God's people became rebellious while remaining religious. However, God called their offerings "worthless" (Isaiah 1:13).

While the people maintained the outward trappings of worship, they lacked sincere, repentant hearts. God desired their obedience more than their sacrifices. The solution for their hypocrisy came through cleansing and repentance:

> "'Come now, and let us reason together,'
> Says the Lord,
> 'Though your sins are as scarlet,
> They shall be as white as snow;
> Though they are red like crimson,
> They will be like wool.

> If you consent and obey,
> You will eat the best of the land;
> But if you refuse and rebel,
> You will be devoured by the sword.'
> Truly, the mouth of the Lord has spoken." (Isaiah 1:18-20)

We also live in a time where we rarely remember what God has done. We often dwell with those who worship the gods of prestige, power, pleasure, and possession. These preoccupations can steal a person's affection for spiritual goods. The concept is simple: God gives us all things—our cars, our children, our wives, our husbands and our jobs. In order to acknowledge the divine priority, we can't forget God's gifts. To acknowledge God, we must remember, obey, seek, and follow Him.

Moses' second warning was to forsake idolatry and worship God alone.

> You shall fear only the Lord your God; and you shall worship Him and swear by His name. You shall not follow other gods, any of the gods of the peoples who surround you, for the Lord your God in the midst of you is a jealous God; otherwise the anger of the Lord your God will be kindled against you, and He will wipe you off the face of the earth. (Deuteronomy 6:13-15)

God says, "Worship Me. Adore Me. Fear Me." The principle here is that God wants first place. Our devotion guides our affection and governs our direction. Our direction will give way to either maturation or deterioration. A. W. Tozer said, "To worship is to be so personally and hopelessly in love with God that the idea of a transfer of affection never even remotely exists."[1]

The Warranty

With this warning, God also gives a guarantee for success and survival. "So the Lord commanded us to observe all these statutes, to fear the Lord our God for our good always and for our survival, as it is today" (Deuteronomy 6:24). The message of Deuteronomy 6 can bring hope to our homes, not harm. Devotion and obedience to God will strengthen the family and help every generation to survive from one generation to the next (See Proverbs 8:32).

God says, "We must worship Him and fear His name." Our obedience guarantees success and survival for the family. For couples, God has to be the priority. Husbands must be brave and introspective enough to ask their wives and children, "Do I behave in a way that shows I put God first?" Wives and mothers must also ask that question. Our family members know better than anyone what our priorities are.

If your spouse says, "Honey, I don't see godly obedience in your life," we must not get defensive or make excuses. We must be willing to say, "Would you pray with me, that God will be my priority because I want to live and lead properly."

Dear Lord, help us to put You first, to acknowledge Your boundless gifts to us. Please remove any rival that steals our affection for You. Make us into humble and obedient partners who serve You and others. Give us magnificent marriages. Amen.

10

God's Counsel for Couples: Personal Integrity

Leo Tolstoy said, "Everybody thinks of changing humanity, but nobody thinks of changing himself."[1] That resistance to change is evident in many Christians. Often when we hear a Sunday sermon, we think that the biblical message is for someone else's benefit not ours. Yet we must also pay attention because sometimes God is saying, "Listen up, because this message is for you!"

As we grow toward spiritual maturity and acknowledge God as the divine priority, we must also commit to developing personal integrity. Integrity is of utmost importance for our daily living and testimony. Whenever one's integrity fails, purity will be damaged, then spirituality will be diminished, and ministry will be demolished. "Many a man proclaims his own loyalty, but who can find a trustworthy man?" (Proverbs 20:6).

Developing integrity begins with one's commitment to his God and working to honor and glorify Him. Living a life that models God, honors Him, and glorifies Him leads to integrity. But once we compromise that commitment, we may find ourselves caught in a downward spiral. So we each must ask ourselves, *"Am I making a daily commitment to live a life of integrity?"*

To fully understand integrity, it's important to examine these five points: the explanation, the essence, the enemy, the emblem, and the end of integrity.

The Explanation of Integrity: Completeness

Integrity can be explained in one word: Completeness. The Psalmist says, "How blessed are those whose way is blameless, who walk in the law of the Lord" (Psalm 119:1). Thus, the Bible describes a man of integrity as a blameless one. A person possessing integrity is not divided or duplicitous. The man or woman of integrity does not pretend or knowingly practice hypocrisy. When people have nothing to hide, they have nothing to fear.

Integrity comes from a Latin word meaning "completeness" or "wholeness." Integrity characterizes an entire person—his heart, mind, and will. Tommy Nelson defined integrity this way: "Simply put integrity is doing what you said you would do."[2]

When we promise to be faithful to our mates, integrity says we'll stay with that person no matter what; for better or worse, for richer or poorer, in sickness and in health. If we promise the Lord that we will give Him glory, integrity means that we do so whether we're reduced to nothing or exalted to the highest pinnacle. If we promise a friend that we'll return a call, integrity guarantees we'll return it. If we promise a child that we'll spend Saturday together, integrity means we keep that appointment. A promise is a holy thing, whether it be to the chairman of the board or to a child.

Integrity is keeping your word:

> Lord, who may abide in Your tabernacle?
> Who may dwell in Your holy hill?
> He who walks uprightly,
> And works righteousness,
> And speaks the truth in his heart. (Psalm 15:1-2 NKJV)

The phrase "he who walks uprightly" describes the Israelites as they offered their sacrificial lamb. The priest would examine that lamb for blemishes to guarantee a fit sacrifice would be offered. In a similar way, the holy man or woman must be able to stand the scrutiny of God. The person of integrity examines his life to see if it is clean, without blemish.

Furthermore, we must be honest and truthful, for out of the heart, man speaks (Luke 6:45). Satan is a liar and the father of lies, but God's people are to be truthful. "Lying lips are an abomination to the Lord, but those who deal faithfully are His delight" (Proverbs 12:22). In some families, telling lies or even little fibs is accepted.

The question arises then for any family: *Is it ever right to lie?* Some use biblical examples as a way to justify deception. For example, in Exodus, to save lives the midwives lied about the birth of the male babies born in Egypt. In Joshua, Rahab lied to protect the spies in Jericho. In Genesis, Rebecca lied to her husband Isaac so that her beloved son Jacob would receive the birthright. Often pastors explain that there is an appropriate time to lie. Authors of theological books also discuss the justification of falsehoods. Yet the Bible says that the Lord detests lying lips. God never lies. He's a God of truth. So do we align ourselves with those midwives, Rahab, and Rebecca, or with the character of God?

Obviously, we align ourselves with the character of God. "Do not lie to one another, since you laid aside the old self with its evil practices" (Colossians 3:9). The Bible speaks clearly about truth-telling. "A righteous man hates falsehood, but a wicked man acts disgustingly and shamefully" (Proverbs 13:5). There is never an occasion where it's right to lie. Sometimes when we lie, despite our falsehoods, the situation works out okay, but that doesn't mean lying is right. It just means that God and His grace are greater than our sin.

It's recorded in Acts 5 that Ananias and Sapphira lied to God and died on the spot. God was not unjust when he killed them for lying, for as sinners, they got exactly what they deserved. Since God is truthful, He expects His children to speak truthfully. It is God's grace that preserves our lives and offers redemption despite our lying and other sins. We need to understand that concept in order to become the kind of people God desires.

The Essence of Integrity: A Clear Conscience

The essence of integrity is a clear conscience before God and before man. There's nothing better in the entire world than a clear conscience. The Puritan Richard Simms said, "The conscience is the soul reflecting upon itself."[3] Through the conscience, one has an innate ability to sense right and wrong. The Apostle Paul asserts that everyone, even the most unspiritual heathen, has a conscience.

> For when Gentiles who do not have the Law do instinctively the things of the Law, these, not having the Law, are a law to themselves, in that they show the work of the Law written in their hearts, their conscience bearing witness and their thoughts alternately accusing or else defending them. (Romans 2:14-15)

Everyone is born with a conscience. Christians must possess a conscience that's clear and clean. It's the essence of integrity. Paul says, "In view of this, I also do my best to maintain always a blameless conscience both before God and before men" (Acts 24:16).

J.I. Packer says,

> An educated sensitive conscience is God's monitor. It alerts us to the moral quality of what we do or plan to do, forbids lawlessness and irresponsibility and makes us feel guilt, shame and fear of the future retribution that it tells us we deserve when we have allowed ourselves to defy its restraints. Satan's strategy is to corrupt, desensitize and if possible kill our consciences. The relativism, materialism, narcissism, secularism and hedonism of today's western world help him mightily toward his goal. His task is made yet simpler by the way in which the world's moral weaknesses have been taken into the contemporary church.[4]

Having a clear conscience before men means that how we live reflects exactly what we believe (See also 1 Timothy 1:5, 2 Timothy 1:3, 1 Timothy 3:9, 2 Corinthians 1:12, 2 Corinthians 4:2, 1 Peter 3:16-17). To possess a clear conscience is to live a harmonious life. It's like the process of making bread. The yeast, flour, water, and salt cannot just be tossed haphazardly into a pan to be baked in an oven. The end result would not be an edible loaf. In order for bread to bake properly, all the ingredients must be mixed together in a specific order to make a whole. That's how we get bread.

Just as bread comes from a synthesis of ingredients, so the essence of integrity is a synthesis of behaviors. What we say matches what we do; how we live matches what we believe. The greatest gift parents can give their children is a life that's complete and true, for such a lifestyle provides a sense of security. Our children must be able to believe us and take us at our word. Children need to know that parents mean exactly what they say. We must have that good conscience before God and man. Others cannot know the inner workings of our souls, but God cares about what's going on inside us.

In the twenty-first century, various ministries emphasize small group gatherings. Often these are accountability groups where members hold one another answerable for certain behaviors or commitments. There's nothing wrong with having an accountability partner. However, the most important accountability partner for each of us should be our spouse. Such accountability promotes complete honesty within the relationship.

Sadly, a lot of husbands don't want their wives to know the truth about them. In accountability groups, it's easy for men to pull the wool over another man's eyes. Women, as well, might not be forthcoming with other women in their group. But I've come to realize that it's hard to fool my wife. In fact, my wife knows everything and that's one of the greatest parts of my marriage. My wife knows where I go, who I meet, and what I see. As a result, she is better equipped to pray for me, to support me, and to stand by me in every situation. We have a rule in our home: "no surprises." I hate surprises like anniversary or birthday parties.

In the same way, couples need to make the husband or wife their highest accountability partner. Transparency and intimacy in marriage depend upon how truthful and honest men and women are with each other. There is nothing wrong with having other accountability partners, but if someone outside the marriage knows more about our personal problems than our spouses, that's a problem because the husband or wife is hiding something.

We should not build walls of protection around ourselves to keep from being totally open and honest. Instead a husband should bare his soul to his wife, sharing as one flesh. I once heard of an incident in which a young woman, who was shopping at the mall one afternoon, ran into a gentleman who was an elder from her church. After a bit of polite conversation, the man said, "I was really sorry to hear that your husband has a problem with pornography and is struggling to overcome it." The wife stared at him in surprise. "My husband has problem with pornography?" The man replied, "Yes, didn't he tell you?" To learn about such a serious matter from another person can be devastating to a wife or husband.

A husband should not hide his problems from his wife. Such actions show a lack of integrity and honesty. How can a wife pray for her husband, stand by him and support him if she doesn't know his struggles? Learning about them during a friendly conversation with an acquaintance at the mall is hardly the way to build trust in the marriage.

When couples go to bed at night, they should not be hiding anything. He puts his head on the pillow. She puts her head on hers and now they are ready for all matters to be in the open. That's how it is with my wife and me. She knows everything about me. I know everything about her. That's a great marriage! Everything is on the table.

The Enemy of Integrity: Compromise

The enemy of integrity is compromise. When we compromise the truth, we violate a very basic biblical principal. Church elders and pastors are called to live "above reproach," blameless. If a leader is someone with a great personality, that's one thing. But if a leader is somebody who is to model a specific standard that we want people to follow, then that leader must be one who models integrity. Most churches choose their leaders on the basis of personality, success, prosperity, or even popularity. Most people choose their spouse on the same criteria.

However, the number one criteria must be trustworthiness. The Christian's actions should match what he says he believes. Warren Wiersbe said, "Many ministers today are governed by popularity and not by integrity, by statistics and not by Scripture."[5] A person who is above reproach deals with issues of sin and temptation. He has no secrets that will discredit his testimony.

Daniel was a key Old Testament figure who modeled integrity. He didn't compromise by eating the king's meat or by yielding to idolatry. No matter what it cost, while in service to the king, he stood firm. Daniel achieved a high position in the Babylonian government. Others tried to discredit him. "Then the commissioners and satraps began trying to find a ground of accusation against Daniel in regard to government affairs; but they could find no ground of accusation or evidence of corruption, inasmuch as he was faithful, and no negligence or corruption was to be found in him" (Daniel 6:4).

Daniel's enemies scrutinized even his private life to see if he was secretly corrupt, but they found nothing. He proved righteous—squeaky clean. Even when his enemies passed a law forbidding prayer, he never wavered. "Now when Daniel knew that the document was signed, he entered his house (now in his roof chamber he had windows open toward Jerusalem); and he continued kneeling on his knees three times a day, praying and giving thanks before his God, as he had been doing previously" (Daniel 6:10). Daniel was so committed to God that no matter what the king or government decreed, he would continue worshipping as he had done before. A man of integrity never compromises his worship.

When I was a boy, my parents said I could not play baseball on Sunday mornings. I couldn't rebel and just go on my own because I relied on them to drive me to the games. My folks taught that the Lord's Day should be reserved for worshipping God. If I played baseball on Sundays, I was going to have problems—not with my batting average or my coach, but with my God. My folks would say, "You don't want to have problems with your God." They trained me never to compromise my worship. When a father tells his boss that he'll work six and a half days a week, but he won't work on Sunday morning because that's time to worship God, his actions speak volumes to his children. They realize that Dad is not going to compromise.

Joseph also exemplifies a great man of God. When Potiphar's wife tried to seduce him, Joseph asked, "How then could I do this great evil and sin against God?" (Genesis 39:9b). He realized that yielding to temptation meant sinning against God. The man of integrity doesn't compromise because God is his priority. Throughout this ordeal, even when Joseph was wrongly imprisoned, Genesis 39 records that "God was with him." The man of integrity knows God is always with him. Joseph was a great man of God.

We need men like Daniel and Joseph both in the church and in the home. God has called men to lead. Abraham compromised when he lied two separate times, saying Sarah was not his wife. His weakness for falsehood was a trait also seen in the generations that followed him. When a man's character is corrupted, his testimony is always tainted and damaged. When a leader or a husband lacks integrity, his followers or family members lose confidence in his leadership.

We are all called to be truthful and forthright each spring when the April tax day arrives. It's our responsibility to be completely honest on our tax returns. I remember a time as a boy when I answered the door and greeted a man in a suit, briefcase in hand, who asked to see my parents. He announced to my mother that he was an IRS agent sent to audit their tax forms. The problem was that my parents charitable giving seemed much higher that it should ever be for a couple with their household income.

Now, my mom is very organized and keeps immaculate records. In fact, she kept a log of every gift I'd ever received for Christmas, birthday, or any other thing, how much it cost, where she bought it—unbelievable bookkeeping. So for the IRS agent, she brought out boxes of documents, pointing out receipts for several years. She told the man, "I want you to feel free to go through all of these. And if you have any questions, please ask."

After examining all the paper work, the agent said, "Mrs. Sparks, in all my years of working for the IRS, I've never met anyone as organized as you. And I have to tell you that you don't owe the government any money. In fact, the government owes you."

I tell that story because my parents modeled truthfulness and integrity in the home, and they made sure I learned to be truthful. When facing the IRS agent, my mom had a clear conscience. She was hiding nothing. Everything was above board. Lot, the Old Testament figure, was a man of great compromise and he lost everything—his home, his testimony, his family. He compromised to meet his own needs and failed miserably.

The Emblem of Integrity: Confession

The emblem of integrity is confession. Some people admit that they haven't been honest. They say, "I am a liar and a hypocrite." The ability to confess our sins, to be forthright about what we really are becomes an emblem of integrity.

> Vindicate me, O Lord, for I have walked in my
>   integrity,
> And I have trusted in the Lord without wavering.
> Examine me, O Lord, and try me;
> Test my mind and my heart. (Psalm 26:1-2)

"Without wavering" is the Hebrew phrase that means "unable to slip, to slide, to shake or to totter." Such trust makes us stable and strong.

In this Psalm, David was saying that no matter the obstacles, he was determined to trust the Lord. He would not slip or slide under the load. Instead, he would ask God to judge him and to vindicate him. He said essentially, "God, give me internal scrutiny and intensive surgery. Examine my life and turn it inside out. Then take Your Word and give me surgery." The phrase "try me" speaks of the act of refining gold or silver. Confession is the refining emblem of integrity.

When Solomon became king, God told him, "As for you, if you will walk before Me as your father David walked, in integrity of heart and uprightness, doing according to all that I have commanded you and will keep My statute and My ordinances, then I will establish the throne of your kingdom over Israel forever" (1 Kings 9:4-5a). David was called a man of integrity because he was a man who confessed his sin: an affair with Bathsheba, the murder of her husband and the cover-up lies. The emblem of integrity is confession. Although David fumbled, faltered, and failed, in his heart, he desired fellowship with his God; therefore he confessed his sins.

So no matter what has happened in our pasts, we can confess all our failings before God. We can ask God to examine, prove, and forgive us. We can pray, "God, take whatever is wicked in me and get rid of it because I want to live Your kind of life." That's what God wants for us.

The End of Integrity: Christian Character

The result of character building goes far beyond anything we could ever imagine. Living with integrity makes a man or woman solid, strong, brave and immoveable. "He who walks with integrity, and works righteousness, and speaks truth in his heart.... He who does these things will never be shaken" (Psalm 15:2, 5b). In Proverbs 11:3, Solomon says, "The integrity of the upright will guide them, but the crookedness of the treacherous will destroy them." And in Proverbs 19:1, we are told, "Better is a poor man who walks in his integrity than he who is perverse in speech and is a fool." Finally, the Psalmist reminds us, "No good thing does [the Lord] withhold from those who walk uprightly" (Psalm 84:11b).

Dear Lord, Purify us. Cleanse us. Try us. Test our minds. Test our hearts. God, do whatever You want to do. But God, vindicate us. Look at our lives. Examine us. See if there be any wicked way in us, and if there is, lead us in the way of everlasting. Amen.

11

God's Counsel for Couples: Meeting Needs

When a man and woman marry, they have a lifetime to get to know each other and gain a better of understanding of each other's strengths and needs. Just as Christians learn more about the nature of God, the more they live for Him, husbands and wives can develop a deeper understanding of their mates with each wedding anniversary. "Do nothing from selfishness or empty conceit, but with humility of mind regard one another as more important than yourselves" (Philippians 2:3).

God has designed a husband to meet the needs of his wife. Likewise, a wife must understand her husband so that she might meet his needs. God has designed the man to be what the wife is not, and the woman to be what the husband is not. Therefore when the two come together, they complete each other. However, problems arise when men and women put their own needs first. A man who acts selfishly is unwilling to sacrifice for his wife. Unmet needs can strain a relationship and eventually push the couple apart.

During the temptation of Christ as described in Matthew 4, Satan approached Christ after He was baptized. He'd been in the wilderness for forty days and nights. That's when the tempter whispered to Him, "If You are the Son of God, command that these stones become bread" (4:3). Here Satan appealed to the physical appetite of the Lord Jesus. Essentially, he was saying, "Son of Man, you can meet your own needs." However, Christ said, "It is written, 'Man shall not live on bread alone, but on every word that proceeds out of the mouth of God'" (4:4). When Christ was tempted, not only did He give an example to follow on handling temptation, but He demonstrated that personal needs are not primary. Instead, God's will is most important for the Christian.

Christ could easily have produced bread, yet He didn't because the will of His Father was more important than His own wishes. When we make serving God more important than pursuing our desires, we can glorify Him. In Satan's last temptation of Christ, he took Jesus atop a mountain and showed Him the glorious kingdoms below. "All these things I will give You, if You fall down and worship me," Satan said (4:9). However, Jesus commanded him, "Go, Satan! For it is written, 'You shall worship the Lord your God, and serve Him only'" (4:10).

In a similar way, Satan appeals to each one's egocentric nature and tempts husbands and wives to put their own wants and needs first. Such self-centered attitudes and motivations keep individuals sidetracked and preoccupied. The marital intimacy a couple shares is directly correlated with their level of commitment to Jesus Christ and obedience to biblical concepts. If the glory of God is the priority, then husbands and wives are willing to meet the needs of the spouses.

Social Needs

Social needs are not related to the desire individuals have to party or go out for a good time. Rather, these needs are the ones met through the nurturing relationships that enrich the personal lives of couples. The social aspect of Christian married couples can be fulfilled within the confines of the body of Christ (the church congregation):

> And all those who had believed were together and had all things in common; and they began selling their property and possessions and were sharing them with all, as anyone might have need. Day by day continuing with one mind in the temple, and breaking

bread from house to house, they were taking their meals together with gladness and sincerity of heart, praising God and having favor with all the people. (Acts 2:44-47)

In the early days of the church, the Christians were committed as a corporate body. Together, they supported the group when each one used his or her strengths and gifts to encourage others. In a similar way, as a husband and wife serve together in ministry, they also meet the social needs of others.

Marital intimacy begins with a worshipful heart:

> One thing I have asked from the Lord, that I shall seek:
> That I may dwell in the house of the Lord all the days of my life,
> To behold the beauty of the Lord
> And to meditate in His temple. (Psalm 27:4)

That's the verse my dad wrote in my very first Bible on March 19, the day I became a Christian. His prayer for me was that the church would be the place where I would long to "dwell." His prayer was answered. Christian couples should understand that the church family represents a faithful community that provides nurturing and spiritual encouragement to meet the social needs of both husbands and wives.

In Paul's letters, he often reminds his readers of a truth, saying, "Brethren, I don't want you to be ignorant or uninformed." He uses the phrase several times (see 1 Thessalonians 4:13, 1 Corinthians 10:1-2, 2 Corinthians 1:8). In 1 Corinthians 12:1, Paul says that he does not want us to be ignorant about spiritual gifts. As couples nurture and develop their spiritual gifts within the church and ministry, the Christian community is edified. People in the church need to see husbands and wives who love one another, doing ministry and modeling good behavior and attitudes at the same time. Children need to see that their Sunday school teachers have good marriages that honor the Lord Jesus Christ. Thus, the church can provide a nurturing environment that demonstrates how Christians ought to live and relate to one another.

Emotional Needs

Every one has emotional needs. Since women's emotional needs cannot be ignored, Peter offers men instruction. "You husbands in the same way, live with your wives in an understanding way" (1 Peter 3:7). Thus, a husband should know every part of his wife's heart and be sensitive to her needs. He should know what makes her tick, what makes her angry, what makes her happy, and what keeps her calm. When a man knows his wife in "an understanding way," it means he can perceive her innermost make-up and discern her deep-seeded fears. Then he can help her work through difficulties.

When Peter addresses women's roles, he stresses their inner development.

> Do not let your adornment be merely outward... rather let it be the hidden person of the heart, with the incorruptible beauty of a gentle and quiet spirit, which is very precious in the sight of God. For in this manner, in former times, the holy women who trusted in God also adorned themselves, being submissive to their own husbands. (1 Peter 3:3-5 NKJV)

The lovers' discourse in Song of Solomon demonstrates how couples can nurture each other: "How beautiful you are, my darling" (4:1). The word "beautiful" is the same Hebrew word used to describe the city of Haifa on the Mediterranean Sea in Israel. It's a beautiful port city on the coast. The term literally means "to shine." So Solomon is telling his bride, "You shine with beauty." The passage shows that he loved everything about her.

Some husbands do not make the effort to compliment their wives. If a man never praises the way his wife cooks or dresses or does her hair and make-up, she may decide that he really doesn't notice or care. It's important for a man to observe and praise his wife. That's one more way to meet her emotional needs.

In the same way, a wife should be "lovesick" for her husband:

> I adjure you, O daughters of Jerusalem,
> If you find my beloved,
> As to what you will tell him:
> For I am lovesick. (Song of Solomon 5:8)

She goes on to praise his looks:

> His appearance is like Lebanon,
> Choice as the cedars.
> His mouth is full of sweetness.
> And he is wholly desirable.
> This is my beloved and this is my friend,
> O daughters of Jerusalem.
> (Song of Solomon 5:15b-16)

This lover describes her husband as one magnificent man. Rather than speaking negatively about a husband, a wife should build her man up, accentuating his great qualities. The Song of Solomon stresses the physical relationship of the lovers. However, it also implies that they were emotionally tied to one another and concerned for one another.

Verbal Needs

The words couples use are important. "Death and life are in the power of the tongue" (Proverbs 18:21 KJV). We can also use words to destroy—to wound a spouse and cause them discouragement or pain. The Bible has much to say about our conversation. "Let no unwholesome word proceed from your mouth, but only such a word as is good for edification according to the need of the moment, so that it will give grace to those who hear" (Ephesians 4:29).

To deepen marital intimacy, couples must use words that demonstrate grace and wholesomeness. Statements should build up others, through encouragement, blessings, and praise rather than criticism, anger and negativity. There are many verses about speech in the book of Proverbs:

> The one who guards his mouth preserves his life;
> The one who opens wide his lips come to ruin.
> (Proverbs 13:3)
>
> A gentle answer turns away wrath,
> But a harsh word stirs up anger....
> A soothing tongue is a tree of life,
> But perversion in it crushes the spirit. (Proverbs 15:1, 4)

Above all, husbands and wives must be open and honest, kind and considerate.

Wayne Mack, in his book *Strengthening Your Marriage*,[1] gives six guidelines to help communication. He suggests that a person ask these six questions before they ever open their mouths to speak.

1. Is what I'm going to say true? Do I have all the facts?
2. Is what I'm going to say profitable, or is it going to hurt the one I am going to speak to? Will it be constructive or destructive?
3. Is this the proper time for me to say it, or would it be better for me to wait?
4. Is my attitude right?
5. Are the words that I will use the best possible way of saying it?
6. Have I prayed about this matter and am I trusting God to help me?

(Adapted from Mack)

Those six guidelines will help conversation. In my own case, I realize that I can use just one word to devastate my wife or lift her up as the most honored person in my life. When I fail, I have to ask forgiveness for the words I've used to harm or hurt her. Then I work to control and modify my speech in the future.

Intellectual Needs

Husbands and wives establish intimacy when they grow in wisdom.

> The words of wise men are like goads, and masters of these collections are like well-driven nails; they are given by one Shepherd. But beyond this, my son, be warned: the writing of many books is endless, and excessive devotion to books is wearying to the body. The conclusion, when all has been heard, is: fear God and keep His commandments, because this applies to every person. For God will bring every act to judgment, everything which is hidden, whether it is good or evil. (Ecclesiastes 12:11-14)

Solomon knew that writing many books is wearisome. So cultivating the intellect in marital relationships is not about how much a person knows (gaining knowledge from books) but about how wise the person is. One aspect of achieving intellectual intimacy in marriage is learning what it means to depart from evil. "'Behold, the fear of the Lord, that is wisdom; And to depart from evil is understanding'" (Job 28:28). This growth as a couple requires that a couple develop understanding and knowledge of God. One man said it this way:

> Since 1955, knowledge has doubled every 5 years. Libraries groan with the weight of new books. In fact, our generation possesses more data about the universe and human personality than all the previous generations put together. High School graduates today have been exposed to more information about the world than Plato, Aristotle, Spinoza or Benjamin Franklin. In terms of facts alone, neither Moses nor Paul could pass a college entrance exam today.
>
> Yet by everyone's standards, even with all our knowledge, society today is peopled with a bumper crop of brilliant failures. Men and women educated

to earn a living, often don't know anything about handling life itself. Alumni from noted universities have massive information about a narrow slice of life but couldn't make it out of the first grade when it comes to living successfully with family and friends. Knowledge is not enough to meet life's problems. We need wisdom, the ability to handle life with skill.[2]

Proverbs helps us understand how to handle life's problems with skill. It teaches about marriage, child rearing, anger, wisdom, knowledge, and instruction. God's directives supply guidance to change our behavior and attitudes, so that we can have profitable relationships in marriage.

Physical Needs

The physical needs of a couple comprise more than sexual aspects. The Song of Solomon contains a brief summary of the wedding night of Solomon and his bride. It's described from the wife's point of view. The passage offers insight into the physical facets of a relationship and how the wife gains security through the husband's actions.

> He has brought me to his banquet hall,
> And his banner over me is love.
> Sustain me with raisin cakes,
> Refresh me with apples,
> Because I am lovesick.
> Let his left hand be under my head
> And his right hand embrace me. (Song of Solomon 2:4-6)

These verses reveal how Solomon would interact with his wife physically. She says that her lover has brought her to his banquet hall. Literally, it's "the house of wine," speaking of a joyful celebration. In addition, it's a common reference to a bridal chamber. Thus, she says that her man has taken her to a house of celebration, his bridal chamber. It's a picture of victory and triumph.

This woman finds herself under the banner of his protection. She has security because of his love. She feels the safety of this man's presence and she says, "His right hand embraces me." That's important, because the word "embrace" is from the Hebrew word which means "to fondle" or "to stimulate sexually." Face-to-face, Solomon is communicating with his wife, as he talks to her and as he touches her. They have not engaged in any sexual union, but he is communicating physically with his wife, which communicates love and security to her.

The description implies that the man cares about his wife's needs and feelings. He is more concerned about how she is responding to the intimate situation than he is about how he feels. Most men never get to that point—of thinking about how their wives feel. However, Solomon understood the importance of putting the woman first. He helped her understand his love.

She speaks of raisins and apples. They are erotic symbols. Because of their sweetness, they suggest that she can only be rescued from her passions by the embraces and the kisses of her lover. She is so enthralled with him that he has enraptured her with his love. She says that she has been sustained and refreshed.

If my wife tells me, "I feel so invigorated in your presence. I feel so safe when I'm with you," such comments inspire me for months and make me feel completely gratified in our relationship. Since the man is the leader in the home, if he leads properly, she'll respond properly. If my wife is having a problem with my leadership, it's probably my fault because I'm doing something wrong. Perhaps I'm not sensitive to her needs or not focused enough on her struggles. I must determine where I am sidetracked if I'm not treating her as a prized possession. God has designed the man to lead and the woman to respond to that leadership.

Sexual Needs

The marriage bed is a sacred place. "Marriage is to be held in honor among all, and the marriage bed is to be undefiled; for fornicators and adulterers God will judge" (Hebrews 13:4). Also Paul explained that in a marriage relationship, the wife's body is no longer her own (1 Corinthians 7:4). In fact, partners are not to deprive one another sexually unless it is for a short time and only for prayer. This commitment ensures that Satan will not get an in-road into a couple's relationship and spark a spirit of bitterness or resentment (1 Corinthians 7:5).

When Paul says that the marriage bed is undefiled, he means that sexual relationships are pure in the confines of marriage. God designed sexual desire. God intends that a man's or woman's physical needs be met in the confines of a marital relationship only. When husbands and wives come together to experience sexual intimacy, they are to focus on what each can give and not what each can get. When couples behave unselfishly, they will reap rewards in a mutually satisfying sexual relationship.

Spiritual Needs

A husband must want his wife to be pure, holy, and unblemished.

> Husbands, love your wives, just as Christ also loved the church and gave Himself up for her, so that He might sanctify her, having cleansed her by the washing of water with the word, that He might present to Himself the church and all her glory, having no spot or wrinkle or any such thing; but that she would be holy and blameless. (Ephesians 5:25-27)

If we love someone, their purity should be our goal. The husband must assume his role as the protector, as the provider, and as the one who puts his wife under a banner of love. He must nurture his wife's holiness, virtue, and righteousness. The man should not put his wife in a compromising situation or induce an argument with her. Furthermore, he should never expose her to anything that would cause her to doubt her faith in God.

It is the wife's responsibility to instill a sanctifying influence in her home. "In the same way, you wives, be submissive to your own husbands so that even if any of them are disobedient to the word, they may be won without a word by the behavior of their wives, as they observe your chaste and respectful behavior" (1 Peter 3:1-2).

A woman's behavior must be chaste, pure, and faithful. Any thought or word or suggestion of impurity can destroy a relationship. "Just as Sarah obeyed Abraham, calling him lord, and you have become her children if you do what is right without being frightened by any fear" (1 Peter 3:6). Thus the godly woman, like the Old Testament wife Sarah, has such respect for God, such awareness of her accountability to God, that she lives in obedience to biblical standards.

So the man in the relationship is concerned about the needs of his wife. Further, the woman lives a chaste life because she understands her accountability to God; she lives in the light of Him as her judge. That's intimacy in the marriage. When couples have a superficial relationship, they do not develop a deep understanding of each other. However, if they choose to follow God's direction, then God can make a couple's relationship so unique that others will observe it, take note, and begin to ask, "How can we have a love relationship like yours that honors God and each person in the marriage?"

Help us Lord, in our marriages. Help men stand strong and take the initiative lead. Help the women understand what it means to submit to that leadership and trust You for the outcome. Amen.

12

God's Counsel for Couples: Sacrifice

Do we want to be like Jesus Christ? In answer to the question, many of us would say, "Yes, I want a successful relationship. I want to be like Christ." Success in marriage requires that individuals become selfless. They must expend themselves in self-sacrificing ministry. "Therefore I urge you, brethren, by the mercies of God, to present your bodies a living and holy sacrifice, acceptable to God, which is your spiritual service of worship" (Romans 12:1).

Christ reminded His disciples about His purpose: "For even the Son of Man did not come to be served, but to serve, and to give His life a ransom for many" (Mark 10:45). Christ was explaining the crux of His ministry. He came to earth to do for us what we could not do for ourselves in order that we might be like Him. We must think of marriage in the same way. Our objective is to do for our spouses those acts they cannot do and to expend ourselves in ministry by giving ourselves away by helping and loving them.

The greatest achievement of Christ came not in the life He lived but in the life that He gave away. For the living of His life never saved anybody. His miracles, though a supreme demonstration of His power, were not the answer. In giving His life away, He did for you and me something beyond comprehension. He modeled what it means to live a sacrificial life. "Have this attitude in yourselves which was also in Christ Jesus, who, although He existed in the form of God, did not regard equality with God a thing to be grasped, but emptied Himself, taking the form of a bondservant" (Philippians 2:5-7a). He emptied Himself. It's the great *kenosis*, the laying aside of His divine attributes to become a man for us: "Being found in appearance as a man, He humbled Himself by becoming obedient to the point of death, even death on a cross" (Philippians 2:8). He's the supreme example of humility. The King of Kings is one who needs to be served not to serve us. Yet our Lord gave His life for the service of man.

The greatest way to demonstrate love to our spouses is to give our lives away. "Greater love has no one than this, that one lay down his life for his friends" (John 15:13). The greatest sacrifice is death, yet in contrast, most of us are not willing to give up a paycheck, a newspaper, or even an afternoon nap for a spouse. Yet Jesus says, "I came to give My life away."

In a world that emphasizes self-preservation and promotion, Christ's admonition runs counter to everything we want to believe or do. However, Christ says that if we abide in Him, then we ought to walk even as He walked (1 John 2:6). As abiders in and followers of Christ, it should be our ambition to walk as Jesus walked. The question is, *what are we giving away so that He might be honored and glorified?*

A great marriage centers on giving one's life away for the spouse. That commitment will model much for children who see parents selflessly give up time, hobbies, monies, even pet peeves to minister to family members. But one might say, "If I do that, won't I just become a door mat? Won't my spouse just walk all over me?" Yes, probably, like they walked all over Christ. But if we're not into self-preservation, if we're into giving our life away instead, there's much we can learn. There are four parts to understanding this process of sacrifice: the overriding principle, the overbearing problem, the overlapping precept, and the overwhelming prospect.

The Overriding Principle

Acts 20 offers Paul's parting words to the Ephesian elders, after he served with them for three years. In Acts 20:35 Paul quotes Christ, "In everything I showed you that by working hard in this manner you must help the weak and remember the words of the Lord Jesus, that He Himself said, 'It is more blessed to give than to receive.'" Thus, the blessed life does not center on how much we get but on how much we give. The Lord Jesus Christ modeled that concept because He came to give His life away.

The reward for this kind of ministry is spelled out in the Acts 20:36-38a, "When he had said these things, he knelt down and prayed with them all. And they began to weep aloud and embraced Paul, and repeatedly kissed him, grieving especially over the word which he had spoken, that they would not see his face again." These people loved and admired Paul. They grieved deeply because he gave his life away.

There are many marriages where the wife would not grieve if her husband left. In fact, she might call out, "Don't let the door hit you on the way out." There is no love lost because the husband never gave himself away for his wife nor did she for him.

John Henry Jowett said, "The ministry that costs nothing accomplishes nothing."[1] We could substitute the word "marriage" for ministry, for the marriage that costs nothing accomplishes nothing. In ministry, Paul essentially gave his life to the people of God, by the Spirit of God, according to the Word of God, for the purposes of God. He recognized a greater purpose in life than serving himself. There's more to life than self-preservation and self-fulfillment. We must give our lives away for the sake of our spouses.

If we husbands or wives are not willing to give 100 percent, the marriage relationship is not going to work. A fifty-fifty relationship will not succeed. However, if we give 100 percent of ourselves to our spouses, we're going to have great marriages even if our spouses give nothing in return because the Lord said that it's more blessed to give than to receive.

God tells the truth. Christ exemplified that truth when He gave His life away. In the same way, God expects us to give. Love is an action verb, a *giving* word. For God *so loved the world* that He gave His dearest possession even to His enemies (John 3:16). Such sacrifice means expending our efforts in selfless ministry as Jesus did. He gave Himself away.

There is a story in Mark where Christ had ministered all day. Then when He returned home at night, people still crowded into His house. In His humanity, He must have been exhausted. Yet the Bible says that He healed all who came to Him (see Mark 1:29-34). He kept giving Himself away, even when He received rejection and ridicule. As time went on, fewer people followed Him. When He was feeding thousands of people and performing miracles, people flocked to Him. However, when He explained what it meant to follow Him, many devotees dropped away. After Jesus' crucifixion, only 120 nondescript disciples gathered in the upper room to pray (see Acts 1). Sadly, it seemed that the more Christ gave, the less the people wanted to follow Him.

Similarly in marriage, as a wife gives sacrificially to her husband, he may reject her love. When rejection occurs, the wife must not stop giving because there's no response. We must not give just to get a positive response. It's like saying, "I gave you flowers so that you would like me." Or "I took you to dinner, so we could have sexual intimacy this evening but you rejected me therefore I am done giving." The bottom line is that we husbands and wives must give ourselves away regardless of the result because it's more blessed to give than to receive. It's sacrificial—that concept is of utmost importance.

My wife understands well the concept of sacrifice. For example, when our children were young, getting everyone prepared for church each Sunday morning proved difficult. I would rise early to get to the church by 5:00 a.m. Meanwhile my wife remained at home getting all our kids ready by herself: feeding them, bathing them, combing their hair, and getting them out the door. After years of doing it all alone, she would sometimes get discouraged. Yet she knew I needed to be at the church during those hours to be fully prepared for the demands of Sunday services—to pray, meditate, and memorize. Willingly she sacrificed so that I could fulfill my responsibilities.

My wife realized that she had to give herself away in order for the ministry to take place at the church and for ministry to happen in the lives of our children. Her actions and sacrificial attitude ministered to me. She made it possible for me to do what was required every Sunday when I faced the congregation. Her willing sacrifice increased my love and respect for her.

In marriage, we must give our lives away because it's more blessed to give than to receive. Are we willing to give something up for the sake of our spouses? The overriding principle is just keep giving.

The Overbearing Problem

In marriage relationships, we crave affirmation and reciprocation. We demand "give and take" in a marriage. Consequently, if we keep giving and giving without any getting, we're tempted to find someone else who will give back to us. That's why people have affairs, commit adultery, and walk out on their spouses.

Our natural tendency is to look out for ourselves, not to look out for someone else. However, Paul says that love "does not seek its own" (1 Corinthians 13:5). True love, biblical love, the *agapaō* kind of love is what believers need to express. If I love somebody the way Christ loved the church, if I love my spouse the way God has designed me to love her, then I'm never going to seek my own desires. Instead, I'm going to give myself away. That's what true love does. It gives itself away.

True love is sacrificial, volitional, unconditional, beneficial, emotional, and ultimately, it's eternal. The Phillips translation of 1 Corinthians 13:5 says, "Love is never selfish." Yet in a me-centered society, we believe that individual rights and demands must be met. Therefore, we expect our spouses to meet our needs.

During the last night of Jesus' ministry, His disciples selfishly argued about who would be greatest in the kingdom. Amidst that argument, Christ never said a word. Instead Jesus demonstrated this principle.

> Jesus...got up from supper, and laid aside His garments; and taking a towel, He girded Himself. Then He poured water into the basin, and began to wash the disciples' feet and to wipe them with the towel with which He was girded. So He came to Simon Peter. He said to Him, "Lord, do You wash my feet?"

> Jesus answered and said to him, "What I do you do not realize now, but you shall understand hereafter." (John 13:3-7)

Jesus washed the disciples' feet—even Judas' feet—an amazing act. He said, "Truly, truly, I say to you, a slave is not greater than his master, nor is one who is sent greater than the one who sent him. If you know these things, you are blessed if you do them" (John 13:16-17). In this scene, Christ's illustration is not that we should wash other people's feet. Rather the act exemplifies a very clear principle: When adversity is present, humility is primary.

Christ was facing adversity. He knew the soldiers were coming to take Him away to be crucified. Yet in this turmoil, Jesus did not say, "Guys we've got to pray. I'm going to be executed tomorrow. Don't you care?" Instead, He girded himself with a slave apron and washed their feet. Then He said that someday Peter would come to understand the principle because the Savior left an example to follow (see John 13:9-20).

Sometime later, Peter wrote of this concept himself. "You younger men, likewise, be subject to your elders; and all of you, clothe yourselves with humility toward one another, for God is opposed to the proud, but gives grace to the humble" (1 Peter 5:5). The phrase "clothe yourself" means to tie in a knot. It refers to the slave's apron. Peter reiterated Christ's message described in John 13. His message was: Don the slave's apron and serve, for God is opposed to the prideful, but He gives grace to the humble.

When relationships are bad, when situations are at their worst, we must serve. We must think about others because it's more blessed to give than it ever is to receive. "Now we who are strong ought to bear the weaknesses of those without strength and not just please ourselves. Each of us is to please his neighbor for his good, to his edification. For even Christ did not please Himself" (Romans 15:1-3a).

To be like Christ, we must give ourselves away. In the marriage context, we please our wives or husbands first. We must ask ourselves, *"What one thing can I do today to please my wife or my husband?"* While the overriding principle is giving, the overbearing problem is getting. The more we give, the better our marriage will be.

The Overlapping Precept

Here's the precept that overlaps everything: "Pursue love" (1 Corinthians 14:1). Instead of standing by waiting for something to happen, we must actually *do* something. Love is an action verb, so we must take the initiative. For God so loved, He gave. God did not remain in heaven calling us to Him. Instead, He came to us. In a similar way, we must pursue love. Don't keep a record of wrong doings because love keeps no record of wrongs (1 Corinthians 13:5). True love is patient, kind, and gentle.

However, we often respond, "Oh, I can't." Yet what we really mean is, "I don't want to." The solution to this dilemma is found in Romans 5:5, "Hope does not disappoint, because the love of God has been poured out within our hearts through the Holy Spirit who was given to us." We have the power to love even in difficulty because God's Spirit is in us making us partakers of the divine nature (2 Peter 1:4). The love of God has been poured out in our hearts. "God has not given us a spirit of timidity, but of power and love and discipline" (2 Timothy 1:7). God has equipped us with the power to love and the power to go. So we can never say, "I can't do that." Instead, we must pursue love.

Jesus Christ is the model. He is the one we pattern our lives after—not our parents, our grandparents, or our best friends. In Colossians 3:14 Paul says, "Beyond all these things put on love, which is the perfect bond of unity." When we married, my wife gave me a gold chain and said, "This chain is a reminder of my love for you because 'love is the golden chain of all the virtues'" (Colossians 3:14, Phillips). I wear that chain continually to remind myself of my wife's love. Pursue love, unconditional kind. That's the cure for a troubled relationship.

We must remind ourselves each day, "Let all that you do be done in love" (1 Corinthians 16:14). Let all we do be characterized by giving our lives away. We can show it in the way we do the laundry, comb the children's hair, or complete household tasks. Giving selflessly makes a great marriage. Christianity is about taking the initiative in every situation. The Great Commission says to go into all the world and make disciples (see Matthew 28:19). It doesn't say to wait for the world to come to us to make disciples.

I understand the challenge of such selflessness. I act in the carnal ways myself. I want my wife to be the one to come through for me. I want my children to affirm me. I need checks and balances in my own life, and I must examine my behavior and attitudes according to the Scriptures. I realize that the less I look at me and the more I look at my wife or my children, the more I realize my responsibility to obey God. I've always found it true that whenever God prompts me to do something and I do it, even though I don't want to, He always blesses my life.

The Overwhelming Prospect

We can't give in order to gain but if we give in obedience to God, we will gain. That's the end product. "Above all, keep fervent in your love for one another, because love covers a multitude of sins (1 Peter 4:8). The word "fervent" means the stretching forth of a hand and an arm forward as far as it goes, reaching as far as one can. We must develop that kind of love for a spouse: to extend or expend oneself, to give our all.

John recounts Christ's triumphal entry into Jerusalem. Everyone wanted to see this King, who rode into Jerusalem. However, Jesus resisted their attentions and explained an important spiritual concept to His disciples in John 12:23-26:

> "And Jesus answered them, saying, 'The hour has come for the Son of Man to be glorified. Truly, truly, I say to you, unless a grain of wheat falls into the earth and dies, it remains by itself alone; but if it dies, it bears much fruit. He who loves his life loses it, and he who hates his life in this world will keep it to life eternal. If anyone serves Me, he must follow Me; and where I am, there My servant will be also; if anyone serves Me, the Father will honor him.'"

In this passage, Christ explains what Christianity is all about. Christ gave His life away for the salvation of a multitude. Loving only ourselves pays no dividends but serving and giving our lives away pays eternal dividends. Men want to be kings in their homes; however, it's not the coronation but the crucifixion that makes a man a king. That's what Jesus was saying.

Matthew 19:16-30 records Christ's encounter with the rich young ruler. Sadly, the man proved unwilling to give his wealth away. It was all about getting for him, not giving. And Christ says, "If you truly love Me, then sell all that you have" (see Matthew 19:21). The rich man wasn't about to sacrifice what he owned. Then Peter asked Jesus, "Behold, we have left everything and followed You; what then will there be for us?" (Matthew 19:27). Peter asserts in this conversation that he's not like the rich man. He and the other disciples *have* given their lives to Christ, so Peter is interested in the rewards for his sacrifice. He was not disappointed, for Jesus replied:

> "Truly I say to you, that you who have followed Me, in the regeneration when the Son of Man will sit on His glorious throne, you also shall sit upon twelve thrones, judging the twelve tribes of Israel. And everyone who has left houses or brothers or sisters or father or mother or children or farms for My name's sake, will receive many times as much, and will inherit eternal life." (Matthew 19:28-29)

In this text, Christ affirms that there is a reward for those who commit to Him. He honors those who follow Him and those who give will always gain more than what they gave. "Give, and it will be given to you. They will pour into your lap a good measure—pressed down, shaken together, and running over. For by your standard of measure it will be measured to you in return" (Luke 6:38). If we give our lives away, the byproduct is so great we'll never be able to comprehend it because God says, "He who honors Me, I will honor."

If a husband gives his life away, God promises, "I will give in return." If a wife gives her life away, God promises, "I will give in

My time and in My way." However, the best news is that we can be assured that we will receive beyond anything we could ever imagine from God (see Ephesians 3:20). His promises are true. He who loses his life for Christ's sake will find it.

Lord, help us to be givers. Train us in the ways of unselfishness and generosity. Help us to take You at Your Word. You will reward those who diligently seek You. Make us seekers and servers to our mates. Train us to be willing servants of Yours.

13

God's Counsel for Couples: Forgiveness

Forgiveness is an essential ingredient in any successful relationship. So it comes as no surprise that the act of forgiveness is a crucial component in making a happy marriage. Chuck Swindoll once said, "Forgiveness is not an elective in the curriculum of servanthood. It is a required course, and the exams are always tough to pass."[1] Jesus explained to His disciples that forgiveness is a process. "Be on your guard! If your brother sins, rebuke him; and if he repents, forgive him. And if he sins against you seven times a day, and returns to you seven times, saying, 'I repent,' forgive him" (Luke 17:3-4).

Jesus' instruction about forgiveness puzzled His disciples. I can well understand their confusion. If I consider the idea that I must forgive someone seven times in the same day, it poses quite a challenge. For every day consists of twenty-four hours, with an average of sixteen hours of awake time. That would mean that every two hours and fifteen minutes during those sixteen hours, if someone offended me, I'd rebuke him. He'd repent and I'd forgive him. If this process continued seven times, the experience would be exhausting. Yet Christ says that I am to continually forgive others.

In their bewilderment, the disciples said to the Lord, "Increase our faith!"(Luke 17:5 NIV). Christ's followers knew that they would need more faith to follow such a command. Christ responded, "If you had faith like a mustard seed, you would say to this mulberry tree, 'Be uprooted and be planted in the sea'; and it would obey you" (Luke 17:6). Essentially, Christ is telling the disciples that they don't need any more faith because forgiveness is not about faith.

Jesus goes on to explain that a slave does not demand service from his master. For the servant knows his role and is expected to work hard and long to complete his assigned tasks. Further, the master is not expected even to thank the slave for doing the work the slave was commanded to do (Luke 17:9). Then comes Christ's application: "So you too, when you do all the things which are commanded you, say, 'We are unworthy slaves; we have done *only* that which we ought to have done'" (Luke 17:10). Christ drives the application home to His men. They are slaves. He is their Master. When He commands, they should obey. In essence, Christ is saying, "Forgiving your brother has nothing to do with faith. It has everything to do with obedience to Me. If I tell you to forgive your brother seven times a day if he comes to you and repents, you are to do it without question."

That's the moral of the story described in Luke 17. That concept sets the groundwork for understanding what it means to forgive one another in genuine humility. When it comes to marriage, however, there are certain offenses that we're not willing to forgive. We hold grudges. We're unwilling to overlook the slights and insults we endure. Yet Christ very succinctly says that forgiving a brother has nothing to do with more faith, for we have all the faith we need. What forgiveness requires is a spirit willing to obey God because He is our master, and we are His servants. There are seven principles that can illustrate the importance of forgiveness in marriage.

Forgiveness Is a Pattern to Follow

Forgiveness is a pattern that we are commanded to follow. "Let all bitterness and wrath and anger and clamor and slander be put away from you, along with all malice. Be kind to one another, tenderhearted, forgiving each other, just as God in Christ also has forgiven you" (Ephesians 4:31-32). It's God's forgiveness that makes it possible for us to forgive our spouses and others in our lives. Because of what God has done, we are able to forgive our brother of his sin.

The question is, *Do we understand the forgiveness of God?* God says that He is compassionate, slow to anger, and forgiving (Exodus 34:6-7, Nehemiah 9:17). Daniel says that forgiveness belongs to God (9:9), and the Psalmist declares that our God is the one who pardons all our iniquities.

> He has not dealt with us according to our sins,
> Nor rewarded us according to our iniquities.
> For as high as the heavens are above the earth,
> So great is His loving kindness toward those who
>   fear Him.
> As far as the east if from the west,
> So far has He removed our transgressions from us."
> (Psalm 103:10-12)

We are to forgive as God in Christ Jesus has forgiven us. D. Martyn Lloyd-Jones said, "Whenever I see myself before God and realize something of what my blessed Lord has done for me at Calvary, I am ready to forgive anybody anything. I cannot withhold it. I do not even want to withhold it."[2] Our God longs to forgive us of all our sins. "If we confess our sins, He is faithful and righteous to forgive us our sins and to cleanse us from all unrighteousness" (1 John 1:9). We must not grieve the Holy Spirit through our bitterness and resistance to forgive others (Ephesians 4:30). Instead, we must use God's Spirit to enable us to be kind, tenderhearted, compassionate, and forgiving just as God for Christ's sake forgives us (Ephesians 4:31-32).

D. Martyn Lloyd-Jones goes on to say that a person's willingness to forgive is an indication of his spiritual condition:

> If you want to know if your sins are forgiven, here is my test. Are you forgiving others? Are you ready to forgive others who have harmed you and sinned against you? Or look at it another way: Does this argument of the Apostle appeal to you? As I read out these words, "Be ye kind to one another, tenderhearted, forgiving one another, even as God for

Christ's sake has forgiven you," are you softened in your feelings? Do you feel melted? Are you ready to forgive at this moment? If you are, I do not hesitate to say that you are a Christian, but if bitterness is still rankling down there, and if you are saying in spite of these glorious words, "But after all, I did nothing and I don't deserve such treatment," you had better go back and examine your foundation. I find it very difficult to see how such a person can be a Christian at all.[3]

Thus Lloyd-Jones gives a short test for Christianity. Are we willing to forgive our brothers' transgressions? It's the pattern we're commanded to follow. Christ was sinless, yet He forgave the ones who ridiculed, mocked, and hung Him on the tree. Our God is a forgiving God. It's a pattern that we are to follow.

Forgiveness Is a Picture of Christ to the World

If we want the world to understand God, we need to be forgiving people. In the book of Matthew, the author is only mentioned as "Matthew, the tax gatherer" (Matthew 10:3). He is the only apostle associated with his occupation. Being a tax collector was a despicable profession. Everybody hated tax gatherers, for they obtained as much money as they could by skimming off the top of the tax bills they collected. Men like Matthew were considered the worse of sinners, but not to Jesus.

> As Jesus went on from there, He saw a man called Matthew, sitting in the tax collector's booth; and He said to him, "Follow me!" And he got up and followed Him. Then it happened that as Jesus was reclining at the table in the house, behold, many tax collectors and sinners came and were dining with Jesus and His disciples. When the Pharisees saw this, they said to His disciples, "Why is your Teacher eating with tax collectors and sinners?" But when He heard this, He said, "It is not those who are healthy who need a phy-

sician, but those who are sick, but go and learn what this means: 'I desire compassion, and not sacrifice,' for I did not come to call the righteous, but sinners." (Matthew 9:9-13)

Matthew records this incident in his life because he, of all the apostles, probably recognized his sinful state more than anyone else. He was a greedy tax collector. Christ rebuked the Pharisees and others who criticized his actions. Jesus used a rabbinical tradition to answer an open rebuke and to expose their error. They had ignored a known command so Jesus told them to go and learn the meaning of Hosea 6:6, "For I delight in loyalty rather than sacrifice, and in the knowledge of God rather than burnt offerings." In essence Jesus was telling His audience, "If you knew Me, you would never ask *why* I am eating with these people."

The book of Hosea is about a man who marries a woman named Gomer who becomes a prostitute and deserts him. Yet God tells Hosea that he is never to abandon his wife. Instead, he is to pursue, love, and forgive her. Hosea's story is meant as a model. His relationship becomes a snapshot, a metaphor for the relationship of God to the nation of Israel. Just as Hosea represents the picture of God to the world, forgiveness is the picture of Christ to the world. The greatest dichotomy between the secular and the sacred is in the area of forgiveness. It's the highest Christian virtue. For never are we more like Christ than when forgiveness is at stake.

Solomon said, "A man's wisdom gives him patience; it is his glory to overlook an offense" (Proverbs 19:11 NIV). Chuck Swindoll said it well, "We are most like beasts when we kill. We are most like men when we judge. We are most like God when we forgive."[4] We must be people who know what it means to forgive. If ever we are to portray our Heavenly Father to others, what better way than when we have been wronged, humiliated, slandered, mocked, ridiculed or abused. Kindly, we must extend the hand of forgiveness to those who have caused us to stumble.

Are we concerned about how we portray Christ to those who don't know Him? If a man or woman is married to an unbeliever, then he or she must be concerned about how that unbelieving partner sees God. Always, in whatever circumstance, we must be the ones who forgive.

Forgiveness Is the Priority in Caring for Others

Christ tells His disciples, "[W]hoever causes one of these little ones who believe in Me to stumble, it would be better for him to have a have a heavy millstone hung around his neck, and to be drowned in the depth of the sea" (Matthew 18:6). This discussion confuses the disciples, so Peter, as spokesman for the group, asks, "Lord, how often shall my brother sin against me and I forgive him?" (Matthew 18:21). Peter remembers the earlier conversation about forgiving "seven times." Peter is thinking, *"So if my brother sins, I forgive him up to seven times, right?"*

However, Jesus replied to him, "I do not say to you, up to seven times, but up to seventy times seven" (Matthew 18:22). If we return to my first illustration about how many times we forgive in 16 waking hours, consider the enormity of forgiving seventy times seven. If such a transgressor existed, he would sin against us every 1.9 minutes in a day, and we would have to forgive him. Christ explains to Peter that there is no limit to forgiveness. There are no boundaries on how much we are to forgive a sinning brother even though in our humanity, we think that there must be a limit!

Christ, knowing what was in the disciples' minds, told a story about a certain king who called a servant to settle his debt (Matthew 18:23-35). This poor slave owed 10,000 talents. That's like owing millions of dollars, so there was no way he could pay. When his lord commanded that he and his family be sold and that he make restitution, the poor man begged for mercy. Fortunately for him, the master showed compassion and forgave the slave's debt. This king was merciful and forgiving.

This slave learned nothing from his master, however, because he demanded that a fellow slave, who owed him 100 denari, pay the debt right away. This man also begged for mercy, but the first slave refused and threw the debtor into prison. When the master learned about the slave's unmerciful behavior, he confronted him. "You wicked slave, I forgave you all that debt because you pleaded with me. Should you not also have had mercy on your fellow slave, in the same way that I had mercy on you?" (Matthew 18:32-33). The angry king ordered the man to be tortured until his debt could be paid. Then Christ concludes, "My heavenly Father will also do the same to you, if each of you does not forgive his brother from your heart" (Matthew 18:35).

That parable doesn't take a Phi Beta Kappa to interpret. Christ says that Peter and the other disciples must forgive as Christ has forgiven them. Similarly God is saying to us, "How dare you withhold forgiveness from another when I am so willing to forgive you all your iniquities, all the debt you cannot pay." The sin others commit against us is nothing compared to the sin we've committed against the Holy God of the Universe.

Forgiveness Is the Prerequisite to Communion with God

Forgiveness is a prerequisite for communing with God. If we have an unforgiving spirit, communion and fellowship with God are negated. In Matthew 6:9-13, Jesus offers a model for prayer. Then after the prayer, Jesus says, "For if you forgive others for their transgressions, your heavenly Father will also forgive you. But if you do not forgive others, then your Father will not forgive your transgressions" (Matthew 6:14-15). In this passage, Christ is not talking about a believer's salvation in Christ. He's talking about forgiveness in a relational sense, not a judicial sense.

For example, if our children sin against us, we forgive them because we love them. However, there's no fellowship or communion between the child and us unless that child asks for forgiveness. Even if we parents forgive our erring children, a barrier remains because that sin has not been settled. So Christ is saying that if we don't forgive our brothers, then there is a barrier between God and us.

Take me, for example. If I have an attitude of resentment and bitterness toward my wife, then I'm unforgiving toward her. "If I regard iniquity in my heart, the Lord will not hear me" (Psalm 66:18 KJV). Christ wants me to understand that if I'm going to commune with Him, I must be a forgiving person to my wife and to others who hurt me. Many Christian families face this difficulty. They're praying and asking God to do a great work, but in their hearts, they are bitter, angry, and resentful toward others. They harbor evil thoughts and speak against their mates or family members. Consequently circumstances and relationships are not working well in their lives. God tells us that an unforgiving spirit becomes an obstacle. "He who conceals his transgressions will not prosper, but he who confesses and forsakes them will find compassion" (Proverbs 28:13). God is not going to bless us if we have an unforgiving spirit.

People come to church and say, "You know, if we had better music or a better facility, worshipping God at church would be better." Yet what truly enhances worship is a forgiving spirit. An unforgiving spirit hinders communion with God. If we're harboring a bitter spirit against another brother or sister, we must make it right. That's why Christ said that if we go to worship Him, and we know that our brother has something against us, we are to leave our gift at the altar and go be reconciled to him (see Matthew 5:23-24). We can't continue our worship until reconciliation occurs. God says that we must first be reconciled with our brother and then we can return to worship Him.

If someone asks forgiveness of another but that person refuses to forgive, that's okay. That's their issue. Further, some will ask, "Well, what if I go and ask forgiveness and the situation gets worse?" That's the bad news. Sometimes situations do get worse despite our best efforts. However, the most important element is our obedience to God. We can't just say, *"I'll think about it or I'll pray about it."* We don't have to pray about what God has commanded. We just have to obey—like the Nike slogan, *just do it*. We must be obedient to God, and let God handle the fallout.

Forgiveness is the prerequisite to communion with Almighty God. If we feel like we're just going through the motions, we must ask ourselves: *"Where have I offended another brother and not sought reconciliation? Or where am I harboring resentment toward another brother or sister?"* Often such examination frees us and situations change in our walk with the Lord.

Forgiveness Is the Process that Clears a Guilty Conscience

In Psalm 32, David speaks of his sin with Bathsheba.

> How blessed is he whose transgression is forgiven,
> Whose sin is covered!
> How blessed is the man to whom the Lord does not
>   impute iniquity
> And in whose spirit there is no deceit!
> When I kept silent about my sin, my body wasted
>   away
> Through my groaning all day long.
> For day and night Your hand was heavy upon me.
> (32:1-4a)

This Psalm was written during the time of David's affair with Bathsheba. Before he acknowledged his sins, he felt God's hand of judgment upon him. He was a sick man without vitality or peace because he had sinned against Bathsheba and her husband Uriah, and ultimately, against God.

Once David confessed, he gained the forgiveness he sought. His guilty conscious was cleansed when he asked God for forgiveness.

> I acknowledged my sin to You,
> And my iniquity I did not hide;
> I said, "I will confess my transgression to the
>   Lord"; and You forgave the guilt of my sin.
> (Psalm 32:5)

Paul warned that when we don't forgive, we offer Satan opportunity to create trouble for both us and for the church (see 2 Corinthians 2:10-11). For if we don't forgive our brothers and sisters, then we can give Satan a foothold. "Be angry, and yet do not sin; do not let the sun go down upon your anger, and do not give the devil an opportunity" (Ephesians 4:26-27). If we don't deal with problems and conflicts, Paul warns, Satan can take advantage of the situation.

Like David, we can know freedom from guilt when we go to God, acknowledge our sin, and ask for forgiveness.

Forgiveness Is a Practice Characteristic of the Christian

The stoning of Stephen is a perfect illustration of forgiveness (see Acts 7). When Stephen preached the Gospel, the people listening grew angry. They clenched their teeth and covered their ears to block out his message. They didn't want to hear any more about how they had killed Jesus, the Messiah. They chased him out of the city and stoned him. Yet Stephen, seemingly unafraid, looked up to glory and said, "Lord, do not hold this sin against them!" (Acts 7:60 NIV). Stephen's behavior exemplifies the practice that's characteristic of the Christian.

Similarly, Christ says that we are to love our enemies and pray for those who persecute us (Matthew 5:43-45). Such an attitude and behavior proves that we're sons and daughters of our Father in heaven. What better way to prove that we're Christians than to reach out to someone who's abused or harmed or ridiculed us and extend to them the right hand of forgiveness. All Steven did was preach the Word, yet the people hated him and killed him for it. Even so, as the stones struck him down, he forgave them.

Forgiveness Predicates our Comprehension of God's Sovereignty

The perfect illustration of God's sovereignty is shown in the life of Joseph. His brothers came before him in Egypt fearing that he would punish them for their cruelty toward him. These men knew that they deserved punishment for their wicked betrayal of their brother. "Joseph said, 'Do not be afraid, for am I in God's place? As for you, you meant evil against me, but God meant it for good in order to bring about this present result, to preserve many people alive. So therefore, do not be afraid; I will provide for you and your little ones.' So he comforted them and spoke kindly to them" (Genesis 50:19-21).

Nothing affirms our belief in God's sovereign control more than when we extend forgiveness to those who have harmed us. Joseph understood God's sovereign control in his life. Do we comprehend God's sovereign control in our lives?

Dear Lord, please forgive us for our transgressions and grant us the grace to continually forgive those who sin against us. Amen.

14

God's Counsel for Couples: Spiritual Warfare

Developing family relationships that are harmonious and fulfilling requires diligence and vigilance. Many pressures exerted on the family come from both visible and invisible forces. The Bible warns that Satan is at work in the world, creating trouble for family members and confounding their relationships. Therefore God's children must guard their hearts and homes against the wiles of the devil.

In order to deal with such spiritual warfare, one must understand Satan's involvement in the world. The book of Job offers insight into this unseen realm. In a conversation between God and Satan, twice God asks Satan, "From where do you come?" Each time, Satan answers, "From roaming about on the earth and walking around on it" (Job 1:7, Job 2:2). So Job reveals that although Satan has access to the earth, God sits on heaven's throne. God is the Almighty One. In fact, the word "almighty" is used thirty-one times in Job to express that God is both in control and all powerful. "But our God is in the heavens; He does whatever He pleases" (Psalm 115:3).

In contrast to God's heavenly realm, Satan roams the earth. Yet he has access to God (as revealed in their conversation from Job 1). Unfortunately, many individuals fail to understand Satan's role and influence in the universe. They have been influenced by John Milton's concept of Satan as portrayed in his epic poem, *Paradise*

Lost. In Milton's work, Satan rules the world from his abode in hell, but the truth is that Satan is not in hell. In fact, hell (the place reserved for Satan and his angels) is unoccupied at present. Eventually Satan will be cast into the lake of fire forever and ever (see Revelation 20:10). But until that time, he roams the earth.

In the Bible, Job is presented as a godly man, but God allows Satan to afflict him. Satan commits evil against Job's family, home, and possessions, and God permits it. That situation reveals that God is in control of Satan, who is not omnipresent. Satan is not able to do whatever he wants. He has to ask permission from God to act. Job is allowed to suffer in order to silence the blasphemous accusations of Satan and prove that a man would honor God, even though he has lost everything. That's the message of the book of Job.

Job's life becomes a spiritual battleground. Job had no Bible to read for perspective. He just had to trust God, believing that God ultimately was at work. As an upright man of integrity, he possessed a reverence for God. The book of Job asks, *"Is Jehovah God worthy of man's worship no matter what happens?"* The answer is a resounding, *"Yes!"*

We must ask the same question. If we are to succeed in this spiritual battle, it's important to understand the motives and methods of the enemy.

Realize Satan's Strategy

Paul says the armor of God allows Christians to stand against the devil's plans. "Put on the whole armor of God, that you may be able to stand against the wiles of the devil" (Ephesians 6:11 NKJV). The wiles of the devil represent his plans for war; they are to devastate lives, divide marriages, and deceive hearts. His secret aim is the destruction of souls.

It's important to understand such evil designs. In 2 Corinthians 2:11, Paul wrote that we should not be ignorant of the devil's devices. Satan has a two-fold strategy: to blind "the minds of the unbelieving so that they might not see the light of the gospel of the glory of Christ, who is the image of God" (2 Corinthians 4:4), and to beguile the mind of the believer by creating distractions that destroy peace of mind and deceive hearts (see 2 Corinthians 11:3).

Satan has been active since the beginning (see Genesis 3-4). He even tempted Jesus Christ even though he knew that Christ was sinless (see Matthew 4). In a similar way, Satan hopes to divide church congregations, paralyze ministries, and ruin Christian leaders through scandal and failure. Christians live in Satan's territory. We are aliens and strangers in a foreign land, fighting on ground where Satan is the prince of darkness. "The whole world lies in the power of the evil one" (1 John 5:19). Therefore, it's important that Christian believers work together in worship (Hebrew 10:24-25). To encourage one another toward love and good deeds, we must come together as a body to study the Bible and discover the truth of God.

Satan seeks to destroy individuals. The Bible contains several verbs associated with Satan. He beguiles, seduces, opposes, resists, deceives, hinders, and persecutes. His first goal is to deceive. Paul tells the Corinthian believers that he fears for them. "But I am afraid that, as the serpent deceived Eve by his craftiness, your minds will be led astray from the simplicity and purity of devotion to Christ" (2 Corinthians 11:3). He goes on to say, "Satan disguises himself as an angel of light. Therefore it is not surprising if his servants also disguise themselves as servants of righteousness, whose end will be according to their deeds" (2 Corinthians 11:14-15).

First, Satan is such a master deceiver and when the one called the Antichrist appears, millions will believe he is the Messiah. In essence, he will deceive the whole world (Revelation 12:9). In fact, the miracles that he will perform during the Tribulation period will appear so astounding that multitudes will be duped. Satan is the father of lies and "there is no truth in him" (John 8:44 NIV). He uses false teachers who misquote Scripture, teach corrupt ideas, and mix truth with error to advance his cause. Satan convinces people that he doesn't exist. Furthermore, he convinces them that evil is good. That's how tricky he is.

Second, Satan is a master divider. In his rebellion, Satan swept away one third of the angels with him. He hoped to divide Heaven and rule there. He couldn't succeed because God, Himself, is the great ruler of the world. Yet his ongoing strategy is to sow seeds of suspicion, intolerance, and criticism. His chief aim is to divide. That's why Paul stresses the unity of the Spirit and the bond of peace among Christians. Satan wants to destroy Christian unity, to destroy purity, to destroy ministry, and to destroy church credibility. That's why when people in the church sow seeds of discord and create divisions, it is clear that Satan is using them to divide the church.

Third, Satan is the master destroyer. In fact, his name in Hebrew is Abaddon and in the Greek, Apolloyon, which "mean destroyer" (see Revelation 9:11). He uses adversity and discouragement to assault the Christian's spiritual nature. He wants us to compromise our vows of commitment. Ultimately he seeks to damage our testimonies and our lives. The Bible says that he was a murderer from the beginning. Satan, the destroyer, divider, deceiver, is active in our world.

Paul says that Satan has plans. He calls them the "flaming arrows of the evil one" (Ephesians 6:16). Revelation 12 gives a picture of the world from the beginning of time to the end when Christ returns. Satan plans to destroy the Messiah, to destroy Israel, and to destroy the believer. His plan will be apparent in the Tribulation with the Antichrist when the whole world will be tempted to worship the beast.

Recognize the Severity of Satan's Schemes

Job lost everything, from family and possessions to his own health (Job 2). He suffered many afflictions that worsened over time, including head-to-toe boils that oozed puss, day and night. He could find no position—sitting, standing, or lying down—that would relieve his pain. Eventually his breath became so diseased that even his wife could not be near him (Job 19:17). Ravaged by chills and fevers, he grew thin. He developed uncontrollable diarrhea and his skin turned black. In fact, he became so pitifully altered that even his friends did not recognize him, and they wept when they saw him (Job 2:12).

His appearance grew so repulsive that he left home for the city dump. Job sat against a putrid ash heap. The city's leading citizen, the world's foremost Christian, the man who walked with God more than anybody else, found himself abandoned amidst poverty and shame. The situation was so awful that his wife suggested that he curse God and die. (It's important to consider that Job's wife lost everything, too. Along with family and home, she also lost her husband, for he was unable to minister to her because of his severe physical affliction.)

Here's the point: Satan wanted Job to do as his wife suggested. Of all the disasters that befell him, the severest temptation Job faced came from his helpmate, the one who loved him the most. That's how Satan works his finest evil in our lives as well. Those closest to us may be used by Satan to draw us away from God. For example, after Jesus predicted His own death, Peter took Him aside and rebuked Him saying, "No, you're not, Jesus! You're the Son of God. You're not going to die."

Then Jesus said, "Get thee behind me, Satan" (Matthew 16:23 KJV). Satan even used the great Apostle Peter to attempt to distract Christ from His ultimate mission, to die on the cross. Similarly in Acts 21, Phillip, the evangelist, begged Paul to stay away from Jerusalem, for prophecy had revealed that Paul would be arrested (vv 8-12). Yet Paul knew that God had called him to Jerusalem, and his eyes were set on fulfilling the will of God. Phillip, a great man of God in his own right, essentially said to the Apostle Paul, "Don't do what God tells you."

Paul responded, "Why are you weeping and breaking my heart? I am ready not only to be bound, but also to die in Jerusalem for the name of the Lord Jesus" (Acts 21:13 NIV). Paul shows the true strength as a man of God. He's my kind of man. He'll do whatever God says even if it costs him his life. Yet this account illustrates how Satan can use sincere people of God to draw someone away from his spiritual mission.

Therefore, we must realize Satan's strategy if we're going to guard our hearts and our families against the enemy. The devil will use the ones closest to us to draw us away from God. Men need to stand strong in the faith, believe God, and know what the Word of God says. Then they can obey God and stand up to their wives and children saying, "Thus sayeth the Lord. This I will do." Wives need to be led by a masculine leader who says, "I am not afraid to do what God says because I am fearful of God Himself. Therefore, I will follow God regardless of what others say." Those kinds of men provide spiritual strength for both their families and their church congregations.

Similarly, Job stood firm and did not take his wife's advice.

> He said, "Naked I came from my mother's womb,
> And naked I shall return there.
> The Lord gave and the Lord has taken away.
> Blessed be the name of the Lord." (Job 1:21)

Through all his suffering, Job did not sin, nor did he blame God. Instead, he looked backward and said that at birth, he came into this world with nothing. Then he looked forward and realized that since he came with nothing, he will leave with nothing. Finally, he looked upward and said, "The Lord has given and the Lord has taken away. Blessed be the Lord." Instead of cursing and blaming, he blessed God. He understood the principle Paul discussed in Colossians 3:1-2, "Therefore if you have been raised up with Christ, keep seeking the things above, where Christ is, seated at the right hand of God. Set your mind on the things above, not on the things that are on earth." It's important that we bless, not blame God, and trust Him for what He's going to do.

God is not going to let anything come our way that is beyond His power. Satan's temptation is not stronger than the power of the Almighty God. "No temptation has overtaken you but such as is common to man; and God is faithful, who will not allow you to be tempted beyond what you are able" (1 Corinthians 10:13). For Job and for us, God provides an escape route. God has power and a plan. God is good.

In the Bible, spiritual warfare is compared to a wrestling match. Such a metaphor suggests that Christians must be strong to prepare for that struggle or they will find themselves pinned to the mat by their evil opponent. My friends often remind me that, as a pastor, I am a warrior engaged in a spiritual battle. A.W. Tozer said, "Men think of the world not as a battle ground today, but as a playground. We are not here to fight; we are here to frolic. We are not in a foreign land; we are at home…and the best we can do is rid ourselves of our inhibitions and our frustrations and live this life here to the full."[1]

Tozer denounced this belief as part of the religious philosophy of modern man.

God says, "If you're a friend of the world, you're an enemy of God" (see James 4:4). Satan entices us to adopt the behavioral standards and the social mores of secular society and to ignore the statutes prescribed for us by a holy God. When Satan successfully deceives us, he keeps us from serving the true and living God.

Remember Your Spiritual Armor

In order to contend with the constant battles happening each day in our spiritual and physical lives, we need God's spiritual armor.

> Finally, be strong in the Lord and in the strength of His might. Put on the full armor of God, so that you may be able to stand firm against the schemes of the devil. For our struggle is not against flesh and blood, but against the rulers, against the powers, against the world forces of this darkness, against the spiritual forces of wickedness in the heavenly places. Therefore, take up the full armor of God, so that you will be able to resist in the evil day, and having done everything, to stand firm. Stand firm therefore, having girded your loins with truth, and having put on the breastplate of righteousness. (Ephesians 6:10-14)

The first piece of armor named is the belt of truth. A Roman soldier going into battle would put his tunic inside his belt, so he could move freely. Similarly, Christians must prepare for spiritual battle by knowing the truth of Almighty God. It's important to understand God's mercy, love, justice, wrath, compassion, and grace. Without this knowledge, believers can't even begin to explain the truth of God. This knowledge of God resides in the Bible.

The warrior's breastplate covers the intestines, the heart, the lungs, and other vital organs. Similarly, the breastplate of righteousness guards the seeds of our emotions. As a man thinks in his heart, so is he (Proverbs 23:7). The center of learning, the center of who we are, is guarded by the breastplate of righteousness. That means,

God declares us righteous. So the breastplate of righteousness is simply living out our righteous position in the world being obedient to God. A holy life defeats Satan. For example, Job lived as an upright, holy man. He feared God. Therefore, Satan could not make an inroad into Job's soul. Job possessed a proper perspective on God that ultimately preserved him from Satan's evil.

Furthermore, when going to war, a soldier must have the right shoes: "having shod your feet with the preparation of the gospel of peace" (Ephesians 6:15). Although many scholars explain that the key to this piece of armor is about sharing the faith with others, that interpretation is inaccurate. Having "shod feet" is not about going but about standing. It's not about sharing faith; it's about fighting a battle. When our hearts have the peace of God, that peace prepares us to fight against temptation. This armor deals with our position in Christ. We are on His side, not Satan's side. God's peace enables us to stand strong because no matter what happens around us or to us, inside we know we can trust the Lord.

No matter how bad events were for Job outwardly, inwardly he had the peace of God. That's why Jesus said, "Peace I leave you; My peace I give to you; not as the world gives do I give to you. Do not let your heart be troubled, nor let it be fearful" (John 14:27). Jesus possessed this kind of peace when He was in the boat with the disciples during a ferocious storm. The boat rocked and rolled so much that the disciples feared for their lives, yet Jesus slept contentedly. The peace that Jesus offers can help us stand against the wiles of the devil, no matter how difficult a situation may become.

The shield of faith allows us to remain strong because we believe in the promises, power, and peace of Almighty God. Next is the helmet of salvation which is also called "the hope of salvation" (1 Thessalonians 5:8 NIV). That helmet gives perspective into the future. I know that one day I will be ultimately glorified with my God. That hope of a future glorification helps me stand firm today against what Satan is going to do.

Then, of course, there's the sword of the Spirit. It's a short dagger, the only offensive weapon described in the battle against Satan and his devices. Using specific passages from God's Word helps us resist temptation. Finally, the weapon of prayer joins all the different pieces of the armor together. If we're going to fight, we need our spiritual armor.

Recite Scripture

The Word of God is quicker and sharper than any two-edged sword. Moses said, "Take to your heart all the words with which I am warning you today....For it is not an idle word for you; indeed it is your life" (Deuteronomy 32:46-47). When Jesus was tempted in the wilderness, He quoted passages from Deuteronomy 6 and 8 that were life to the nation of Israel. When He recited those words, Satan could not conquer Him (Matthew 4:1-11). When we have scripture in our minds and ready on our lips, we will have greater trust in God. That's why reciting Scripture is vital for the Christian.

> Incline your ear and hear the words of the wise.
> And apply your mind to my knowledge;
> For it will be pleasant if you keep them within you,
> That they may be ready on your lips.
> So that your trust may be in the Lord,
> I have taught you today, even you. (Proverbs 22:17-19)

Resist Satan

The Apostle Peter warned that the devil is a fierce adversary calling him, "a roaring lion, seeking someone to devour" (1 Peter 5:8). So Peter urges his audience to resist the devil and to remain steadfast in the faith. The word "steadfast" is a military term, describing the Greek phalanx. In a phalanx, the soldiers joined together arm-in-arm. This human shield could stretch a mile long with soldiers five to ten men deep, marching all together. If at any time that phalanx was broken, the army would be defeated. However, if they stood strong together not allowing any gaps in that phalanx, then they would be able to conquer their enemy.

Similarly, Peter is urging Christians also to be "steadfast" in the faith. That is, we develop a spiritual phalanx so strong that there are no chinks in our spiritual armor, no gaps in our faith. By doing so, we resist the devil, and he flees from us. Further, James says, "Submit therefore to God. Resist the devil and he will flee from you" (James 4:7). When you resist the devil and draw near to God, and He will draw near to you. Drawing near to God requires submission. We can't draw near to God if we are unwilling to resist Satan.

Rely on the Savior

Unless we rely upon the Lord Jesus Christ, we will not be able to guard our homes and our hearts against the enemy. "Finally, be strong in the Lord and in the strength of His might. Put on the full armor of God" (Ephesians 6:10-11). Proverbs 18:10 says, "The name of the Lord is the strong tower; the righteous runs into it and is safe." Martin Luther's classic hymn, "A Mighty Fortress Is Our God"[2] captures well the truth that God's power of God can sustain us:

> *A mighty fortress is our God,*
> *A bulwark never failing;*
> *Our helper He amid the flood*
> *Of mortal ills prevailing.*
> *For still our ancient foe,*
> *Doth seek to work us woe;*
> *His craft and power are great,*
> *And armed with cruel hate,*
> *On earth is not his equal.*
>
> *Did we in our own strength confide,*
> *Our striving would be losing,*
> *Were not the right man on our side,*
> *The man of God's own choosing.*
> *Dost ask who that may be?*
> *Christ Jesus it is He;*
> *Lord Sabaoth, His name,*
> *From age to age the same,*
> *And He must win the battle.*

To guard hearts and homes against the enemy, we must realize the strategy, recognize its severity, remember our spiritual armor, recite Scripture, resist Satan, and rely on the Savior.

Dear God, we cannot succeed alone. We are incapable of fulfilling Your call. We are incapable of standing strong against temptation. We need Your Spirit to lead and guide us. You are the strong tower. Make us strong in the power of Your might. We will run to You for safety. Amen.

15

God's Counsel for Couples: Money Matters

What does it mean to honor God? It is a matter often discussed in Scripture. God declares, "Those who honor Me, I will honor" (1 Samuel 2:30). Clearly, we must make service to God our priority as we worship and adore him: "If anyone serves Me, he must follow Me; and where I am, there My servant will be also; if anyone serves Me, the Father will honor him" (John 12:26). This truth is vital if Christians are to have successful family relationships. When a man or woman's relationship with God is out of line, then everything around that person, including the marriage relationship may suffer.

If truth were known, we honor God in certain ways and dishonor Him in others. We think if we can honor Him in more ways than we dishonor Him, then we are on the good side of God. However, God wants to be honored in all areas. So it's important to understand what it means to put God first, specifically with our finances.

We need to honor God with our money. Otherwise, we inhibit our spiritual fellowship with God and open the door for conflict with our husbands or wives. Most of us know first hand that conflict arising from financial matters destroys many marriages. In order to have an effective relationship with a spouse or be an effective leader in the family, we must honor God with our money. Giving consideration to biblical guidelines will help us understand more fully God's plan for us and our money.

The Precept

God insists that we honor Him:

> Honor the Lord from your wealth
> And from the first of all our produce;
> So your barns will be filled with plenty
> And your vats will overflow with new wine. (Proverbs 3:9)

The Proverbs passage doesn't say, "Wait until the end of the month and see if there's any money left to honor Me." Instead, the precept is to honor the Lord by giving the first fruits of our wealth. In another proverb, Solomon says, "The reward of humility and the fear of the Lord are riches, honor and life" (Proverbs 22:4). God makes a promise that if we, in humility and fear, honor Him with our talents and resources, then He will honor us. Further, Paul says, "But my God shall supply all your need according to His riches in glory by Christ Jesus" (Philippians 4:19 KJV). God supplies not *out* of His riches, but *according* to His riches.

In Genesis, we learn that God prospered Jacob. In the 20 years that Jacob worked with Laban, God increased his herds and flocks. "So [Jacob] became exceedingly prosperous, and had large flocks and female and male servants and camels and donkeys" (Genesis 30:43). Jacob grew prosperous because God transformed Jacob's life. Jacob made a vow, saying, "If God will be with me and will keep me on this journey that I take, and will give me food to eat and garments to wear, and I return to my father's house in safety, then the Lord will be my God. This stone, which I set up as a pillar, will be God's house, and of all that You give me I will surely give a tenth to You" (Genesis 28:20-22). Jacob made a vow to give ten percent of all that he had even when he had nothing. So later, when Laban deceived Jacob and tried to take advantage of him, God still remembered Jacob's vow and blessed him.

Many Christians have trouble letting go of those dollars. However, my father used to say, "If we were supposed to hold onto our money, God would have put handles on the bills." Yet money was never meant for hording. Believe it or not, that's exactly why God increased Jacob's wealth—because Jacob kept his vow and gave to God. Abraham made the same commitment when he gave a tenth of all that he had to Melchizedek (Genesis 14:17-24). There was no law that said Abraham had to give a tenth. Yet his offering represented his sacrifice to God. If we wonder why God hasn't blessed us, we must consider how much we're giving. God says that if we honor Him with the first fruits of our increase, He will bless us so much that our vats will overflow. As Christians, will we trust God or not? If we want to move forward in our Christian growth and commitment, we must be willing to say, "I'm going to obey God. I'm going to give from my 'first fruits.' From the weekly or monthly check I get, right off the top, I'm giving to God."

The Problem

God says through the apostle Paul that the reason we don't want to honor God with the "first fruits of our increase" is because we love money.

> But godliness actually is a means of great gain when accompanied by contentment. For we have brought nothing into the world, so we cannot take anything out of it either. If we have food and covering, with these we shall be content. But those who want to get rich fall into temptation and a snare and many foolish and harmful desires which plunge men into ruin and destruction. For the love of money is the root of all sorts of evil, and some by longing for it have wandered away from the faith and pierced themselves with many griefs. (1 Timothy 6:6-10)

The verb meaning "love for money" is a phrase that means "affection for silver." The term speaks of our selfish attitudes, our sin of greed. Often we are beset by the desire to have more and more. We don't want to admit our love for money. However, that desire prevents us from giving freely to God. We can't serve both

God and money (Matthew 6:24). In fact, as Paul says, the love of money is the root of all kinds of evil.

1. *How do we know we have a love for money?*
We must ask ourselves these questions:

- Am I thinking more about how to get money than about how to pursue excellence in my work?
- Am I always looking for a bigger, better job with a larger salary?
- Am I concerned more about my testimony in the work place or more about my place on the pay scale?

The answers may reveal our true motivations. Our quality of service should mean more than the amount of money we earn. Our vocation, our calling, is to be a representation of Jesus Christ in the market place. But somehow the motivation of our jobs or careers ceases to be enough. Instead, we seek money to supply increasing and often insatiable cravings for possessions and status.

Certainly a husband must work to support his family. However, individuals work for another reason as well. "He who steals must steal no longer; but rather he must labor, performing with his own hands what is good, so that he will have something to share with one who has need" (Ephesians 4:28). God provides us jobs so we can meet the needs of our brothers. This principle gives a whole new perspective on work. We may think, *"Man, I've got a better job, so now I can get a bigger house or a newer car or nicer clothes."* Yet the Ephesians passage clearly states that we labor to give that which is good to others who have needs. When we have such a perspective on work, our priorities change.

2. *We know we love money if we never seem to have enough.*
Once we get a raise, we increase our standard of living. It's the American dream to live better next year than we did this year. Otherwise, we think we have an achievement problem. Popular magazines like *GQ*, and *Fortune 500* reinforce that value system by featuring slick images and stories of wealth. Yet Christians must

live as aliens and strangers, who work for a heavenly hope rather than for tangible goods. Furthermore, Paul says that godliness with contentment is great gain (1 Timothy 6:6).

3. *We know we love money if we flaunt what we have.*

We derive inordinate pleasure from showing off our new merchandise. The new suit, new car, or new house becomes a source of personal pride.

4. *We know we love money if we resent giving to others.*

We dislike pastors who teach about tithing. We avoid mission presentations that remind us of financial needs around the world. We begrudge giving to other people even for a worthy cause. Yet the reality is that it's God's money, not ours.

When people come to my door asking for donations, I say, "Listen, my sole ambition is to give to the church where I serve. I don't give to other organizations or charitable groups. Instead, all my money goes for ministry because I want to honor God more than anything in the world." Most people don't stay on my doorstep long enough to hear the end of my speech. Yet I want them to know that I give. Even though my gifts don't go to a drug abuse program, police project, or school fundraiser, I'm still giving to ministry. The world's needs are not material but spiritual. Since the church meets people's spiritual needs, I'm giving toward a cause that is eternal, not temporal.

5. *We know we love money if we'll sin (lie, cheat, steal) to obtain it.*

Some people lie on their income tax returns. Others like to cheat on their expense accounts, steal from the till at their jobs, or otherwise compromise in order to get their hands on more funds. Anytime we sin to get ahead, we prove that our love of money is more important than our love for our righteous and holy God.

Be warned, the love of money produces all kinds of evil:

> My son, do not reject the discipline of the Lord
> Or loathe His reproof. For whom the Lord loves He
> reproves,

> Even as a father corrects the son in whom He delights.
> (Proverbs 3:11-12)

Some of us are being disciplined, but we don't know it. We face difficulty, maybe it's financial, relational, or professional, but still we won't subject ourselves to the mighty hand of God. Yet God will bless us when we honor Him:

> How blessed is the man who finds wisdom
> And the man who gains understanding.
> For her profit is better than the profit of silver
> And her gain better than fine gold. (Proverbs 3:13-14)

God disciplines those who do not honor Him with their resources.

However, God says, "I want you to love Me. I want you to be committed to Me. I want you to understand what I can do for you. I want you to trust Me and realize that your relationship with Me is more important than anything money can buy, or the world can offer." Sadly, most people never understand that point. They endure the Lord's discipline, struggling from week to week, satisfied with merely trudging through life. God wants us to understand that money can't buy us happiness or peace.

The Perspective

God is the great gift giver: "What do you have that you did not receive?" (1 Corinthians 4:7). Everything we have is from God. "Furthermore, as for every man to whom God has given riches and wealth, He has also empowered him to eat from them and to receive his reward and rejoice in his labor; this is the gift of God" (Ecclesiastes 5:19). In this passage, Solomon says that even our jobs are a gift from God.

God makes days of prosperity and days of adversity:

> In the day of prosperity be happy,
> But in the day of adversity consider—
> God has made the one as well as the other
> So that man may not discover anything that will be

after him. (Ecclesiastes 7:14)

We're not prosperous because of our ingenuity, our education, or our own talents and skills. God gave us these gifts.

God gives us the power to make wealth. "But you shall remember the Lord your God, for it is He who is giving you power to make wealth, that He may confirm His covenant which He swore to your fathers, as it is this day" (Deuteronomy 8:18). Unfortunately, we often say, "It's not good enough" while God is waiting for us to say, "Thank you for what we have." We don't thank God for leaky faucets, running toilets, chipping paint, or junky cars. Most of us don't want to thank God for those annoyances. Yet we are stewards of all God has given. Our circumstances could be much worse. We could be homeless with no food or shelter. We are household managers of God's possessions. Whatever God has given us is His gift. It is He who has given us the power to make wealth. It's all about God. That's a heavenly perspective.

The Priority

The Macedonian church described in 2 Corinthians was poor.

> Now, brethren, we wish to make known to you the grace of God which has been given in the churches of Macedonia, that in a great ordeal of affliction their abundance of joy and their deep poverty overflowed in the wealth of their liberality. For I testify that according to their ability, and beyond their ability, they gave of their own accord, begging us with much urging for the favor of participation in the support of the saints, and this, not as we has expected, but they first gave themselves to the Lord and to us by the will of God. (2 Corinthians 8:1-5)

In their poverty, they begged for the opportunity to give more. Paul says that they were generous because they first gave themselves to God. In a similar way, if we're not looking for more ways to give our money to ministry, then we have not given ourselves first to God. Of course, we might ask ourselves, *"If I give all this to God, will there be enough left over for me to take care of my needs? How will I pay my rent? How do I maintain my standard of living?"* The solution may be that we need to lower our standard of living. However, that's not a message we like to hear. Yet if we first give ourselves to God, then our standard of living will seem less important to us. I recall that God owns me. All that I have, I received from Him. My body is the temple of the Holy Spirit therefore God dwells in me. So if I'm all God's, then all I have is His. That means everything is God's not mine, even my money.

However, we often have the wrong perspective. We view our salary as something we earned and deserve, like a child's chore allowance. Yet if all we have belongs to God, we must hold it loosely. God's far more interested in the giver than He is the gift. That's why He says we should present our bodies as a living sacrifice, holy and acceptable to God, which is our reasonable service (Romans 12:1).

Many Christians serve faithfully, doing church ministry, Bible study, and prayer groups. Yet these same servants resist the idea of tithing or contributing to ministry needs. They won't release the reins, thinking if they keep their coins, they'll prosper in the end. However, God urges an opposite view: the more we give, the more we receive. God says, "Honor Me first and your vats will overflow" (see Malachi 3:6-12). Once we decide to surrender our funds and ourselves, we can then gain an understanding of the principles of giving.

The Principles

First, God says we should give *bountifully*.

> Now this I say, he who sows sparingly will also reap sparingly, and he who sows bountifully will also reap bountifully. Each one must do just as he has purposed in his heart, not grudgingly or under compulsion, for God loves a cheerful giver. And God is able to make all grace abound to you, so that always having all sufficiency in everything, you may have an abundance for every good deed; as it is written, 'He scat-

tered abroad, He gave to the poor, His righteousness endures forever.' Now He who supplies seed to the sower and bread for food will supply and multiply your seed for sowing and increase the harvest of your righteousness. (2 Corinthians 9:6-10)

God says He will both supply and multiply like seeds sown in the field if we give bountifully. Will we let Him do so?

Second, we must give *individually*. "Each one must do just as he has purposed in his heart, not grudgingly or under compulsion, for God loves a cheerful giver" (2 Corinthians 9:7). A husband and wife should say, "We are going to honor God with our money. We are going to give every week or month. It's just between us and the Lord." None of us is too poor. We all have something to give.

Third, we must give *systematically* as we have purposed in our hearts. The word "purposed" means "to choose before hand." To succeed, we need a plan for giving with a heart-felt willingness. When I was just a young boy, I saw my parents give week after week to the Lord through the church. Then I saw God provide week after week for my parents in amazing ways. So I said to myself, *"I want to be a part of that blessing process."* My mom and dad also taught me how to develop a giving strategy. They explained that any allowance I earned was really God's money, so they showed me how to manage it properly. My parents would always say, "If we don't manage our finances properly, God's going to discipline us. So we give first to ministry, right off the top, before we do anything." While growing up, my folks held me accountable to that standard every week.

At age sixteen, I would toss my lawnmower into the trunk of my Ford Galaxy 500. The trunk lid flapped wildly as I drove from house to house to mow lawns. I earned six dollars per yard. As I counted my earnings, I would say, "Okay, this is the Lord's money, and the rest is what I can spend." As a result of that systematic plan, I never missed an opportunity to give to God.

Fourth, we must give *joyfully*. "God loves a cheerful giver" (2 Corinthians. 9:7). Every Sunday, when ushers pass the offering basket, Christians ought to laugh and laugh. Giving ought to be the high point of a service, not the singing or preaching. Christians should ask themselves, *"What would happen if we gave the fifty-dollar bill rather than the five-dollar bill?"*

Fifth, we must give *proportionately*. "Now concerning the collection for the saints, as I directed the churches of Galatia, so do you also. On the first day of every week each one of you is to put aside and save, as he may prosper, so that no collections be made when I come"

(1 Corinthians 16:1-2). Giving proportionately means we ought to consider various levels of wealth. If a person makes $20,000 per year and gives a ten-percent offering of $2,000, he has $18,000 left for living expenses. If another person earns a $100,000 salary, her tithe of $10,000 leaves $90,000 to live on. Perhaps both these individuals live in a community where the average annual income is $40,000 per year. The person with the lower income has far less discretionary income than the person earning six figures. So those with larger incomes should give proportionately, out of their abundance. When God gives more, He expects us to return more. So the next time we get a raise, we need to give it away rather than spend it and see how God blesses such an offering.

Sixth, we must give sacrificially. Jesus was pleased with the widow who gave her two mites because she gave all she possessed. Though her offering seemed far less than the amount the Pharisees could give, hers represented true sacrifice. When she gave everything she had, God honored her (Mark 12:41-44). Similarly, Jesus gave up everything for us by dying on the cross. For most, sacrificial giving is a foreign concept. God asks, "Why don't you give until it hurts and see what happens?"

The Promise

The generous man will be blessed. "Give, and it will be given to you. They will pour into your lap a good measure—pressed down, shaken together, and running over. For by your standard of measure it will be measured to you in return" (Luke 6:38). The law of the harvest is a very important law to understand. If we sow little, we reap little. If we give bountifully, we reap bountifully (2 Corinthians 9:6). We simply can't reap a crop if we don't sow seed. It's the same principle whether we sow corn, wheat, lettuce, or money. "He who is generous will be blessed, for he gives some of his food to the poor" (Proverbs 22:9).

When a farmer puts a crop into the ground, he sows tiny seeds but reaps a product far larger. In addition, the plants don't spring up the minute those seeds hit the soil. It takes time to reap a harvest. In the same way, as we invest in God's kingdom, we may not see results for a long time. God tests us to see if we're going to trust Him. However, we must not forget His promise. God says, "I'm going to bless the generous. If you honor Me, I will honor you. If you give to Me, I will give to you." If we sow bountifully, we will reap bountifully. We can trust God. Watch and see what He does.

Lord, our relationship to You is most important. You tell us that if we honor You, You will honor us. We do want to honor You with our lives and our resources. Help us to take You at Your Word, to become generous servants. Please give us the will to believe and the strength to trust. Amen.

16

God's Counsel for Couples: Communication

For most people, communication is hard work. The difficulties are apparent when parents give their teenager daughter directions on how to clean her room, or a wife tries to explain to her husband how to organize the garage the way *she'd* like it. Often a teen's concept of "clean" doesn't match the parents' ideas nor does the man's sense of organization coincide with what his wife envisioned. The results of those instructions are rarely satisfying! Furthermore, communication is usually about more than exchanging information. Many conversations have an emotional undercurrent that influences not only *what* is said but also *how* it's said. That's why we must pray with the Psalmist, "Let the words of my mouth and the meditation of my heart be acceptable in Your sight, O Lord, my Rock and my Redeemer" (Psalm 19:14).

The good news is that communication doesn't have to be risky. The Bible can help us understand the elements of communication, so that marriage partners can understand each other better. Husbands and wives can buffer the disappointment that comes from unrealistic expectations or misunderstandings or the damage done by harsh statements.

Commitment

The most difficult verse in the Bible to apply to daily living is from Ephesians: "Let no unwholesome word proceed from your mouth" (Ephesians 4:29a). The word "unwholesome" means "rotten." To illustrate that concept, I just picture a rotten banana. If I peel an over-ripe banana, the soft fruity pulp oozes out through the thin, dark skin. It looks, feels, and tastes terrible. I wouldn't want to eat anything rotten. In the same way, I don't want to utter sentences that are going to be rotten to those who hear them. For unwholesome speech, characterized by off-color jokes, profanity, or crudeness, should never be part of the Christian's manner of speaking. We must daily pray, "Set a guard, O Lord, over my mouth; keep watch over the door of my lips" (Psalms 141:3).

Here's a good rule of thumb: When husbands prepare to communicate with their wives about anything at all, they should pray four or five times: *"Lord, please guard my mouth; You keep my words wholesome."* It's important that God control our language whenever we speak.

Paul urges the Colossians to put off anger, wrath, malice, blasphemy, and filthy communication from their mouths (3:8). Like dirty garments, we must discard corrupt speech. Paul goes on to say, "there must be no filthiness and silly talk, or coarse jesting, which are not fitting, but rather giving of thanks" (Ephesians 5:4). So no coarse jesting, no silly talk, no worthless expressions, no rotten words are suitable for us.

Paul sums it up by saying that we should speak "only such a word as is good for edification according to the need of the moment, so that it may give grace to those who hear" (Ephesians 4:29). In this passage, Paul is offering guidelines for effective communication. When a person speaks, three elements should be evident in his conversation.

First, his speech must be edifying. It must be able to build somebody up. It must be able to add strength to the other person in the conversation. As we communicate with the boss, spouse, or children, do our words have a positive effect? Have we edified them? Negativity doesn't encourage or build up, negativity tears down. A negative person should ask the Lord not only to guard the door of their lips but also to seal their lips shut, so that they don't spread the negativity around.

Furthermore, Paul says to speak "according to the need of the moment" (Ephesians 4:29). So it's important to speak only when necessary. Sometimes we talk just to hear ourselves, thinking that we are adding wisdom to the conversation. Or we tell an interesting story hoping to impress someone or get attention using our witty sense of humor. However, the "need of the moment" means we should emphasize the listener's needs or concerns in a process that builds others up. In addition, our speech should be gracious: "that it will give grace to those who hear" (Ephesians 4:29). Our words ought to bless our hearers. It was said of Christ, "All were speaking well of Him [Jesus], and wondering at the gracious words which were falling from His lips" (Luke 4:22).

Second, if God's Word is in our hearts, then our speech will reflect godliness: "For out of the abundance of the heart the mouth speaks" (Matthew 12:34). The mouth reveals what attitudes lurk in the heart. Our language indicates our spiritual condition. We must let God's Word dwell in our hearts so that our speech ministers grace to those who hear us. Our speech must not only be gracious, but also "seasoned with salt" (Colossians 4:6). This seasoning represents the words that preserve goodness, words that keep the conversation pure. These salty words have a preserving, purifying influence. They are conversations sprinkled with pleasantness and kindness.

Command

There's a command we need to follow: "Do not grieve the Holy Spirit of God, by whom you are sealed for the day of redemption" (Ephesians 4:30). The Holy Spirit is grieved when our speech is unwholesome. When we use words that are sinful, we're going to hurt those who hear us. However, the primary emphasis here goes way beyond that. The deeper problem is grieving the Spirit of God. We Christians have been sealed unto the day of redemption as the Spirit indwells us. He now resides within us to strengthen and enable us. When we speak in ways contrary to His character, He is dismayed. When Peter confronted Ananias and his wife Sapphira in Acts 5:1-9, he didn't ask, "Why did you lie to the church and to me?" Instead, he asked, "Why did you lie to God?" The command for us is don't grieve the Spirit of God with our words.

Paul gives us a list of the types of words that will grieve the Spirit of God in Ephesians 4:31, "Let all bitterness, wrath, anger, clamor, and evil speaking be put away from you, with all malice" (NIV). When we examine our conversations with our husbands or wives or even our children, we must face the truth. Do we speak out of anger, resentment, or bitterness? Violent outbursts, whether public or private, grieve the Spirit of God. We should not relate with one another with wrath, anger, slander, and malice. Instead, we are to be kind, tenderhearted, and forgiving. Paul reminds us that God Himself is tenderhearted, kind, and forgiving. God forgave us when we didn't deserve forgiveness: "the kindness of God leads you to repentance" (Romans 2:4).

To those who yell at us and slander us, we must turn the tables and offer tenderness and kindness in return. In so doing, we give them what they don't deserve. That's what makes a great marriage. When a spouse is yelling, we need to respond as the Bible teaches: "A soft answer turns away wrath" (Proverbs 15:1 NKJV). When she is bitter, he must be forgiving. When he is cruel, she must be kindhearted. In that way, we imitate Christ in giving something that the other person doesn't deserve.

Marriage is a picture of Christ to a lost world and His relationship to the church. So when we understand that concept, we can give unselfishly for Christ's sake. Others must see God in our marriages; therefore we must imitate God. This is the command: don't grieve the Spirit of God.

Considerations

Spoken words indicate a person's spiritual condition. James said, "If anyone thinks himself to be religious, and yet does not bridle his tongue but deceives his own heart, this man's religion is worthless" (1:26). His point is that a Christian ought to control his words; if not, the person is deceiving himself. Such self-deception shows a person's hypocrisy or false religion. The bottom line is that if the Gospel transforms a person into a new creation, then that transformation should show in a person's speech.

I'm always taken aback when I hear church people using swear words. It happens quite frequently. During phone conversations or face-to-face discussions, they cuss openly as they talk to me. If they feel comfortable swearing around me, their pastor, I wonder how they speak in their homes. When I will call such language to their attention, they seem surprised and ask, "What did I say?"

Sadly, for some individuals, using foul language has become so routine that they no longer realize how they sound. The same can be said for those who yell and criticize. Such negative speech unfortunately becomes a normal mode of communication for some. Yet the Bible says that life and death are in the power of the tongue (see Proverbs 18:21).

For effective communication, we must consider the following guidelines: First, when communicating with a spouse, be a ready listener. "He who gives an answer before he hears, it is folly and shame to him" (Proverbs 18:13). The Bible says that if a person gives an answer before she hears the whole story, that's foolishness. Yet how many times do we, in the course of conversation, fail to listen to what our husbands or wives say? We already have a preconceived answer in mind because we are anxious to make our own point. Most of us are ready talkers but not ready listeners. It's good to let our spouse finish his or her sentences and strive to be a good listener. We ought not give an answer before we hear the full question.

The second consideration is to be slow to speak. "A man has joy in an apt answer, and how delightful is a timely word!" (Proverbs 15:23). A timely word delivers wholesome speech at the precise moment it's needed. In addition, a righteous person considers his answer before speaking. "The heart of the righteous ponders how to answer, but the mouth of the wicked pours out evil things" (Proverbs 15:28). A wise answer requires forethought. "Do you see a man who is hasty in his words? There is more hope for a fool than for him" (Proverbs 29:20).

The third consideration is that we must speak the truth in love. "Speaking the truth in love, we are to grow up in all aspects into Him who is the head, even Christ....Therefore, laying aside falsehood, speak truth each one of you with his neighbor, for we are members of one another. Be angry, and yet do not sin; do not let the sun go down on your anger, and do not give the devil an opportunity" (Ephesians 4:15, 25-27). Many people end the day angry at something or someone. However, Paul warns that if we go to bed angry, we give the devil an opportunity to tempt us with bitterness and resentment. Instead, we must deal with conflict before the sun goes down. We must put aside falsehood and speak the truth.

Fourth, we must not involve ourselves in quarrels. "The beginning of strife is like letting out water, so abandon the quarrel before it breaks out" (Proverbs 17:14). Often small arguments can escalate into something surprisingly huge and unproductive. Sometimes it's good to abandon the quarrel and just walk away from it. "Keeping away from strife is an honor for a man, but any fool will quarrel" (Proverbs 20:3). If we always have to win an argument, then we have a problem with pride and arrogance. What's at stake is the Lord Jesus Christ and His reputation lived out through our lives. It would be better to say, "Let's take a time-out here for a minute. Let's go pray about this disagreement individually. Then come back and talk about it together like two Christians who love the Lord Jesus Christ."

It's important to remember that Jesus Christ must be at the center of our conversations. Whenever our discussions depart from scriptural guidelines, our own sentimental feelings or our frustration or our anger wells up inside. Instead, we can keep Christ as the focal point by saying to ourselves, *"You know, the Lord Jesus Christ would have us make peace."* If we quote Scripture, the Spirit of God will calm our hearts and attitudes, allowing us to communicate freely with one another. When we are wrong, we should confess it and ask forgiveness. We should practice these words: "I'm so sorry. Please forgive me." We shouldn't just say, "I apologize." That response doesn't mean anything. Nor should we just say, "I'm sorry." That's a game by Parker Brothers. We should express both these statements: "I'm so sorry. Please forgive me."

Saying, "Please forgive me" is the biblical way. Furthermore, it's important to give your spouse time to reply, "Yes, I do forgive you." If the wife doesn't forgive but goes on with the conversation, the husband should say, "Excuse me, before we go any further, I need you to hear me. Would you please forgive me?" Once the wife forgives the husband, the barriers come down, and there's renewed freedom to communicate one with the other.

Fifth: rather than get in a "last word," we need to forgive our husbands or wives, be tenderhearted, forgiving one another, just as God for Christ's sake has forgiven us (Ephesians 4:32). Communication is never difficult if Jesus Christ is at the center of the conversation. When He's the focal point, when His Word is quoted, communication becomes easier because it becomes biblical. We must put aside our own agendas and behave God's way. If I had a nickel for every time I was right and my wife was wrong, I'd be very poor. I like to think I'm always right, but of course, that's not true. Often, I have to admit my mistake and seek forgiveness. Fortunately, I have a wife who loves to extend forgiveness.

The sixth consideration is to avoid nagging; we must remember that "the contentions of a wife are a constant dripping" (Proverbs 19:13b). People who nag don't know how to pray, but people who know how to pray don't need to nag. We nag in an effort to control others. The constant naggings of a wife are like the faucet that drips and drips and drips and drips. However, nagging never brings change. We must substitute prayer for nagging. God is the one to bring change.

Confrontation

In marriage, we cannot be afraid to confront a spouse. Some individuals avoid such conflicts. They say, "Oh, I could never say that to my husband. Oh, he'd be so hurt, or he'd be devastated." Yet for true communication and growth to take place, a husband or wife must be willing to discuss difficult issues. If a husband is doing something wrong or sinful that needs to be corrected and the wife doesn't confront him, then that couple doesn't have a good marriage. They are afraid to do what the Bible says.

Husbands and wives must be willing to discuss difficult matters. Using the excuse, "I can't confront my wife because she won't be able to handle the truth," only contributes to the problem. The ability to negotiate conflicts and confront sin between husbands and wives is vital to a healthy relationship:

> Better is open rebuke
> Than love that is concealed.
> Faithful are the wounds of a friend,
> But deceitful are the kisses of an enemy. (Proverbs 27:5-6)

It's important that marriage partners approach problems through prayer and love and humility. In so doing, they will contribute to the other's spiritual growth. "Iron sharpens iron, so one man [or woman] sharpens another" (Proverbs 27:17).

Christ in His dealings with the Pharisees warned, "Do not judge so that you will not be judged" (Matthew 7:1). Sometimes our own self-righteousness keeps us from being what God desires for us. We look at someone else's sin, which is small as a speck, while ignoring our big failures that blind us like a log in our own eye (Matthew 7:3). Further, without a spirit of judgment, we are better able to confront our own sin as well as confronting a spouse about their sin. There are many wives who know their husbands are into Internet pornography or they have a drinking problem, yet the women say nothing. They avoid dealing with the problem, but it's critical that they do. Husbands and wives must be helpmates to each other. Therefore, it's the spouse's responsibility to confront her partner about sin.

Consider another example, perhaps a wife has a problem in her speech; perhaps she talks too much. So the husband might say, "Honey, it's time for you to stop dominating conversations and stop using hasty words. Consider being more quiet, my dear." During these times of confrontation, husbands and wives should share scriptural concepts with one another. That helps make a marriage strong and brings couples closer. The goal is to reach a place where husbands and wives can communicate about the most intimate details of their lives, even the sinful details. Once the discussion opens up, the couple can talk to God about the problems together and seek solutions.

Concession

Couples must concede to the other one. One person doesn't always have to be top dog. "Let love be without hypocrisy. Abhor what is evil; cling to what is good. Be devoted to one another in brotherly love; give preference to one another in honor" (Romans 12:9-10). In other words, prefer the other one. We honor our spouses by allowing them to voice their opinions and their criticism.

For me, I secretly dread it when my wife asks, "Honey, can I talk to you about something?" When she says that, I know it's going to be negative. So I take a big breath and reply, "Sure Babe, go ahead." Of course, the biggest critic of my sermons is my wife. She sits in the service attentively, taking notes. Then later at home, she'll ask, "Honey, can I give you a suggestion?" Once I swallow my pride, I agree and wait for her response. Then in this sweet tone, she'll say, "You know, maybe you could make your point this way, instead of saying it that way."

My initial thoughts are usually something like, *"What do you know? You don't look at those people every week like I do. How do you know what to say? Why do you think that wasn't the right way to make my point?"* I realize that my first responses are not good. The point is that I don't care if others criticize my preaching, but it's painful when my wife criticizes my work. However, I've developed a more appropriate response. "Thanks, Honey, I'll take that into account." In spite of all the pain it causes me, I know I must listen to my wife. Is she a preacher? No. Is she ever going to be preacher? No. However, she is my helpmate. God gave her to me for "such a time as this." So I should listen to what she says and heed her suggestions. In so doing, I grow personally and I also give preference and honor to her.

The Bible says that we are to honor our wives. "You husbands in the same way, live with your wives in an understanding way, as with someone weaker, since she is a woman; and show her honor as a fellow heir of the grace of life" (1 Peter 3:7). Husbands serve the Lord first and then serve their wives. Likewise, wives first serve God and then their husbands.

Compassion

We must clothe ourselves with compassion; we must put it on like a garment. "So, as you have been chosen of God, holy and beloved, put on a heart of compassion, kindness, humility, gentleness and patience" (Colossians 3:12). My Father-in-law shared this verse with me the day Laurie and I married. A heart of compassion makes a marriage vibrant. When we care sincerely for a spouse, we will be kind, not harsh. Christ used the same word for "harsh" when he said, *"My yolk is easy"* (Matthew 11:30). In other words, His yolk is not harsh; it is kind. This kindness leads us to repentance.

When we put on a heart of compassion, not only do we respond kindly, we also respond humbly and gently. The word "gentleness" means, "one who is willing to suffer injury instead of inflict injury." A heart of compassion says, "I will allow you to inflict me with a problem rather than allowing myself to injure you with my words or my actions." That's the gentle spirit. That is *macrothumia*, a word that means "to bear up under, " as in bearing with one another and forgiving one another. As I've mentioned before, I wear a neck chain that my wife gave me the night we were married: it is a reminder of this verse, that love, as the Phillips translation says, is the "golden chain of all the virtues" (Colossians 3:14).

Lord, help us to love one another by showing compassion. God, may You give us the strength to communicate in a way that glorifies Your name. Amen.

17

God's Counsel for Couples: Dangers of Compromise

Marriage is a journey. It should be a joyful journey; but for many, it is not. Sadly, some husbands and wives struggle year after year without finding solutions to their conflicts. However, Christian couples don't journey alone; they travel with the Master, Jesus Christ. If on the road together, couples can gain the strength of commitment and learn obedience to God, then they will find success in marriage, making their lives together the joyful one God had in mind.

On this road with the Master, there are two parameters to consider. First, we must journey with Him without questioning. Second, we must resist the urge to compromise. For example, consider Zacharias and Elizabeth, the parents of John the Baptist. When the Angel Gabriel announced that the couple would have a child, Zacharias was very confused. He doubted the angel's divine message. "Zacharias said to the angel, 'How will I know this for certain? For I am an old man and my wife is advanced in years'" (Luke 1:18). Zacharias' wife Elizabeth could not have children. Yet Zacharias was a priest, who knew well the Old Testament accounts of such miraculous events. He knew that Abraham's wife Sara had been barren, yet God blessed her with a child. He knew that Isaac's Rebecca had also been childless, but God gave her twin sons, Esau and Jacob. Further, he knew how God answered Hannah's fervent prayers by providing a baby boy, Samuel.

However, Zacharias could not conceive that he and his wife would receive the same blessing. So the Angel Gabriel made him deaf and mute. (Striking a priest dumb is like telling a preacher he can't speak for nine months. That's a hard situation.) Zacharias's question did not come from his desire to understand the situation, but because he doubted the veracity of Gabriel's message.

We can learn from Zacharias's experience, so that when we journey with Jesus, we follow Him without question. Our response should be, "Yes, Lord, whatever You say." When we doubt God, we question Him. Our queries arise because we don't believe that He's going to do what He says. Such disbelief hindered Zacharias and it can hinder us, too.

When a person doubts, he becomes vulnerable to compromise. Abraham and Sara were led to compromise when they doubted that God would fulfill His promise to give them a son. The couple grew impatient and decided that their maidservant Hagar would be the one to produce Abraham's heir. Their actions set in motion a conflict among groups of people that continue in each generation. Although Abraham and Sara are mentioned in the Hebrews 11 "Hall of Faith" passage as people who honored God, they were imperfect sojourners. Their story demonstrates clearly the danger of compromise.

Such failure is also evident in the story of David and Bathsheba. King David knew the law, yet he yielded to temptation. Other kings demonstrated power by having a large harem, and David followed their example, a mistake that cost him dearly. Because of his illicit relationship with Bathsheba, he first lied and then committed murder. Even though the Bible says that David was a man after God's own heart, his compromise caused several tragedies.

To avoid such tragic consequences, we can follow a better biblical model. The prophet Hosea exemplifies a man who didn't compromise. His wife Gomer deserted him to become a prostitute. Hosea had every right to leave her. Yet he obeyed the Word of the Lord. He pursued Gomer and redeemed her from the slave market. There she stood, naked, degraded, and shamed, but he willingly bought her back. God was using him as a living illustration for the wayward nature of the nation of Israel in contrast to God's faithfulness. Similarly, God wants our marriages to be living illustrations of Christ's relationship to the church (see Ephesians 5).

The lyrics of Will L. Thompson's traditional hymn, "Jesus Is All the World to Me" emphasizes our friendship with Jesus:

> Jesus is all the world to me.
> I want no better friend;
> I trust Him now, I'll trust Him when
> life's fleeting days shall end.

Each verse ends with the line, "He's my friend." The song reminds us that nothing matters except Jesus Christ. He's our friend, the one to journey with. The songwriter understood what it means to journey with the Master, unquestioningly and uncompromisingly.

How can we journey with the Master without question or compromise? We can find guidance in the admonition and clarification we are given in 1 Thessalonians 5. Paul offers warnings and instructions that can show us how we ought to live on our "road of life."

The Admonition

The admonition deals with an attitude of the inner life; it is set forth in three commands—rejoice, pray, and give thanks. "Rejoice always; pray without ceasing; in everything give thanks; for this is God's will for you in Christ Jesus" (1 Thessalonians 5:16-18). Paul rattles off these commands confidently, knowing that his Thessalonian audience would be receptive to such truths. "For this reason we also constantly thank God that when you received the Word of God which you heard from us, you accepted it not as the word of men, but for what it really is, the Word of God, which also performs its work in you who believe" (1 Thessalonians 2:13). So like the Thessalonians, when we read the Bible, we must accept its truths. When we do so, it's like putting out a welcome mat for God to visit us.

The Clarification

As we accept God's work in our lives, we must also consider some biblical clarification. First, with humility, we must receive the "implanted" word which is able to save our souls (James 1). It's important to understand that life was not easy for the Thessalonians. "For you, brethren, became imitators of the churches of God in Christ Jesus that are in Judea, for you also endured the same sufferings at the hands of your own countrymen" (1 Thessalonians 2:14). These people were suffering, so when Paul asked them to "Rejoice always," it seemed paradoxical.

Be Joyful Continually: When Paul speaks of joy, it is not some emotional high but an inner attitude that glorifies the Lord Jesus Christ. Paul testifies of the hardships in his life, "but in everything commending ourselves as servants of God, in much endurance, in afflictions, in hardships, in distresses, in beatings, in imprisonments, in tumults, in labors, in sleeplessness, in hunger" (2 Corinthians 6:4-5). He says, "We're hungry. We don't get enough sleep. We are beaten. We are imprisoned. We are persecuted. Yet, we are always rejoicing." Thus, Paul demonstrates that he was a man committed to serving God no matter what.

In the middle of suffering, how is it possible to be joyful continually? Paul says, "For I consider that the sufferings of this present time are not worthy to be compared with the glory that is to be revealed to us" (Romans 8:18). When Paul says we should "consider," he is speaking of a numerical calculation. It's a word that refers to reaching a settled conclusion by careful study or careful reasoning. Paul strongly affirms that any time a person suffers for Christ's sake, it's a small price to pay for the dividends they will reap in eternity. So it's important to calculate the temporal. No matter how difficult one's condition or situation, it will not last forever. When in difficulty, we only see pain, not the proverbial "light at the end of the tunnel." If we're suffering difficulty because of our own sin, that's our fault (see 1 Peter 2 and 4). However, if we suffer difficulty and hardship because of our commitment to Christ, then Paul says we can "calculate" the temporal. The suffering lasts only for a limited time.

We can declare with the Psalmist, "I will bless the Lord at all times; His praise shall continually be in my mouth" (Psalm 34:1). Paul continues this thought in Romans 5:3, "And not only this, but we also exult in our tribulations." As difficult as it may seem, we benefit from tribulation and persecution because such trials bring about "perseverance; and perseverance, proven character; and proven character, hope; and hope does not disappoint, because the love of God has been poured out within our hearts through the Holy Spirit who was given to us" (Romans 5:4-5). Paul says that he is never disappointed because his hope is in God, and God never disappoints.

Many times, we find ourselves disappointed because what we hoped would happen in our family doesn't happen. What we hoped for in our jobs doesn't materialize. What we hoped would happen in our marriage doesn't occur. We are tempted to give up. We want to get rid of the disappointments. Yet Paul urges us to reevaluate our temporal situations. Such difficulties are brief compared to eternity. Satan wants us focused horizontally on our problems. He doesn't want our affections set on eternal values. He sends discouragement so that we question God. However, joy comes when we consider eternity.

Contemplate the Eternal: During his life, Paul experienced much hardship. He didn't have an easy life. People hated the man. They wanted him dead. However, Paul remained confident in his God. "Therefore we do not lose heart, but though our outer man is decaying, yet our inner man is being renewed day by day. For momentary, light affliction is producing for us an eternal weight of glory far beyond all comparison, while we look not at the things which are seen, but at the things which are not seen; for the things which are seen are temporal, but the things which are not seen are eternal" (2 Corinthians 4:16).

It may be difficult to understand the rejection and isolation that Paul experienced because we can usually find somebody to be kind to us—a person says, "Hi," or buys us a coffee. However, some people refused to travel with Paul because they feared for their safety. When the physician Luke accompanied Paul, he did so to offer his medical services. Paul needed help because he was beaten so often. Luke would treat his wounds so Paul could continue his ministry. Yet Paul never gave up because he considered his suffering a momentary affliction.

Celebrate the Trial: Trouble doesn't last forever. When we focus on the eternal, we are better able to celebrate within the trial. Like Paul, when we are weak, God demonstrates His strength (see 2 Corinthians 12:10). Once when Paul boarded a ship as a prisoner, a great storm arose. All aboard feared for their lives. Over 270 men panicked as water poured onto the deck, and the boat pitched wildly on the waves. Yet Paul said, "Therefore, keep up your courage, men, for I believe God that it will turn out exactly as I have been told" (Acts 27:25).

We don't experience good cheer in a crisis because at the deepest level, we don't believe God. If Jesus is with us, why do we fear or question? When we trust the Lord for everything, we can experience peace. God will protect us, watch over us, and supply all of our needs because He is our tender shepherd and cares more for our souls than we do. That's why Paul could say, "Rejoice in the Lord always; again I will say, rejoice!" (Philippians 4:4).

We may say, "I can't rejoice about the tragedy I'm facing." But we must. In Galatians 5, Paul talks about the fruit of the Spirit being love, peace, and joy. The Spirit of God produces the joy in us, "for the kingdom of God is not eating and drinking, but righteousness and peace and joy in the Holy Spirit" (Romans 14:17). That's the kingdom of God, and we're part of that kingdom if we're children of God. A.J. Mason said, "The Christian who remains in sadness and depression really breaks a commandment; in some direction or other he mistrusts God—His power, providence, forgiveness."[1]

Individuals who live in despondency, always down in the dumps, are people who doubt God. In fact, a simple definition of depression is "misplaced dependency." If depressed individuals were reliant upon God Almighty, they would find encouragement. However, because they're dependent upon someone else, when that person betrays or disappoints them, they become discouraged.

When we face difficulties, imminent tragedies, or immense failures, we must understand that God is still in complete control of everything. God works all things together for good to those who love Him and are called according to His purpose (Romans 8:28).

God's going to orchestrate the events of our lives for His own glory and our own good. That truth should lift us out of the dumps where we've fallen. We must choose to trust God and His promises; otherwise we live in painful doubt and discouragement.

Be Prayerful Constantly: What does it mean to "pray without ceasing"? (1 Thessalonians 5:17 KJV) We can't pray every moment. The phrase describes a reverential attitude, not a specific time given to petition. It refers to one's heavenward consciousness as it is focused on God and our communication with Him, living moment by moment in His presence. J.B. Lightfoot said, "It is not in the moving of the lips, but in the elevation of the heart to God that the essence of prayer consists."[2] We must develop a growing awareness that God is always with us.

In Genesis 39, we learn of Joseph's story. The statement, "And the Lord was with him" is repeated four times in the chapter. Despite the betrayals and injustices that Joseph experienced, the man recognized the presence of Almighty God in his life. So much so that it says that his employer, Potiphar knew that Joseph's God was with him. Later in Acts 7, Stephen commented on Joseph's experience. "The patriarchs became jealous and sold him into Egypt. Yet God was with him, and rescued him from all his afflictions, and granted him favor and wisdom in the sight of Pharaoh, king of Egypt, and he made him governor over Egypt and all his household" (Acts 7:9-10).

If we can pray without ceasing, like Joseph, we can sense the presence of God's Spirit at work in us. We can reflect the light of His glorious presence every moment. Leon Morris said, "We are to live in the spirit of prayer, realizing our dependence on God for all we have and are, being conscious of His presence with us wherever we may be, yielding ourselves continually to Him to do His will."[3]

Be Thankful Consistently: While the two previous commands (be joyful and be prayerful) relate to time, giving thanks is more universal in scope. The Christian is to meet difficulties with a spirit of unfailing gratitude and give thanks for everything (Ephesians 5:20). Paul and Silas were singing and praising God and giving glory to His name, even though they had been beaten and imprisoned. Similarly, Peter and the apostles were also counted worthy to suffer shame for

Jesus' name (Acts 5). Those people understood what it meant to give thanks consistently. That's a perspective we Christians must learn.

To move forward in our spiritual attitudes, we must ask ourselves three questions:

- *Today, did I rejoice always?*
- *Today, did I pray without ceasing?*
- *Today, did I give thanks in and for everything?*

At the end of the day, it's important to evaluate our actions and answers. A husband could with his wife and ask, "Was there something you couldn't rejoice in today? Let's talk about it." Our goal should be to live in the light of God's presence, recognizing that He is with us.

The Justification

D. Edmond Hiebert said, "If the dove of Christian joy is continuing to mount upward it must fly on the wings of prayer and thanksgiving."[4] Everything that we encounter in a day, we encounter because God has us in mind. As a result, He wants us to face obstacles and difficulties in order that we might rejoice, pray, and give thanks to Him. That's His will for each of us. God wants to make us into something better than we are today. Husbands must demonstrate to their wives that they know that God is with them as He was with Joseph in Egypt.

In my personal life, I want those whom I visit with everyday to know that God is with me. To do so, I must rejoice, pray, and give thanks in everything. I understand that such behavior is God's will for me. Everything that happens to me doesn't just happen. There are no accidents in life. God is the controller and designer of everything. Therefore, He has a perfect plan for me, specifically designed to shape me and mold me into the kind of person He wants me to be. In God's plan, He gives each of us the power to complete the tasks He calls us to perform.

The Examination

The story of Mary and Joseph shows the virtue of trust and obedience to God. If we put ourselves in Mary's sandals, we can understand the complexity of her dilemma. An angel tells her she will conceive a child through the Holy Spirit. How could she explain such an event to her friends? It wasn't easy for Mary. Telling Joseph the news must have been even more difficult. She must have feared that Joseph would not believe her.

Such fears were not unfounded because the story explains that Joseph did have doubts. He hoped to "put her away privately," to divorce her because she was pregnant. However, an angel also came to explain the truth:

> But when he had considered this, behold, an angel of the Lord appeared to him in a dream, saying, "Joseph, son of David, do not be afraid to take Mary as your wife; for the Child who has been conceived in her is of the Holy Spirit. She will bear a Son; and you will call His name Jesus, for He will save His people from their sins."...And Joseph awoke from his sleep and did as the angel of the Lord commanded him, and took Mary as his wife, but kept her a virgin until she gave birth to a Son; and he called His name Jesus. (Matthew 1:20-25)

Later on, Simeon told Mary, "Your soul is going to be pierced through until the end. Your whole life's going to be in turmoil, Mary. Oh sure, you birthed the Messiah, but it is going to bring havoc on you and your family from this day until the end" (paraphrased from Luke 2:28-35).

The real situation with Mary and Joseph wasn't as easy as seems in the Christmas story. However, Mary gave a willing response to the angel's message: "may it be done to me according to your word" (Luke 1:38). Even her cousin Elizabeth said, "Blessed is she who believed that there would be a fulfillment of what had been spoken to her by the Lord" (Luke 1:45).

Mary didn't compromise or question the Lord's message. She journeyed with the Master unquestionably and uncompromisingly. Neither did Joseph compromise the Word of the Lord. "Now when they had gone, behold the angel of the Lord appeared to Joseph in a dream and said, 'Get up! Take the Child and His mother and flee to Egypt, and remain there until I tell you; for Herod is going to search for the Child to destroy Him.' So Joseph got up and took the Child and His mother while it was still night, and left for Egypt" (Matthew 2:13-14). Again, these individuals responded unquestioningly, uncompromisingly. God said, "Leave." Joseph said, "We're out of here."

That's where we need to be. If God says, "This is what you do. Rejoice always. Pray without ceasing. In everything give thanks," we must answer wholeheartedly, "Yes." That's what we will do because in our marriage relationships, we want to journey with the Master unquestioningly and uncompromisingly:

> Rejoice in the Lord always; again I will say, rejoice! Let your gentle spirit be known to all men. The Lord is near. Be anxious for nothing, but in everything by prayer and supplication with thanksgiving let your requests be made known to God. And the peace of God, which surpasses all comprehension, will guard your hearts and your minds in Christ Jesus. (Philippians 4:4-7)

Dear Lord, We rejoice that You are near. Continually remind us that we live in Your presence, Almighty God. We know You are with us. Thank You, for Your plan, for Your will, and for Your strength. Amen.

18

Hallmarks for Husbands

"Husbands, love your wives, just as Christ also loved the church and gave Himself up for her" (Ephesians 5:25). Great lovers make great leaders. The biblical duty and responsibility of a man is not only to be a leader but also to be a lover of his family. A man's ability to lead is determined by what kind of lover he is. To understand what it means to love his wife and family, a man must understand what God's Word says about love.

The Apostle Paul outlined a comprehensive description of love in 1 Corinthians 13:4-8. In this passage, Paul emphasizes the utter selflessness of love, its kindness, gentleness, and total concern for another's welfare. Paul relies on verbs to describe love's duties: it suffers long, rejoices always, bears all things, believes all things, hopes all things, and endures all things. In fact, "Love never fails" (1 Corinthians 13:8). Love is not passive but active. When a husband understands God's hallmarks of love, he can be transformed into the spiritual leader that God desires.

Honor Your Wife

You husbands in the same way, live with your wives in an understanding way, as with someone weaker, since she is a woman; and show her honor as a fellow heir of the grace of life, so that your prayers will not be hindered" (1 Peter 3:7). The Bible says that husbands are to grant honor to their wives. That's the opposite of putting her down. The word "honor" means to lift up or to elevate. It is the same word that is translated "precious" in 1 Peter 1:19, "but with the *precious* blood, as of a lamb unblemished and spotless, the blood of Christ." In this passage, Peter is describing how man was redeemed through the "precious" blood of the Lamb. So if a man is to "honor" his wife, he is to treat her as the most "precious" possession that he has. She is not just any woman, but rather God's chosen instrument given specifically to him.

The Bible says that it was not good for man to be alone, so God made for him a suitable helper (Genesis 2:18). A man's wife should occupy a highly respected position in the family and hold top priority in his schedule. When a husband honors his wife and respects her, then the children also realize how important she is. Conversely, if children treat their mother with little respect; if they interrupt her, speak down to her, or openly criticize her, then chances are they have observed that behavior modeled in their father in his relationship with the mother.

When Peter describes women as the "weaker vessel," he speaks of physical characteristics (1 Peter 3:7). She's not weaker spiritually but physically. It's quite obvious that women are not as physically strong as men. They do not possess the same muscle mass. Furthermore, because the wife is the weaker vessel, a man can be tempted to dishonor his wife through intimidation and domination.

However, the Bible warns that if a husband doesn't honor his wife, if she's not his number one priority, his prayer life is hindered. Sometimes when men have a weak spiritual life, it's not because they don't pray or read the Bible. It's because they dishonor their wives. Learning how to honor a wife can transform a man's prayers. In fact, his ministry could change once he learns how to truly honor his mate. So because the woman is that weaker vessel, a man must go overboard to elevate her, praise her, bless her, and grant her honor. "We are heirs together," Peters says, "of the grace of life." We're equal in the eyes of God. Therefore, we men need to lift our wives up in the eyes of our children and the community because she is our most prized possession.

It's fascinating that the Lord says, "Husbands, love your wives and do not be embittered against them" (Colossians 3:19). Does the statement suggest that bitterness primarily tends toward the husband more than anybody else in the home? Paul's admonition is very clear; don't be harsh, don't be resentful, and don't be preoccupied with her flaws. Such actions and attitudes produce bitter feelings toward her. Instead, the husband is to love her with a love that suffers long and endures all things. Love never fails because love is full of action.

Understand Your Wife

"Live with your wives in an understanding way" (1 Peter 3:7). That's an amazing statement because the most difficult person to understand in the world is a wife. The phrase "to live" or "to dwell" means to be at home with. Unfortunately, many men do not feel "at home" with their wives. They don't know how she is put together. Husbands must be students of their wives to perceive their innermost makeup, to discern their deep-seeded concerns, and to apprehend their fears.

A few years ago, my wife mentioned that the cozy house we occupied had grown a bit small. Its spaces shrunk as the kids grew older and bigger. She said, "Maybe we ought to pray about finding a house with more room."

So I prayed, "Lord, if you want us to you move, then open the door and show us where to go." Just two days later, our landlord announced that he was selling the house that we were renting. We would definitely have to move and in only thirty days. So I sat with my wife and said, "You asked for a new place to live, and God has granted your request. You see, He's closed the door here and is moving us. He just hasn't told us where we're going yet."

She could see that I wasn't worried about the situation because I knew that thirty days was an eternity for God. I said, "I remember the time when, on a Wednesday, our church congregation didn't have any place to meet for the following Sunday services, yet God provided a place by Friday so that we could worship together that weekend. God always knows the timetable. Everything is in his timeframe. My job is just to trust Him and to pray and to live in the light of His glorious presence."

Moving is more stressful for a wife than a husband. She's often responsible for the packing, cleaning, and organizing. Men can sleep anywhere; it's no big deal. But for women, it's a different matter. Women care about where they live, and they must like the environment.

In an "understanding way," men must remind their families that God will provide and will take care of them. A woman needs a sense of security. She wants to hold on to something sturdy that will keep her from falling. That's the way God designed it. As helpmates, we must be strong for our wives in a period of uncertainty. If we worry about what's going to happen next or where the next paycheck is coming from, then we don't provide the security that wives require. Wives (and children, too) must know that we trust God unquestionably, uncompromisingly, and that we believe absolutely that God is in control. Some times, though, we have to wait for Him to show us that plan.

In this process of gaining understanding, there are two subjects a man needs to study—his Bible and his bride. Peter says that there are some things hard to understand in the Scripture, and that's true (2 Peter 3:16). Therefore, men must pray for insight in order to grasp the complex concepts in the Bible. The same is true with wives. "To study a bride" means a man must pay attention. He must read her like a book: What are her weaknesses? What makes her sorrowful? What delights her? What are her hopes and dreams? "Wife study," like Bible study, means the man prays for insight from God to learn to meet her needs and spends time contemplating her personality and character.

Sanctify Your Wife

"Husbands, love your wives, just as Christ also loved the church and gave Himself up for her, so that He might sanctify her, having cleansed her by the washing of water with the word, that He might present to Himself the church in all her glory, having no spot or wrinkle or any such thing; but that she should be holy and blameless" (Ephesians 5:25-27). Christ sanctifies the body of the believer. In a similar way, He wants husbands to help sanctify their wives.

Love seeks purity. Therefore, the Lord set men and women apart to be used for greater spiritual purposes. For example, if a woman had an abusive father, the husband can encourage her emotional healing from that abuse. If she can learn forgiveness, she might have a ministry with her father as never before. Or maybe the wife had a domineering mother, who ran the home and would ramrod her choices through in every family decision. Whatever the case, the husband can be a "cleaner upper" by helping his wife to understand what the Bible says about relationships with God and others.

Husbands can assist their mates in maintaining holiness, purity, virtue, and righteousness. The man should not incite an argument or defile his wife by putting her in a compromising situation. Christ sanctifies by cleansing us with the "washing of water by the word, that He might present to Himself the church in all of her glory, having no spot or wrinkle or any such thing" (Ephesians 5:26b-27). The husband's job is to minister to his wife in such a way that she heals and grows spiritually, replacing broken attitudes and behaviors with godly ones.

So the man must ask himself, *"Is my wife more sanctified today than last month or last year? How have I contributed to that transformation?"* That's a hallmark for a husband. He must honor, understand, and sanctify his wife. True love does not rejoice in iniquity. It rejoices in purity. It rejoices in the truth (1 Corinthians 13:6). The Lord God gives men strength and wisdom and insight to meet their wives' needs.

Bless Your Wife

"Her children rise up and bless her; her husband also, and he praises her, [or he blesses her] saying: 'Many daughters have done nobly, but you excel them all'" (Proverbs 31:28-29). Her husband has much admiration for her.

Every woman wants to receive such approval. She wants acknowledgment for the work she does with the kids, keeping the household, and loving her husband. As she juggles all kinds of activities that occupy busy families at church services, sporting events, and after school programs, she needs her husband's support. The virtuous woman is praised by her husband. Her daughters want to be like her. Her boys want to marry women like her. Her husband commends her.

The concept sounds easy enough. However, the problem is that typically men seek glory for their own deeds. Yet the wife is to be the glory of the husband (1 Corinthians 11:7). She deserves to be honored and prized. Husbands should practice phrases like, "Wow honey, you're doing a great job with the kids." Or, "Sweetheart, that was a great meal," even if it didn't taste the greatest. My mom always said that burnt toast was good for the complexion. Perhaps she made up that story because she often burned the toast. Yet, the blacker the bread, the more my dad would praise Mom. As a kid, his compliments didn't make sense to me. But now that I'm married, I understand. My dad always spoke well of my mom. This praise was sweet music to her. A loving husband can communicate important statements, such as "You are my best friend. You are my confidante and intimate soul mate." These expressions bring wives pleasure. It's important to praise her openly.

Unfortunately, during casual conversations with friends, some husbands jokingly ridicule their wives. Perhaps she's too short, too tall, too thin, too heavy, too slow, or too silly. Such public criticism, even in jest, undermines relationships. Husbands should never speak down to their wives or anybody for that matter—not even in a joking manner.

Children should not hear negative or demeaning words about their mother. If they do, they may emulate such behavior, not only with their own mother but with their future spouses. Husbands must set forth a positive pattern. It's vital for husbands to bless their wives.

Accept Your Wife

"For this reason a man shall leave his father and his mother, and shall cleave to his wife; and they shall become one flesh. And the man and his wife were both naked and were not ashamed" (Genesis 2:24-25). The man and woman were one flesh. That is, they were so entwined that they accepted one another just as they were.

After the honeymoon period, a husband suddenly decides that he wants his wife to look or act a certain way—a different way. The husband's fault finding may arise because he fails to accept her attributes and personality. When the Genesis passage says that Adam and Eve were both naked, it speaks of more than a lack of clothing.

The statement suggests a spirit of honesty and openness between the couple. They had nothing to hide. True acceptance of another suggests exposing everything rather than hiding it all.

Instead of rejoicing with the wife of his youth, a man sometimes becomes disillusioned and makes comparisons. "Well, my first wife didn't shop constantly like you do." Or, "My mother didn't cook turkey that way." Or, "Wow, that gal at church sure is a sharp dresser. Too bad you don't dress like that." Making such comparisons reveals that the husband does not accept his wife, her talents, or tastes. It may also reveal a double standard. The husband may want his wife to lose weight while he puts on the pounds and never considers his own problems or appearance. If there are some ways in which a wife needs change, then the husband has a responsibility to converse lovingly with her about the matter. Comparisons always demean an individual, but encouragement brings hope.

It's important to remember that Christ accepted us when we were unworthy and unacceptable. Christ died for us when we were sinners (Romans 5:8). There was nothing acceptable or worthy about us. Therefore, if the perfect one, the Lord Jesus Christ, accepted the imperfect sinner, to demonstrate His love toward us, how much more are we, then, to picture Christ's love to the world through our relationship with our mates.

A lot of men are really into cars. They sometimes even name them. Every week, they wax the body, shine the chrome, and polish the interior. They study their car manuals and auto magazines over and over. Sadly, they spend all their time pampering a prized car in the garage while the wives in the house are virtually ignored. Consider how the marriage relationship would improve if the husband spent time reading the manual of his wife, and tenderly pampering her as he does his special car.

Nourish Your Wife

"So husbands ought also to love their own wives as their own bodies. He who loves his own wife loves himself; for no one ever hated his own flesh, but nourishes and cherishes it, just at Christ also does the church" (Ephesians 5:28-29). A wife is not merely a personal maid, babysitter, or sex partner. A wife is someone to be treasured as one treasures his own body. She is to be nourished and cherished.

We take care of ourselves. If we're hungry, we eat. If we're thirsty, we drink. If we're tired, we sleep. If we're disheveled, we clean up. In the same way, husbands should treat their wives as they want to be treated, to care for them as they care for themselves. This care is motivated by the love the couple share.

The word "nourish" means "to bring up," literally *to listen* and *to feed*. Nourishing a wife, then, is feeding and providing for her: "Fathers, do not provoke your children to anger; but bring them up in the discipline and instruction of the Lord" (Ephesians 6:4). The word "instruction" is the same word as "nourish" in Ephesians 5:29. These are the only passages that use the term in the New Testament. In these verses, Paul doesn't name the mother as provider but the father. The biblical standard establishes the husband as breadwinner. Christ gave His life for us and husbands are to follow that example by sacrificing for their wives. A couple might ask, "Well, does that mean a wife shouldn't work outside the home?" That is a choice each family must make. However, the Bible asserts that the husband plays the role of primary provider.

Wives are also to be "cherished." The word means "to warm with body heat." The term emphasizes tenderness and the intimacy that a man has with his wife. Husbands ought to provide secure environments for their brides. A wife should be able to say, "I am completely secure in my relationship with my husband and completely secure in his ability to provide for me and my family." That is a goal which each husband should seek. It may take time, but it is worth the effort. It is often difficult because Satan fights against husbands, yet it is the man's responsibility to provide and protect.

Desire Your Wife

The Song of Solomon is a book describing the physical affection of lovers. It describes desire in a relationship, not only sexual affection and physical affection, but also emotional affection.

> Let your fountain be blessed,
> And rejoice in the wife of your youth.

> As a loving hind and graceful doe,
> Let her breasts satisfy you at all times;
> Be exhilarated always with her love. (Proverbs 5:18-19)

A man may complain that he no longer desires his wife. There are usually two reasons why a man might lose desire. First, he is driven by selfishness caring more for himself than his mate. Second, he develops desire for someone else. However, love never seeks its own interests or its own benefit. Instead, love is always giving itself away (1 Corinthians 13:5). The Bible reminds us that we must deny ourselves. The good news is that we can ask God to forgive us for our selfish attitudes, then take steps to foster renewed desire for our mates.

Rather than cast blame on a spouse, it is important to believe that God can supply the love the husband needs to once again desire his wife. There is nothing too hard for God (see Jeremiah 32:17). Further, we are not to love only in words but with actions and with truth (see 1 John 3:18). A loving husband listens to his wife, overlooks her faults, and values her input. Such actions are tangible expressions of love. True love meets the needs of others. In addition, a husband must satisfy his wife. No man ever hates his own body; he loves himself (Ephesians 5:29). Yet husbands must learn to satisfy their wives as well as themselves.

Understanding these hallmarks can aid men in becoming better and stronger husbands. Women want romance. Women want security. Women want leadership. When their men provide those elements, wives will be satisfied. Their relationship will be blessed, and together they will also bless others.

Dear Lord, give us Your supernatural ability to be the loving men and women You've designed us to be. Help us men to honor, understand, sanctify, bless, accept, nourish, and desire our wives. Strengthen us husbands so that our wives will become the most satisfied women on the face of the earth. Amen.

19

Wisdom for Wives

In God's plan for the family, each member plays a unique role. While God intends that husbands be leaders of their families, the Lord designed the wife to be a suitable helper. "Then the Lord God said, 'It is not good for a man to be alone; I will make him a helper suitable for him.'...The man gave names to all the cattle, and to the birds of the sky, and to every beast of the field, but for Adam there was not found a helper suitable for him" (Genesis 2:18, 20). The woman becomes a suitable helper for the man in several ways.

Honorable Helpmate

Wives and husbands should be best friends. A wife should ask, *"Is this the man I want more than anybody else?"* A wife can do for her husband what nobody else can. Such friendships in marriage also involve dependency. "However, in the Lord, neither is the woman independent of man, nor is man independent of woman. For as the woman originates from the man, so also the man has his birth through the woman; and all things originate from God" (1 Corinthians 11:11-12). Sometimes wives strive for independence, which can make husbands feel that their assistance is not needed. In marriage, though, spouses need a healthy dependence on one another.

Developing a healthy friendship requires that a woman esteem her husband, showing the man that he is important to her. In so doing, she exercises love for her mate (see 1 Corinthians 13). A wife must also pray for her man. He should be the first one on her prayer list, as she asks God to make him into the man he ought to be.

Next, a wife should look for ways to minister to her husband and learn to accept his personality and temperament as part of who he is. Such action is different than accepting his sinful behavior or attitudes. Lastly, a wife commits fully to her spouse since true love endures to the end (1 Corinthians 13:7). Thus an honorable helpmate is one who thinks of her spouse and works to meet his needs. "Nevertheless, each individual among you also is to love his own wife even as himself, and the wife must see to it that she respects her husband" (Ephesians 5:33).

Submissive Servant

Submission is an attitude, not necessarily an action. It's possible for individuals to do outwardly what is expected of them while inwardly, they harbor resentment. However, submission is having a manner that honors Christ and glorifies His name. "Be subject to one another in the fear of Christ. Wives, be subject to your own husbands, as to the Lord" (Ephesians 5:21-22). The ultimate act of submission is to sacrifice one's life for another. Husbands are to give their lives as Christ gave Himself for the church (Ephesians 5:25). Wives, likewise, are to be submissive to their husbands as unto the Lord. Submitting to a husband is not primarily for his benefit. Rather it represents service to Christ, showing a woman's obedience and honor to the Lord.

Servant-hood is part of a Christian's identity. Jesus Christ took upon Himself the form of a servant, for His death on the cross was an act of ultimate service (Philippians 2:5-11). Christ, before His death, explained to His disciples that He did not come to be served but to serve and to give His life as a ransom for the lost (Mark 10:42-45). When a woman becomes a servant, she takes on Christ's identity because the Spirit of God dwells within her. She is a partaker of the divine nature. Also her acts of obedience influence not only her husband but also other people within her sphere.

Being a submissive servant requires that a wife follow her husband's lead. Problems develop if the husband is not a very good leader. How can a wife go along with a man who, for all intents and purposes, is a loser and totally inept? In such cases, a wife can aid her husband by being a supportive, honorable helpmate.

However, a woman is not obligated to follow her husband if he asks her to disobey the divine law of God, for she submits to her husband as unto the Lord (Ephesians 5:22). So submission is primarily to God and secondarily to the husband. Therefore, if a husband says, "We're not going to church because we have to watch the Laker's basketball game instead," the wife has the freedom to respectfully disagree. She can say, "Well honey, I'm going to church because God doesn't want me 'to forsake the assembling of ourselves together as some do'" (Hebrews 10:25 KJV). The biblical concept of submission applies to both partners. Both must strive to be obedient to God's will.

In some cases, a wife may face a more serious dilemma. Perhaps the husband announces that he's going to mortgage everything to make a risky investment. The wife may become fearful and think to herself, *"We're going to lose everything if I obey him. How am I ever going to influence him? If I let him make bad decisions, continue with his plans, our family will be financially destroyed."* It's important for wives to know what to do when such situations arise.

In the biblical example of Abraham and Sara, both partners made mistakes. The passage in Genesis 12 recounts how Abraham made a poor choice by going to Egypt without seeking God's guidance. When a crisis occurred, he was willing to lie about his wife in a deceptive scheme to spare his own life. Later on, Sara doubted that she would have a child as God had promised, so she took matters into her own hands. Women are tempted to take charge if their husbands display poor judgment or make hasty choices. In this case, Sara orchestrated what she thought was an adequate solution to conceiving an heir by giving the maidservant Hagar to her husband Abraham. (Thus Ishmael was born and the racial and political conflicts between the descendants of Abraham's two sons still exist.)

Yet Peter says, "For in this way in former times the holy women also, who hoped in God, used to adorn themselves, being submissive to their own husbands; just as Sara obeyed Abraham, calling him lord, and you have become her children if you do what is right without being frightened by any fear" (1 Peter 3:5-6). In this passage, Peter explains that Sara eventually learned submission, to obey and follow her husband's lead, despite the conflicts she faced.

Another instructive example is found in the book of Esther. A beautiful young Jewess became queen to King Xerxes. During his reign, a high prince, Haman, conspired to destroy the Jews by convincing the King to sign an execution order for all the Jewish exiles in the kingdom. When Esther's cousin Mordecai discovered the plan, he warned Queen Esther of the danger and challenged her to intercede for her people.

The King was about to destroy his own wife because he unwittingly signed the decree. So how could Esther make the most powerful man in the kingdom understand that he'd made a big mistake in advocating the extermination of her people? It's the same dilemma many wives face: How does she make her husband understand that he's making the biggest blunder of his life? Or how can a wife persuade a husband to make the proper choice or rethink an action or decision?

Esther provides an insightful example. "Then Esther told them to reply to Mordecai, 'Go, assemble all the Jews who are found in Susa, and fast for me; do not eat or drink for three days, night or day. I and my maidens also will fast in the same way. And thus I will go in to the king, which is not according to the law; and if I perish, I perish'" (Esther 4:15-16).

Esther's first action was to call for a fast. The request implied that she was asking the people to pray. She didn't run immediately to the King's court to tell him about the impending crisis. Nor did she confront him with the gravity of his actions. Instead, she first elected to fast and pray. She made herself ready because as the book of Proverbs says, "The king's heart is like channels of water in the hand of the Lord; He turns it wherever He wishes" (Proverbs 21:1).

In the same way, God can change a husband's heart. Sometimes, we pray doubting that God will answer. We grow skeptical, not sure He's going to provide help or send guidance. We pray like a double-minded man who's unstable in all of his ways (James 1:8). Yet God repeatedly tells us, "Give your concerns to Me. Let Me provide direction." Sometimes God doesn't answer prayer the way we want because God hopes to work change in us before He works on the other person. You see, our prayer life is more about us than about anyone else. God uses many circumstances to teach and develop us. But above all, we must pray and not faint. In Esther's case, she declared a fast and waited on the Lord.

When Esther did approach the king, she put on her best dress.

> Now it came about on the third day that Esther put on her royal robes and stood in the inner court of the king's palace in front of the king's rooms, and the king was sitting on his royal throne in the throne room, opposite the entrance to the palace. When the king saw Esther the Queen standing in the court, she obtained favor in his sight. (Esther 5:1-2)

Similarly, if after prayer, a wife really needs to confront her husband about an important issue, she shouldn't approach him in old shorts and a t-shirt. For even Esther, a truly beautiful woman, made special preparation before meeting her husband and presented herself in her most appealing aspect.

In the same way, when a woman talks to her husband, she must strive to please him rather than make him angry. It's unwise for her to rush in and declare, "You're making a huge mistake!" or ask in a panicked tone, "Oh, what are you doing?" Instead, she must win his admiration, so that he will be more likely to ask, "What do you need, Babe?" Esther understood the importance of a considerate appeal. There's more to solving a dilemma than through prayer alone. Wives also must be responsible in how they respond to their husbands. In Esther's case, she found favor in the eyes of the King.

Next, Esther took time to choose the proper day. "It came about on the third day" (Esther 5:1). It's important that a woman select the right opportunity for confronting her husband. It helps if he's in the right mood and not in a hurry to go golfing. If necessary, a couple may have to arrange a time to talk. Esther chose the right day. Her timing was crucial. Similarly, wives must look for the right time to influence their husbands.

Then Esther prepared a banquet.

> [T]he king extended to Esther the golden scepter which was in his hand. So Esther came near and touched the top of the scepter. Then the king said to her, "What is troubling you, Queen Esther? And what is your request? Even to half of the kingdom it will be given to you." Esther said, "If it pleases the king, may the king and Haman come this day to the banquet that I have prepared for him." (Esther 5:2-4)

The king promised her half the kingdom, so she made plans to deliver her enemy into his royal hands. With humility, meekness, and a quiet spirit, she begged her husband to reconsider his decree. With God's help, she changed the heart of her husband. God used Esther to save a nation.

Sometimes, because of fear and exasperation, a wife just wants to tell her husband what to do. In an emotional outburst, she may say he's a fool or a loser. She may declare he's making a huge mistake. However, the truth is that we men already know the truth about ourselves. No one has to tell us what we really are. To remind us men of our weaknesses and failures does not help the romantic relationship. It's important for wives to respectfully intercede for their husbands in a biblical manner. Just as God had a great plan for Esther, He also has a great plan for today's women of faith. A wife with a submissive attitude has a heart like Esther, one that desires to please God, to seek His face first, and obey God above anything else.

Loyal Lover

Older women are to teach younger women how to respond to the needs of their families and specifically how to love their husbands. "Older women likewise are to be reverent in their behavior, not malicious gossips nor enslaved to much wine, teaching what is good, so that they may encourage the young women to love their husbands, to love their children, to be sensible, pure, workers at home, kind, being subject to their own husbands, so that the Word of God may not be dishonored" (Titus 2:3-5).

The order of the verb phrases in the Titus passage is significant. Paul lists "love your husbands" before "love your children."

Yet some women love their children more than their husbands. It's obvious when a man sees his mate affectionately giving time to the children, reaching out to them, but not to him. Husbands know when they don't come first. However it's vital for wives to love their husbands and put him first.

When a woman doesn't love her husband, it may have nothing to do with him being the wrong man or an unsuitable mate. Rather, it may have everything to do with the woman's relationship with God. Once a woman understands the love of God, then she understands what it means to love her husband and be devoted to him. Without that relationship with God, it's difficult for someone to be a loyal, committed lover. However, if a wife gives herself to God, then she is empowered to do what God has asked of her as a wife.

The Apostle Paul asserts that Christian women are to be sensible, pure, and kind (Titus 2). Thus women should execute sound judgment. They must display purity in motives, thoughts, and marital faithfulness. They should openly show kindness and concern for their mates. When husbands disappoint, and they will, women can be tempted to dream about how life could be better with a different man. Perhaps a wife thinks she could find a guy who would be more considerate, better at investing, or more adept at meeting her needs. Such desires are pure fantasy, but if nurtured, they can produce a growing sense of discontentment in the marriage. So it's important that a wife be a loyal lover.

In the Song of Solomon, the writer describes what it's like for a woman to be completely lovesick for her husband.

> Like an apple tree among the trees of the forest,
> So is my beloved among the young men.
> In this shade I took great delight and sat down,
> And his fruit was sweet to my taste.
> He brought me to his banquet hall,
> And his banner over me is love.
> Sustain me with raisin cakes,
> Refresh me with the apples,
> Because I am lovesick. (2:3-5)

"I'm lovesick," the speaker says. It is possible for women to pray that God makes them feel this same kind of desire for their own husbands. Furthermore, the woman praises her man.

> My beloved is dazzling and ruddy,
> Outstanding among ten thousand.
> His head is like gold, pure gold;
> His locks are like clusters of dates
> And black as a raven. His eyes are like doves
> Beside streams of water,
> Bathed in milk,
> And reposed in their setting....
> This is my beloved and this is my friend.
> (Song of Solomon 5:10-12, 16)

The speaker compliments her lover's appearance. Everyone needs praise; why not offer compliments freely to the ones we love? Such actions strengthen commitment. The priorities of the godly wife are to love God, then her husband, then her children.

Humble Homemaker

Women must understand that as homemakers, they establish a home environment for their families. Older women are to teach younger women to be "workers at home" (Titus 2:5). That phrase "workers at home" is made up of two words, *oikos*, which means house and *ergon*, which means "work." Thus the intent is that women are household workers or homemakers.

That term *ergon* also appears in John 4:34 when Christ says, "My food is to do the will of Him who sent Me, and to accomplish His work." The Lord Jesus had a mission, to do what God said. He spent His life fulfilling that calling. Unfortunately, in today's society, the role of homemaker is disregarded as an outmoded concept. For some, such a role may even be regarded as a taboo—a role that undervalues women. Yet Paul asserts that work at home is an important and honorable responsibility. Creating a pleasant home environment ought to remain a priority. Some men avoid their homes by working late or going to the gym. However, if a wife creates a welcoming, safe environment for her husband, then he will skip the gym routine to come home and exercise with her instead.

Thus, the Bible says that the primary responsibility of the wife is to be a homemaker. It does not say that the woman's place is only in the home but that it is the woman's priority. It is possible for a woman to stay home, but still not create a loving environment for her family. Wives must ask themselves, *"Does my home provide a sense of refuge for my husband and children? Does my home offer a sense of security?"* Such considerations are important because the homemaker controls the environment of her house.

Excellent Example

God's wisdom for wives is that they be excellent examples. Peter speaks to women who are married to the unbelievers when he says, "In the same way, you wives, be submissive to your own husbands so that even if any of them are disobedient to the word, they may be won without a word by the behavior of their wives, as they observe their chaste and respectful behavior" (1 Peter 3:1-2). If a husband is not a Christian, he needs to see his wife's excellent example. Her behavior should reflect her unwavering commitment to God. For if she is committed to Christ, she will also be committed to her mate.

Her behavior and attitudes are key to the process of winning her husband so that, without even speaking a word, he may see something about her godly life that's worth imitating. Thus a husband may comment, "You know honey, I have noticed how patient and forgiving you are. I am so pleased that you behave in such kind and thoughtful ways." Such an excellent example draws men closer to God.

Sweet Spirit

Clothing, jewels, youth, and beauty all fade with age. Yet what is imperishable is the inner quality of a meek, quiet spirit. "Your adornment must not be merely external—braiding the hair, and wearing gold jewelry, or putting on dresses; but let it be the hidden person of the heart, with the imperishable quality of a gentle and quiet spirit, which is precious in the sight of God" (1 Peter 3:3-4). Esther understood that a woman's power and appeal wasn't merely from outward adornment. Her humble entreaty influenced the King's heart more than her beautiful appearance.

It's the spirit that Peter speaks about in 1 Peter 2:21-25, that meek spirit. The meekness Peter describes is like that gentleness associated with Christ, who said the meek shall inherit the earth (Matthew 5:5). He's not saying that women should sit in the corner, silent and invisible. This spiritual meekness represents one's tranquility of heart. The meek spirit is the opposite of the vengeful, retaliatory spirit. Instead, God asks us to be like Jesus Christ. "Take My yolk upon you and learn from Me, for I am gentle and humble in heart" (Matthew 11:29).

A Wonderful Woman

Proverbs 31 outlines the qualities of a virtuous wife:

> An excellent wife, who can find?
> For her worth is far above jewels.
> The heart of her husband trusts in her,
> And he will have no lack of gain. (Proverbs 31:10)

A husband's most valued treasure is his woman because "She does him good, not evil all the days of her life" (v 12). She encourages and strengthens her man. She doesn't demean him or criticize him openly.

She cares for her husband and her household. Clothing her family is a priority. "She looks for wool and flax and works with her hands in delight" (v 13). The virtuous woman plans and shops wisely. She finds the right items at the right prices for her family. Further, her family's sleep is more important than hers. "She rises also while it is still night, and gives food to her household and portions to her maidens" (v 15).

She earns money and invests wisely. "From her earnings she plants a vineyard" (v 16b); "She makes linen garments and sells them, and supplies belts to tradesmen" (v 24). She prepares in advance and is unafraid of a storm because her children are properly clothed. "She is not afraid of the snow for her household, for all her household are clothed with scarlet" (v 21). She also makes coverings for herself of fine linen and purple. "Strength and dignity are her clothing, and she smiles at the future" (v 25). That's the wonderful woman. She feels no anxiety, worry, or fear of tomorrow because she trusts God for the future.

The Bible says that a wonderful woman is wise and kind. She takes care of her family and is motivated, not idle. Her husband and children are grateful for her efforts and are inspired by her godly character. The Proverbs 31 passage ends with the reminder that, "Charm is deceitful and beauty is vain, but a woman who fears the Lord, she shall be praised" (v 30).

Lord, our prayer is that women of God will embrace Your plan with enthusiasm and obedience—to love and care for their husbands and children joyfully and willingly. Amen.

20

God's Priority for Parents Obedience and Discipline (Part 1)

God has to be the central focus of family life so that we can make an eternal impact on our children. Without God, there is no hope, but with Him, there is great hope indeed. The Psalmist tells us,

> Unless the Lord builds the house,
> They labor in vain who build it;
> Unless the Lord guards the city,
> The watchman keeps awake in vain. (Psalm 127:1)

If the Lord God is not the architect and builder of our homes, then everything we do is futile. Children are part of the Lord's building process in our lives. Children are designed as God's gifts, rewards and blessings to their parents.

> Behold, children are a gift of the Lord,
> The fruit of the womb is a reward.
> Like arrows in the hand of a warrior,
> So are the children of one's youth.
> How blessed is the man whose quiver is full of them;
> They shall not be ashamed

When they speak with their enemies in the gate.
(Psalm 127:3-5)

Some time ago, someone gave me parent preparation exercises for couples who are planning to have children. It's a battery of tests actually for different aspects of child rearing.

The first one is the messy test: To prepare for having children in your home, wipe peanut butter on the sofa and on your curtains. Place a stale fish stick behind the couch and leave it there all summer.

The second is the toy test: Obtain a fifty-five-gallon box of Lego's or substitute roofing tacks for Lego's. Have a friend dump them in various rooms of the house. Put on a blindfold. Then walk barefoot to the bathroom or the kitchen, but do not scream because too much noise will wake a sleeping child.

The third is the grocery store test: Borrow one or two small animals, goats are best. Take them with you to the store. Always keep them in sight and pay for anything they eat or damage.

The fourth is the dressing test: Get one large, unhappy octopus. Stuff it live into a small net bag making sure that all the arms stay inside.

The fifth is the feeding test: Fill a large plastic milk jug halfway full of water. Suspend it from the ceiling with a cord. Swing the jug back and forth; then insert spoonfuls of soggy cereal into the jug while pretending the spoon is a flying airplane. Afterward, dump the contents of the jug on the floor.

Sixth comes the night test: Fill a small cloth bag with 12 pounds of wet sand. From 3-9 p.m. hold the bag while you waltz and hum. Lay the bag down for two hours, then carry and sing to bag again. Continue this exercise every three hours through the night. Set the alarm for 5 a.m. Get up. Make breakfast. Keep routine going for five years while looking perennially cheerful.

Seventh is the ingenuity test: Using scissors and craft paint, turn an egg carton into an alligator. Make an attractive Christmas candle from a toilet paper tube, scotch tape, and aluminum foil. Then, from a milk carton, a ping-pong ball and an empty cereal box make an exact replica of the Eiffel Tower.

Last is the automobile test: Forget about sports cars, get the mini-van instead. Let a chocolate ice cream cone melt in the glove compartment. Stick a dime into the CD player. Break a jumbo package of chocolate chip cookies into the back seat. Drag a rake along both car doors to create the perfect family vehicle.

Surviving those tests will prepare any couple for the challenges of parenthood. Children change the lives of couples profoundly. Most of us are never ready for the shift in focus and responsibility. Once the children come, it's a whole different ballgame. Sometimes parents are unwilling to cheerfully adapt to those changes. Children are an inheritance from God, part of His gifts and rewards. In addition, God wants us to train our children in the "nurture and the admonition of the Lord" (Ephesians 6:4 KJV). While we are training our children, God is training us.

Unfortunately some of us don't want to deal with our children. We see them as a burden, not a blessing. Sometimes, we wish we had somebody else's kids instead of our own. Yet, God has given us children specifically designed in eternity past to be the ones that God uses to influence us for His good purposes.

God has set down some guidelines to help parents. Without guidelines based on biblical principles, parents will face problems in child rearing. Even when we follow the biblical principles, it doesn't mean our kids will turn out perfectly, like evenly formed treats stamped from Bible cookie cutters. God designs each child with his or her own personality and way of handling situations. Our job as parents is to understand how God has designed our children, then train them to know and love God and live according to biblical values.

Proverbs describes a disobedient child: "A wise son makes a father glad, but a foolish son is a grief to his mother" (Proverbs 10:1). From experience, we know that many a mother has grieved for a wayward child who takes a self-destructive path. In Proverbs 15:5 we see that, "A fool rejects his father's discipline, but he who regards reproof is sensible." A rebel doesn't listen to anyone, but those who accept correction become prudent adults. In other verses, Solomon writes that a foolish son elicits grief, bitterness, sorrow, and disgrace (see Proverbs 17:25, 21:17, and 19:13). When the rebel loses a sense of conscience, the consequences bring greater suffering. "He who robs his father or his mother and says, 'It is not a transgression,' is the companion of a man who destroys" (Proverbs 28:24). The rebellious or foolish son brings bitterness to his mother and disgrace to his father.

When parents fail to properly nurture and train their children, those children may bring shame to the family. "The rod and reproof give wisdom, but a child who gets his own way brings shame to his mother" (Proverbs 29:15). It's important that the "rod" (punishment) go along with the "reproof" (training for correction). Children must not be allowed to decide for themselves how they will behave or be left to make important choices on their own. Both punishment and correction are important aspects of child rearing. To give reproof without the rod or the rod without reproof, represents incomplete parenting. The two must go together.

There are many families who don't believe in spanking. However, the Bible says that if we spare the rod, we'll spoil the child. Just as God disciplines us to show He loves us, we must discipline our children. Our heavenly Father disciplines us. "He scourges every son" that is His (Hebrews 12:6). Some decades ago, the Minnesota Crime commission stated,

> Every baby starts life as a little savage. He is completely selfish and self-centered. He wants what he wants, when he wants it: his bottle, his mother's attention, his playmate's toys, his uncle's watch....Deny him these once and he seethes with rage and aggressiveness which would be murderous were he not so helpless. He's dirty, he has no morals, no knowledge, no developed skills. This means that all children, not just certain children, but all children are born delinquent. If permitted to continue in their self-impulsive actions to satisfy each want, every child would grow up a criminal, a thief, a killer, a rapist.[1]

The Bible stresses the concept of human depravity. Left to our own devices, we human beings tend toward evil rather than righteousness. Children require love, guidance, and discipline. Such nurturing helps a child become a contributing member of society. Well-trained children demonstrate a character that honors and glorifies the Lord. To offer proper guidance and instruction, Christian parents can be aided by two important biblical priorities when working with their children

Demonstrate the Character of Christ

Parenting techniques break down when the mother and father fail to reflect God's character and compassion when guiding their children. These major breakdowns happen because a child looks at his parents and thinks, *"You're supposed to represent God to me. Yet you are often harsh, angry or unfair. Is that how God behaves too? If so, I'm not interested in that kind of God or belief system."* It's imperative that we understand the character of God, so that as parents, we model a positive reflection of the heavenly Father. "Therefore be imitators of God, as beloved children; and walk in love, just as Christ also loved you, and gave Himself up for us, an offering and a sacrifice to God as a fragrant aroma" (Ephesians 5:1-2). We must ensure that our lives are accurate representations of God Himself, that we're good imitators. Then we can demonstrate to our children the integrity of Christ through the way we act.

We are not to grieve or sadden the Spirit of God. He lives within us and empowers us. "Let all bitterness and wrath and anger and clamor and slander be put away from you, along with all malice" (Ephesians 4:31). In other words, we must have self control and patience, behaving in kind ways as Jesus models for us in the Gospels. If we're continually angry with our children, if malice is a part of our behavior, that represents evil and wickedness. Further, if we become bitter, then our bad attitude will hinder our parenting. Instead, we must practice kindness, tender-heartedness, and forgiveness (see Ephesians 4:32).

Expectant parents like to go to a bookstore and buy all kinds of books on childbirth and parenting. They also question friends and family asking, "What are we supposed to do once the baby comes? How do we care for our child?" However, it's not about what we're supposed to do. It's about who we're supposed to be because what we do flows from what we believe and what we value. "As obedient children, do not be conformed to the former lusts which were yours in your ignorance, but like the Holy One who called you, be holy yourselves also in all your behavior; because it is written, 'You shall be holy, for I am holy'" (1 Peter 1:14-16). Peter doesn't say that we should be holy in some behavior, but rather, he urges us to be holy in all behavior. It's an inclusive statement. We are to be perfect as our Father in heaven is perfect (Matthew 5:48).

The Bible is God's self-disclosure. Therefore, as we study the Bible and grow in our knowledge of God, we inevitably become a better parent. We become kinder, more graceful, more merciful, more forgiving, and more just as we imitate God. Employing a good example is our most powerful technique in parenting.

> "I have manifested Your name to the men whom You gave Me out of the world; they were Yours, and You gave them to Me, and they have kept Your word. Now they have come to know that everything You have given Me is from You; for the words which You gave Me I have given to them; and they received them and truly understood that I came forth from You, and they believed that You sent Me." (John 17:6-8)

At the end of His ministry, on the eve of His crucifixion, Christ prays and all of His men are around Him. He prays out loud about the fact that He has manifested His Father to His men. They have seen God because they have seen Him. And because He has accurately represented His God in the flesh, He operated as a human being under the complete control of the Spirit of God in His life. Consequently His men believed God's Word, obeyed God's commands and essentially changed the world. In the same way, mothers and fathers must pay attention to what's happening in their families. If the children have a hard time accepting, understanding, and believing the Word of God, the parent needs to ask, *"Am I accurately representing God the Father to my children?"*

During a conversation with His disciples, Phillip said to Jesus, "Lord, show us the Father, and it is enough for us" (John 14:8). In response, Jesus posed an insightful question: "Have I been so long with you, and yet you have not come to know Me, Phillip? He who has seen Me has seen the Father" (John 14:9).

Jesus explained to His disciples that He was one hundred percent man and one hundred percent God. He laid aside His divine attributes. That feat is the *great kenosis* (see Philippians 2). In fact, Jesus explains even more in His discussion with Phillip. "Do you not believe that I am in the Father, and the Father is in Me? The words that I say to you I do not speak on My own initiative, but the Father abiding in Me does His works" (John 14:10). There we have it. Christ is essentially saying, "The Father is abiding in Me, and the Father is working through Me that you might see Him in Me." So Christ could say in John 17, "I have manifested Your name to the men whom You gave Me out of the world" (v 6). In a similar way, our responsibility is to demonstrate to our children the character of Christ so that they would see God's good influence in our lives. Nothing should come between us and God. Our great challenge is to demonstrate a Christ-like example.

The story of Moses and his family provides an insightful example of godly obedience. Moses' parents, Jochebed and Amram are mentioned in the Hall of Faith chapter, Hebrews 11:23. "By faith Moses, when he was born, was hidden for three months by his parents, because they saw he was a beautiful child; and they were not afraid of the King's edict." Their story is recounted in Exodus 1 and 2. When Moses was born, the Israelites served the Egyptians in bondage. To control the Israelite population and maintain his power, the Pharaoh of the day decreed that all the male babies should be thrown into the river to be drowned. Without exception, all the boys were sentenced to die. Such a threat might have frightened some couples so much that they would not even have children, but not Jochebed and Amram. They already had two, Miriam and Aaron, and they proceeded to have a third. Without wavering, they served the Holy One of Israel.

When Jochebed's son was born, the death decree was in full force. The family hid the baby for three months. When they could no longer conceal him, they put their son afloat in a little basket at the edge of the Nile River. In this action, the couple obeyed the letter of the law. Jochebed did put her baby in the river, but she made sure he wouldn't drown. She knew that the Egyptian princess would come and bathe in the place where the basket was tethered. Miriam, the baby's sister, watched out for her brother and when the princess saw the Hebrew child, she fell in love with him. God orchestrated the events of Moses' life and performed amazing wonders. The princess drew the baby from the water and adopted him as her own. Jochebed did not call her son Moses. The Egyptian princess did because the name Moses means "to draw out." The child who was drawn out of the river became the one who would draw out the nation of Israel from slavery in Egypt.

The family didn't hide Moses because he was a handsome baby, but because he was lovely in the sight of God (Acts 7:20). God had set His affection on Moses and somehow communicated that truth to his parents, for the writer of Hebrews says that by faith, his parents risked their lives to protect the child. "So faith comes from hearing, and hearing by the word of Christ" (Romans 10:17). God revealed to Amram and Jochebed that He had a special plan for Moses.

They put their faith in the Word of God and believed it and hid the baby, and that's why they were unafraid of Pharaoh's edict. Their actions demonstrated their godly faith to their other children, Miriam and Aaron. Moses' siblings witnessed God's protection of the baby, so those two children would come to understand that God, Yahweh, was the Holy One of Israel and that He could be trusted.

Jochebed cared for Moses because little sister Miriam would recommend her mother to the Egyptian princess as a competent nurse. Thus, God returned Moses to Jochebed for those early years of Moses' life. She took every opportunity to teach her child about God's calling and protection. Moses didn't discover God's leading as an adult when he lived in the desert. He knew about it as a boy.

Moses believed and followed his God because his mother taught him how to do so. "By faith Moses, when he had grown up, refused to be called the son of Pharaoh's daughter" (Hebrews 11:24). When Moses reached age forty, he asserted himself as an Israelite, not an Egyptian, "choosing rather to endure ill-treatment with the people of God than to enjoy the passing pleasures of sin, considering the reproach of Christ greater riches than the treasures of Egypt; for he was looking to the reward" (Hebrews 11:25-26).

Like his parents before him, Moses left Egypt without fear. "By faith he left Egypt, not fearing the wrath of the king" (Hebrews 11:27). Like father, like son. Moses believed in the Word of God and obeyed in faith. Every child needs to see a demonstration of what it means to follow God, to honor and serve Him. Similarly, our children need to know that Mom and Dad are trusting God no matter what the circumstances. In Moses' case, Egyptian slavery and death sentences for babies were bad circumstances. Yet Amram and Jochebed lived by faith and did not fear, though death would stare them in the face.

Moses chose to suffer ill-treatment with the people of God because he looked to his eternal reward. His mother had taught him about the Holy One of Israel. He was in the line to be the next pharaoh and was the most educated, well-trained, athletic man of his day. Although he enjoyed a position of power and influence, he would forsake it all to follow God's plan. In a similar way, we parents can teach our sons and daughters about courage, strength, stability, faith, and commitment to God. We convey these truths by what we say and do.

Demonstrate the Compassion of Christ

The Lord's compassion never fails. In following Christ's example, we are to be kind, tenderhearted, and forgiving to our children even when they don't deserve it. "Be kind to one another, tender-hearted, forgiving each other, just as God in Christ also has forgiven you" (Ephesians 4:32). When we demonstrate to our children the compassion of Christ, we teach them about His character as well as his conduct.

We sometimes have to resist the urge to give our children what they deserve. In their disobedience and immaturity, our children often test our patience and endurance. They probably deserve punishment, but we must be careful not to provoke them. It's easy to aggravate our children, to irritate them and make them angry.

Paul warns us about this tendency. "Fathers, do not provoke your children to anger, but bring them up in the discipline and instruction of the Lord" (Ephesians 6:4). The word "fathers" in this passage is the Greek word *pateres*. The same word appears in Hebrews 11:23 to describe Moses' parents. The word is also used in a parallel passage in Colossians. "Fathers, do not exasperate your children, so that they will not lose heart" (Colossians 3:21). In these passages the word *pateres* denotes parents.

It's important to understand the various ways that parents can aggravate, infuriate, or otherwise provoke their children. One is by overprotection. It's very easy to frustrate children by overprotecting them, confining them, fencing them in, never trusting them, or always questioning whether they're telling the truth. Such control prevents the child from developing independence. Little by little, boys and girls need to face the conflicts of school or siblings and learn to care for themselves.

Another detriment to children is favoritism. In Genesis we learn that the father Isaac preferred his son Esau over Jacob. Yet the mother Rebecca favored her son Jacob over Esau (Genesis 25-28). The parents' failures caused agony in the family for generations. Later on, Jacob would favor his wife Rachel over his other wife Leah. That action also created tensions that affected the sons, who would produce the twelve tribes of the Nation of Israel (Genesis 37). Jacob showed obvious favor toward his younger sons Joseph and Benjamin, which created resentment among the other ten brothers. Showing favoritism to one child puts him or her above others in the family. Preferences can destroy a child's self-esteem, making the son or daughter feel inferior to a brother or sister. A daughter may not feel she's smart or pretty enough. The son may lack confidence.

Another way to exasperate children is to push them into achievement. A father who wasn't a great academic can pressure his children to achieve high grades. The non-athletic parent may sign his sons up for every sports program available and root for them incessantly from the sidelines. Or maybe the strong academic, athletic mother wants her children to be just like her. So she enrolls them in numerous sports leagues and pressures them to enter academic competitions. However, parents' continual pushing frustrates children.

Another form of provocation is discouragement. Parents may criticize their daughters or sons, pointing out their flaws and failures, but never encouraging or praising them. Mothers may recount how they had to sacrifice a college education or a career for the sake of her children. Yet these comments can make the children feel like they are an intrusion or a burden. We must never blame our children for our unfulfilled goals or objectives in life. Such comments make it seem that the children are unwanted and make them feel unloved. Parents must give of themselves freely to love their children.

Furthermore, some parents completely neglect children. In the Old Testament account, King David neglected his son Absalom, and that prince brought extreme heartbreak to David's life and kingdom. Sometimes parents are so wrapped up in themselves that they spend little time with their children. At other times, parents are busy with mundane tasks like washing the car or watching television. Some even withhold love telling children, "If you disobey, I'm not going to love you any more." Such actions are unacceptable. Withholding love doesn't move children toward Christ or inspired them to follow Him.

Finally, using bitter words to berate children or giving cruel punishment or beatings that hurt children are unacceptable behaviors for any parent. We must not provoke our children to wrath but demonstrate a Christ-like character instead. Our first priority must be to demonstrate the compassion of Christ. That's what we must believe. That's what we must do.

Dear Lord, keep us mindful of Your example, of Your loving, sacrificial character and never ending compassion, so that we might follow Your example. Help us to teach our children to love and serve You. Amen.

21

God's Priority for Parents Obedience and Discipline (Part 2)

In Chapter 20, I shared several humorous tests that preview the perils of parenthood. Here's the final exercise to ensure that all couples preparing for parenthood are well prepared. Find a couple who already have a small child. Lecture them on how they can improve their toddler's discipline, patience, tolerance, toilet training, and table manners. Suggest many ways they can improve. Emphasize to them that they should never allow their children to run wild in public places. Enjoy this experience. It will be the last time you will ever have all the answers about parenting.

There's a bit of truth in that funny tale, for many think they have all the answers before they become parents, but none of us has all the answers to child rearing. We can talk to our local psychologist, politician, preacher, priest, or pediatrician. But only God has all the answers. In the Bible, He details everything moms and dads need to know this side of eternity that will make them godly parents and grandparents. "The unfolding of Your words gives light; it gives understanding to the simple" (Psalm 119:130). God's Word offers wisdom about life. "Your word is a lamp to my feet and a light to my path" (Psalm 119:105). God's Word illuminates our life paths, influences our choices, and shows us what direction to take. The Bible builds, instructs, strengthens, and provides all the tools needed for men and women to become responsible parents.

Sometimes we look at our children and wonder why God gave us that whiney baby girl or that hyper little boy. Yet we are to praise God boldly for all types of children, whether they are one or twenty-one. Further, God gives parents the responsibility to prepare children biblically. Every good warrior prepares sharp arrows. Every child is like a little arrow ready to engage in spiritual warfare. Those arrows can combat our declining cultural values. Those arrows can infiltrate society to bring transformation at its most crucial level. So when parents teach children, it is like the process of sharpening arrows.

Demonstrate a Godly Example

Parents have a responsibility to model the character and compassion of Christ to children. David says,

> The God of Israel said,
> The Rock of Israel spoke to me,
> "He who rules over men righteously,
> Who rules in the fear of God,
> Is as the light of the morning when the sun rises,
> A morning without clouds,
> When the tender grass springs out of the earth,
> Through sunshine after rain." (2 Samuel 23:3-4)

God instructed David to deal justly and righteously with people in the fear of God. In the same way, we must follow, serve, and honor. God's righteousness and holiness must be uppermost in our thinking. With that focus, we become like morning sun shining through the window, brightening the day. We can be people whom others follow. Great leadership functions like a sunny morning. Great parenting has a similar effect. When parents manage their homes through righteous character and in the fear of God, they bring refreshment to their homes. If parents honor and glorify the Lord, then their children are more apt to follow that example.

Dedicate Children to Christ

In church, we often have a dedication service for babies. The parents bring their newborn child to the front. The congregation admires the baby with "oohs" and "ahs," and then prays for the little one and his family. The church gives the infant a gift. Then as a pastor, I exhort the mother and father to fulfill their Christian responsibility. That ceremony is not a trivial practice. Rather it is a biblical model that we're following. A similar ceremony is described in Luke.

> And when eight days had passed, before His circumcision, His name was then called Jesus, the name given by the angel before He was conceived in the womb. And when the days for their purification according to the law of Moses were completed, they brought Him up to Jerusalem to present Him to the Lord. (Luke 2:21-22)

Mary and Joseph knew exactly what the law said. On the eighth day, they named and circumcised their baby boy. They went to the temple to present this child to God, to the Master. Jesus Christ did everything according to the law of God in the Old Testament. His parents were instrumental in following the Word of God, presenting Him to Simeon in the temple at the proper time. "And he came in the Spirit into the temple; and when the parents brought in the child Jesus, to carry out for Him the custom of the Law, then he [Simeon] took Him into his arms, and blessed God" (Luke 2:27-28). When parents publicly say, "I'm giving my child to the Lord," they make a monumental statement. They declare before the church that their child belongs to God. Parents often don't want to release their children to God. But when they do, they're saying, "God, he's yours. Our children are a gift and a reward. Therefore, Lord, we dedicate this child to You. You are in charge; we are not." Once parents make this statement, their actions and attitudes must be consistent with their commitment.

When I look into the eyes of one of my children, I am reminded that this child is the Lord's. If my child is sick and hospitalized, I must say, "Lord, I dedicated this child to you. He is Yours. You can do whatever you desire. You can take him home, or You can heal him, because he is Your child." My children are merely gifts to my wife and me. That process of releasing them to God is very important in a parent's development.

In the Old Testament account in 1 Samuel, the mother Hannah dedicated her first son Samuel to the Lord:

> Now when she had weaned him, she took him up with her, with a three-year-old bull and one ephah of flour and a jug of wine, and brought him to the house of the Lord in Shiloh, although the child was young. Then they slaughtered the bull, and brought the boy to Eli. She said, "O my lord! As your soul lives, my lord, I am the woman who stood here beside you, praying to the Lord. For this boy I prayed, and the Lord has given me my petition which I asked of Him." (1 Samuel 1:24-27)

Hannah was a barren woman. Therefore, she endured disgrace in Jewish society. She had prayed, "O God, please give me a child," and God eventually granted her request. After Samuel was born, Hannah fully dedicated him to God's service. "'For this boy I prayed, and the Lord has given me my petition which I asked of Him. So I have also dedicated him to the Lord; as long as he lives he is dedicated to the Lord.' And he [Samuel] worshipped the Lord there" (1 Samuel 1:27-28).

When Hannah prayed for a child, she promised to give him to the Lord's service (1 Samuel 1:11). She didn't renege on her commitment once her son was born. As soon as she weaned her son, she traveled to the temple. She kept her vow, dedicating Samuel to God for life, to serve the Master of the universe. God rewarded her commitment to him. Hannah gave God one child and God gave her five. Hannah's story models the idea of child dedication. Christian parents must dedicate their children to the Master and to ministry. The trouble is that parents have their own plans for their children—to be athletes, lawyers, doctors, or to fulfill some other dream. Some parents go so far as to formulate their retirement plans based on the intentions and location of their children and what's happening with their lives.

Most importantly, children who are dedicated to the Lord must live life committed to the vocational ministry of serving Christ no matter what their occupation is. Sons and daughters will have different occupations because not all can be preachers, missionaries, doctors, or athletes. But whatever their area of ministry, wherever God puts them, that field becomes their area of spiritual existence. No matter what department or company or organization he or she works for, that becomes the place where each one is salt and light.

When Mary and Joseph dedicated Jesus to the Master and to the ministry that God had ordained; they didn't know what would happen next. However, they received a hint because when Simeon saw this Child, he became excited. "And Simeon blessed them and said to Mary His mother, 'Behold, this Child is appointed for the fall and rise of many in Israel, and for a sign to be opposed—and a sword will pierce even your own soul—to the end that thoughts from many hearts may be revealed'" (Luke 2:34-35).

Simeon prophesied that this child would be the light of revelation to the Gentiles. He would reveal the motives and thoughts of people. When Jesus Christ came to earth, He set aside His divine prerogatives. He was a baby who still needed to be diapered and potty trained. He cried when He was wet and hungry. But Luke says this child was growing in wisdom, growing in His understanding of His responsibility before God, the Father. Jesus Christ developed like our children develop and mature. "The Child continued to grow and become strong, increasing in wisdom; and the grace of God was upon Him" (Luke 2:40).

The difference is that Jesus was sinless. The Bible says that He knew no sin. None of us has such an opportunity as Mary and Joseph in raising a sinless child. Can you imagine being one of Jesus' brothers? They could never blame Jesus, saying, "He's the one who broke the pot. Or he's the one who lied." Mary and Joseph knew that Jesus always told the truth. Jesus' siblings had to live with a brother who was always right. That situation must have been frustrating, for sure.

Mary and Joseph went to Jerusalem every year at the Feast of the Passover. During Jesus' twelfth year, they traveled there according to the custom of the feast. "And as they were returning, after spending the full number of days, the boy Jesus stayed behind in Jerusalem. But His parents were unaware of it, but supposed Him to be in the caravan, and went a day's journey; and they began looking for Him among their relatives and acquaintances. When they did not find Him, they returned to Jerusalem looking for Him" (Luke 2:43-45).

Now consider the panic that Mary and Joseph must have felt. If we lose track of our children in a store or other public place, we start calling their names and asking people, "Have you seen a little boy in a red shirt?" Mary and Joseph must have been asking, "Have you seen Jesus?" Jesus was missing for three days. Mary and Joseph were unable to find him amid the caravan, so they returned to Jerusalem. "Then, after three days they found Him in the temple, sitting in the midst of the teachers, both listening to them and asking them questions. And all who heard Him were amazed at His understanding and His answers" (Luke 2:46-47).

Jesus laid aside His divine prerogative, His omniscience, and omnipotence in order to live a life like we regular people live. However, the Bible says that He grew in wisdom. He was able to talk with the teachers of the law based on His understanding of Scripture even at age twelve.

> When they saw Him, they were astonished; and His mother said to Him, "Son, why have You treated us this way? Behold, Your father and I have anxiously been looking for You." And He said to them, "Why is it that you were looking for Me? Did you not know that I had to be in My Father's house?" (Luke 2:48-49)

(Some translations say, "Don't you know I have to be about My Father's business?") Before Jesus made these statements, no one in the Old Testament had ever called God, "My Father." In the thirty-nine books of the Old Testament, fourteen times God is referred to as the Father of the nation of Israel. God was Abraham's father, but

Abraham never called God, "My Father." Yet Jesus Christ refers to God as "My Father" over sixty times in the Gospels. In fact, He called God My Father every time but when He was on the cross. As He bore the sins of the world, He said, "My God, My God, why have You forsaken Me?" (Matthew 27:46).

Jesus Christ understood His mission in life. When He attended the Passover Feast, He realized that He was the Passover Lamb. He entered God's house to do His Father's work. Mary and Joseph had spoken to Jesus about the Old Testament and His miraculous conception. At that Passover Feast, those aspects came into focus for the boy Jesus, but His earthly parents did not fully understand the future. "But they did not understand the statement which He had made to them. And He went down with them and came to Nazareth, and He continued in subjection to them; and His mother treasured all these things in her heart. And Jesus kept increasing in wisdom and stature, and in favor with God and men" (Luke 2:50-53). Jesus grew physically and intellectually. The more He matured, the more He understood God's plan. His mission was to be the sacrificial Lamb for the world. He followed that mission to the cross.

Similarly, even at the age of twelve our children should realize that they have a mission in life. God has declared from the very beginning that they should serve Him in some capacity. We should help them in their developmental process. Sons and daughters also must grow in biblical wisdom and understanding. To dedicate them to the Lord and to the ministry means that no matter what they do, they can glorify God. "Whether, then, you eat or drink or whatever you do, do all to the glory of God" (1 Corinthians 10:31). Our number one priority as parents is to demonstrate to our children the character of Christ. We must realize that our job is to magnify the Lord, to glorify His name, and to put Him on display so our children see Him reflected in our lives.

Discipline Children

It's important for parents to know that demonstrating godly character comes first, dedication second, and discipline third. "Fathers, do not provoke your children to anger, but bring them up in the discipline and instruction of the Lord" (Ephesians 6:4). The King

James Translations says, "Bring them up in the nurture and admonition of the Lord." The word "nurture" or "discipline" is the Greek word *paideia,* which is also used in Hebrews 12:5-8:

> My son, do not regard lightly the discipline of the Lord, Nor faint when you are reproved by Him; For those whom the Lord loves He disciplines, And He scourges every son whom He receives. It is for discipline that you endure; God deals with you as with sons; for what son is there whom his father does not discipline? But if you are without discipline, of which all have become partakers, then you are illegitimate children and not sons.

God's children are all in the nurturing process. God is training and developing the life of the Christian. He gives rules and regulations. The parameters for behavior are clear in the Bible, and the concepts of reward and punishment are plainly revealed. In the same way, parents must raise children with discipline and instruction. The rules and expectations should be clear from the start. Susanna Wesley, mother of nineteen children, (including John and Charles Wesley) wrote, "The parent who studies to subdue [self-will] in the child works together with God in the renewing and saving of his soul. The parent who indulges it, does the devil's work, makes religion impracticable, salvation unattainable and damns his child, body and soul forever."[1] Susanna Wesley felt that children's willfulness needed to be subdued. The child must understand that his will needs to yield to God's will.

No one outgrows the need for discipline. It is God's way of preventing us from having wrong attitudes toward authority and to make us mature and responsible. God wants us to be disciplined ourselves and to discipline our children.

Six Principles of Proper Discipline

The Bible teaches that when someone steps outside the bounds of God's law, there must be a consequence for that disobedience. When the consequence is delayed, the individual may continue in disobedience which leads to rebellion. "Because the sentence against an evil deed is not executed quickly, therefore the hearts of the sons of men among them are given fully to do evil" (Ecclesiastes 8:11). That's why Solomon, the man of wisdom says, "But it will not be well for the evil man...because he does not fear God" (Ecclesiastes 8:13).

Parents face two struggles: being lazy and being confused. When children disobey, some parents say, "Forget it. I'm just not going to deal with that problem today." They become lazy in their correction and weary of the conflicts. Children soon learn that they can wear their parents down and essentially win the power struggle to get their own way. Parents are never off duty. In my household, my wife and I know we are going to be father and mother for a long time. Eventually we'll be grandparents. We can't take a break because parenting is a twenty-four-seven responsibility. Every time we get lazy in discipline or try to avoid confrontation, our children know it and they test the limits in their rebellious state.

Other times parents are not necessarily lazy but are just at a lost as to what to do. A parent may say, "I don't know how to deal with Johnny. I've tried everything, but he won't obey. I want to give up." The avoidance strategy of just ignoring a problem is not a productive solution either.

We must remember that discipline has a purpose, the first of which is to remove foolishness from the child. "Foolishness is bound up in the heart of a child; the rod of discipline will remove it far from him" (Proverbs 22:15). A child might look cute, but she is corrupted because she is born into sin—even the most adorable, curly-headed toddler. Some parents brag, "My boys are so good." When I hear such comments, I'm tempted to say, "Ask their school teacher how well they behave in class before you brag that they're angels." We parents want to believe that that our children can do no wrong. Such ideas appeal to our egos, making us think we're perfect parents. However, Proverbs says that children are full of foolishness, and it takes proper discipline to correct it.

What is foolishness? The Bible explains that the naive one loves simplicity and scoffers delight in scoffing. Furthermore, fools will hate knowledge (Proverbs 1:22). The characteristics of a fool include one who hates God's knowledge, truth, and wisdom. A fool doesn't want rules or to be told what to do. "Doing wickedness is like sport to a fool" (Proverbs 10:23). In fact, "it is an abomination to fools to turn away from evil" (Proverbs 13:19). Foolish ones love evil so much that they don't want to change. That's why when a parent looks at his toddler and says, "Don't touch that box," the little boy puts his hand on the box and smiles. Even young children rebel and such rebellion can cause them harm. Fools mock sin; their consciences don't make them feel bad for disobeying. "The wisdom of the sensible is to understand his way, but the foolishness of fools is deceit. Fools mock at sin" (Proverbs 14:8-9). Sin doesn't bother a fool. "A fool is arrogant and careless" (Proverbs 14:16). Such individuals exhibit pride and extreme recklessness.

In addition, fools don't often speak kind, sweet, gentle words. "Excellent speech is not fitting for a fool" (Proverbs 17:7). Children will make the most rotten, most perverse, and nastiest comments they can think of because that's what fools do. "The foolishness of man ruins his way, and his heart rages against the Lord" (Proverbs 19:3).

The first principle of proper discipline is to drive that foolishness from children through appropriate punishment and loving discipline.

The second principle of proper discipline is to realize it rescues our children from judgment.

> Do not hold back discipline from the child,
> Although you strike him with the rod, he will not die.
> You shall strike him with the rod
> And deliver his soul from Sheol. (Proverbs 23:13-14)

If children disregard authority, "raging against the Lord," they are headed for hell (see Isaiah 37:28-29). Yet discipline can rescue them.

The third principle is that such discipline brings wisdom:

> The rod and reproof give wisdom,
> But a child who gets his own way brings shame to his
> mother. (Proverbs 29:15)

A child receives wisdom through discipline. Proper discipline consists of complementary elements: the rod and reproof; punishment and instruction; nurture and admonition. Discipline must be balanced.

The fourth principle is that discipline relieves parental anxiety. "Correct your son, and he will give you comfort; he will also delight your soul" (Proverbs 29:17). Parents won't have comfort in their homes without proper discipline. It will be a place of conflict.

Lastly, discipline reflects God's character. Our fathers "disciplined us for a short time as seemed best to them, but He disciplines us for our good, so that we may share His holiness. All discipline for the moment seems not to be joyful, but sorrowful; yet to those who have been trained by it, afterwards it yields the peaceable fruit of righteousness" (Hebrews 12:10-11).

God disciplines us because He loves us as a Father. Therefore, we understand that as we discipline our children, we reflect the character of God. If young Christians grow up without instruction and correction and suddenly face discipline from God, they don't understand it because their parents didn't train them in the ways of God. When parents exercise proper discipline, they reflect the character of God. Consequently their children better understand God's ways of molding Christians as they mature. We must understand and remember the purpose of discipline. As God shows us in His Word what He wants us to do, we realize discipline is our responsibility, and it becomes a priority for parenting.

Lord, give us the wisdom we need to raise our children to love and serve You. Bring us the support of loving family members and Christian friends, who can help and encourage us on this parenting journey. Amen.

22

God's Priority for Parents Obedience and Discipline (Part 3)

It's important to understand God and His purposes for His children. Paul tells the Ephesians that parents are to both instruct and nurture children (Ephesians 6:4). From a divine point of view, God's responsibility is to discipline us, so that we might be the sons and daughters He wants us to be. In fact, the Bible says in Hebrews 12 that if we are *not* being disciplined by God, we are illegitimate children, meaning that we are not true children of God but children of the devil. God disciplines us as His children because He is more concerned about our welfare than we realize.

Biblical Authority

An important aspect of discipline concerns reliance on the Bible for guidance and authority. When we discipline children, we must be guided by biblical truth. This familiar verse in Proverbs can offer insight into this concept. "Where there is no vision, the people are unrestrained, but happy is he who keeps the law" (Proverbs 29:18). This passage is usually mentioned in leadership seminars. Aspiring leaders learn that without a vision, the people perish. The Hebrew word for vision is "revelation." So the text literally says that without revelation—without the revelation of God—the people are unrestrained.

In the same way, without the revelation of God, our children are unrestrained. That is, our children go in all kinds of directions—perhaps the wrong direction. So we need to practice biblical discipline so our children can see the reality of Scripture played out in our lives and theirs. The essence of successful parenting is not based on how many parenting books we read. In fact, success is all about knowing God's character, pursing God's will, and living for God's purposes. The greatest parent is a godly parent, the one who walks and talks with God and has a passion to honor God in all that he says and does. Children need to have those kinds of godly, humble, obedient parents. Teenagers might not *want* those kinds of parents because those parents won't let their children pursue sin. However, they *need* those kinds of parents, ones who stand for what is right. That's where the Proverbs come in to play.

We cannot rely upon the local radio psychologist, TV sociologist, or televangelist. Instead parents should memorize the Proverbs. The book was written from a father to a son about the wisdom, instruction, and knowledge necessary to understand and reverence God. Proverbs offers truths; many concern instruction and discipline. Mastery of the book is vital. When God's Word is central in a family, then everybody knows the guidelines and directions because they're reading from the same manual.

Consequences of No Discipline

There are predictable consequences for parents who fail to discipline their children. "He who spares his rod hates his son, but he who loves him disciplines him promptly" (Proverbs 13:24 NKJV). The proverb doesn't say that he who spares the rod is a wise, compassionate parent. No, he is an unloving parent. The model, of course, is Jesus Christ because He disciplines us. When He does, we understand His love for us (Hebrews 12). Our children understand our love for them but it is not because we buy them expensive toys or we give them cars on their sixteenth birthday. It is not because we offer them credit cards on their eighteenth birthday so they can buy the latest technological gadgets. When moms or dads fail to discipline their sons and daughters, there is a cost both for the parents and the children.

The first consequence of inadequate discipline is a lack of love. The Bible governs our code of conduct. Whenever children violate proper boundaries, they realize discipline is required. Such training teaches them to follow God and His righteousness.

In our home, we want our children to understand that we obey God's commands. So when my wife and I correct our children, we tell them what the Bible says so that they understand the purpose for the discipline and the reason for the correction. We do not respond from anger or frustration. Proper discipline teaches children to understand the character of God.

If parents don't practice discipline, they reveal a lack of love for their children (Proverbs 13:24). God said don't spare the rod. The godly parent who loves his child will discipline promptly, diligently, and lovingly, just as our heavenly Father disciplines us.

The second consequence is family shame. "The rod and reproof give wisdom, but a child who gets his own way brings shame to his mother" (Proverbs 29:15). I've seen a lot of mothers who have endured great shame. Some have thrown up their hands in surrender saying, "I don't know what to do." Often, parents let their kids do whatever they choose. They fear that restraint will prompt their children to rebel. If parents fear they're children are going to rebel, it means that the children are already rebellious. The parent's job is not to fear their children's rebellion but to fear God.

In such cases where children lack discipline and express out-of-control behavior, people may ask, "Why does your son misbehave? Why does he act so wild?" To find solutions parents consider reading a different parenting book or trading in their child for a nicer one or resigning their jobs as parents. Yet the truth is that parents must take responsibility for training their children.

The third consequence of insufficient discipline is the loss of God's blessing. Could it be that if we don't discipline our children, God's blessing will be removed from our lives? We must consider the account of Eli and his sons as told in 1 Samuel. Eli served as priest at the time of Samuel's birth. There's a great contrast between Samuel, who obeyed the Lord, and the two sons of Eli who disregarded the law. In fact, the Bible explains that the sons of Eli were "worthless men" (1 Samuel 2:12).

The two sons, Hophni and Phinehas, didn't care about the Lord, the law, or righteous living. Their dad was a priest, dedicated to God's service, yet his sons lived immoral lives: "Thus the sin of the young men was very great before the Lord, for the men despised the offering of the Lord" (1 Samuel 2:17). These men defiled the priesthood. Further, their sin was blatant and disgraceful. "Now Eli was very old; and he heard all that his sons were doing to all Israel, and how they lay with the women who served at the doorway of the tent of meeting" (1 Samuel 2:22). These men committed immoral acts openly with the women of the tabernacle.

Then Eli asked his sons, "Why do you do such things, the evil things that I hear from all these people?" (1 Samuel 2:23). Eli's sons brought the family shame; their evil deeds were known all across Israel. Yet there was no point in Eli asking Hophni and Phinehas, "Why are you behaving so shamefully?" The issue is not the *why*, but the *what* because they violated the law of God, they would face God's penalty. When parents don't discipline children, the kids assume they won't pay any real price for their actions. So they do their own thing, repeatedly sinning without any awareness that they are violating the law of God and that consequences will ensue.

Eli grew concerned because everyone was talking about him and his boys. Then he told them, "'If one man sins against another, God will mediate for him; but if a man sins against the Lord, who can intercede for him?' But they would not listen to the voice of their father, for the Lord desired to put them to death" (1 Samuel 2:25).

When Eli tried to reproach his sons, they disregarded his warnings. Eli dishonored God by not fathering his sons properly therefore God declared both his sons would die. A messenger brought Eli the bad news. "Far be it from Me—for those who honor Me I will honor, and those who despise Me will be lightly esteemed…and all the increase of your house will die in the prime of life. This will be the sign to you which will come concerning your two sons, Hophni and Phinehas: on the same day both of them will die'" (1 Samuel 2:30b-34). That's a pretty strict punishment. If Eli would have dealt with his boys forthrightly, he would have measured them not against himself, not the priesthood, but specifically against God's commands. Likewise, we don't want to measure a child against siblings or another family's children. Instead their measure is against a biblical standard. When we violate God's principles, there are consequences for our rebellion. Because Eli did not exercise the rod of discipline upon his boys, God removed His blessing from Eli's family.

God has said very clearly, "You honor Me, so I'm going to honor you. But if you treat lightly My Word, despise My name, there will be consequences." God is serious. We don't want our children to live unrestrained lives, and we don't want to lose the blessing of God. Instead, we want to honor the Lord.

Recognize the Importance of Discipline

In Proverbs 10, Solomon again links the concept of understanding with the need for discipline. "On the lips of the discerning, wisdom is found, but a rod is for the back of him who lacks understanding" (Proverbs 10:13). Further, in Proverbs 19:29 we're told, "Judgments are prepared for scoffers, and blows for the back of fools." When the Bible speaks of the "back of fools," it means the middle of our backs—the buttocks or behind. That's God's ordained spot for spanking. That's why God gives us all that padding back there because He wants to make sure we're not damaged, that nothing's broken, that nothing gets out of whack. When Mom or Dad gives their child a spanking, they know that God has designed that ample place as the spanking spot.

Proverbs also employs an animal metaphor to reinforce the point. "A whip is for the horse, a bridal for the donkey and a rod for the back of fools" (Proverbs 26:3). Horses need the whip so they can be kept in line, and just as the donkey needs to be bridled, the child needs the rod. The Bible speaks of the rod because it's important that parents not slap children with their hands. A parent's hand should offer tenderness, giving children the touch of kindness, love, and compassion. A flexible instrument should be used in spanking, so the child associates discipline with the rod and not a parent's hand. Hands offer comforting care for the child after the rod has been applied.

More and more child rearing experts assert that spanking children is harmful. Often child psychologists and other experts give interviews on TV in which they wax eloquently on the dangers of spanking. Yet the Bible says that the results of spanking a child are positive and good. That method of discipline drives foolishness out of the child. Proper discipline relieves anxiety in the life of the child and the parent, bringing comfort to the family. However psychologists warn that if a parent spanks a child, he or she will become more aggressive.

That conclusion is false. Often experts take various studies of parents who abuse their children and don't apply discipline properly or biblically to say, "If parents spank their children, the children become angry, aggressive, or antisocial. Therefore, spanking is unacceptable." However, we need to recognize the importance of God's commands and the truths and principles inherent in them.

Avoid Provoking Children

In Ephesians 6:4 Paul warns, "Fathers, do not irritate and provoke your children to anger [do not exasperate them to resentment], but rear them [tenderly] in the training and discipline and the counsel and admonition of the Lord" (AMP). A child can become angry toward his mother or father or become very discouraged about the relationship with his parents. A parent who's angry should never spank a child. Sometimes it's difficult to control emotions. A son makes a smartaleck remark or the toddler disobeys for the fifth time in a row. Dad shouts, "Get up to your room right now because I'm going to teach you a lesson!" Then he marches after the child and spanks him in haste, frustration, or exasperation.

We provoke our children to wrath when we fail to discipline them out of a spirit of love and concern for their well being. If we're disciplining them because we are angry that they disobeyed us, then we're failing to exercise discipline properly. Discipline is necessary only when children have violated the law of God. If parents can keep that standard in mind—the child's violation of God's law versus their disobedience to the parent—then handling disciplinary issues can be carried out in a biblical manner with a sense of objectivity and perspective.

Parents should calmly explain, "Johnny, this is how you've violated the rules. And God's law says that as your father, my responsibility is to train you about right and wrong. Therefore you will suffer the consequences of your wrongful actions. Do you understand?" Of course, children understand those principles. My dad used tell me, "I punish you because I love you." Yeah, right. I never believed him when he gave me that explanation. But as time went on, I realized my father really did love me because he wanted me to be an honest, trustworthy, Christian man who obeyed God sincerely. I learned that concept and I want my children to learn obedience as well.

I wish I could say I've never provoked my children to anger, that I've always disciplined them in a proper, biblical manner. But I haven't. My kids know that I'm not perfect. However, I realize my responsibility, so I move in that direction to honor and glorify the Lord.

Discipline Offers Affection and Acceptance

We need to discipline children with love and acceptance:

> [Y]ou have forgotten the exhortation which is addressed to you as sons, "My son, do not regard lightly the discipline of the Lord, nor faint when you are reproved by Him; For those whom the Lord loves He disciplines, and He scourges every son whom He receives." It is for discipline that you endure; God deals with you as with sons; for what son is there whom his father does not discipline? (Hebrews 12:5-7)

A father knows when he's disciplined his child properly. He has that firm sense of doing the right thing. For me, I don't like spanking my children but I know that I need to correct them. When I really discipline in love I go to bed at night feeling good, knowing that God has been pleased with my parenting and obedience. Always when we discipline, we must respond with affection and acceptance, helping children to understand the dangers of sin and the love of God.

Develop Your Child

A child's development is the last of the priorities for parents. The Apostle Paul says in Ephesians 6:4 that we are to bring our children up in the "discipline and the instruction of the Lord." Every great parent must help her child learn God's ways. The New Testament affirmed that Timothy had known the Holy Scriptures from his childhood. Evidently Lois and Eunice, his mother and grandmother, helped that young boy so he knew exactly what the Bible said.

There are six principles to consider when guiding a child's moral development.

First, teach your child correctly. Solomon remembered how his father David taught him, so he passed the information on.

> Hear, O sons, the instruction of the father,
> And give attention that you may gain understanding,
> For I give you sound teaching;
> Do not abandon my instruction.
> When I was a son to my father,
> Tender and the only son in the sight of my mother,
> Then he taught me and said to me,
> "Let your heart hold fast my words;..." (Proverbs 4:1-4)

Solomon is saying that biblical truth is something to be grasped—God's guidance—because it gives us life. Such knowledge is the true blood of our family life.

Our children need to know what God says on every subject from dating, sex, marriage, and peer pressure to doctrines about God, Satan, and the end of the world. They need to understand everything, and our job as parents is to teach them. Every great man and every great woman must be a teacher of the Bible. "Whoever then annuls one of the least of these commandments, and teaches others to do the same, shall be called least in the kingdom of heaven; but whoever keeps and teaches them, he shall be called great in the kingdom of heaven" (Matthew 5:19). If we behave as if the Bible is not important, then we're least in the kingdom. We need to make sure that we parents understand our responsibility. "Train up a child in the way he should go, even when he is old he will not depart from it" (Proverbs 22:6).

The Bible does not say it's the church's responsibility to teach children, but we are to teach and equip moms and dads in the work of ministry and understanding the Bible. We cannot let primetime television or Hollywood movies teach children about manhood and womanhood. Sometimes parents say, "But I don't know the answers to all those questions about life." The solution to spiritual ignorance is to study the Bible. The best thing parents give children is a godly life. The best way to develop a godly life is to study God. By understanding the Bible, parents will discover answers to life's vital questions.

Second, teach your children convincingly. "Hear, O Israel! The Lord is our God, the Lord is one! You shall love the Lord your God with all your heart and with all your soul and with all your might. These words, which I am commanding you today, shall be on your heart" (Deuteronomy 6:4-6). In this passage, Moses is saying, "Listen, I'm going to teach you so you can teach future generations. "Now this is the commandment, the statutes and the judgments which the Lord your God has commanded me to teach you, that you might do them in the land where you are going over to possess it, so that you and your son and your grandson might fear the Lord your God, to keep all His statutes and His commandments which I command you, all the days of your life, and that your days may be prolonged" (Deuteronomy 6:1-2).

We must write Bible truths on our hearts to make it part of us. When we're convinced in our beliefs our children will catch our confidence, for the gospel of Christ "is the power of God for salvation for everyone who believes" (Romans 1:16 NKJV). Every time we are hungry, it feeds us. When we're broken, it heals us. God's Word is profitable for teaching all things (see 2 Timothy 3:16). Sunday school and children's programs can teach principles and stories, but the minute children return home, we parents can be a big spiritual detriment if we behave in ways contrary to the Bible. What makes Sunday school teachers effective is that they build on what children learn at home. The congregation can say, "Man, that Sunday school teacher is great! Look what our kids are learning!"

But children learn best when parents aren't living an inconsistent, contradictory life. We compliment the truth when we live the truth. We'll never teach Christian truths convincingly unless we ourselves are committed to them.

Third, teach them continually. "You shall teach them diligently to your sons and shall talk of them when you sit in your house and when you walk by the way and when you lie down and when you rise up" (Deuteronomy 6:7). The term diligently is the Hebrew word *shanan*, which means "to sharpen." Our job is to sharpen our children by continually whittling, honing, and helping them to understand themselves and their purpose. Every time an arrow is used it needs to be sharpened so it sticks deeper the next time. If children are like arrows, they need to be sharpened. We sharpen our children by teaching them, day-by-day, moment-by-moment in a continual process.

Some parents might say, "Well, I've already failed. It's too late." Yet from God's viewpoint, it's never too late. It's always the right time to do the will of the Father. A dad can say, "Well, all those years I blew it." Yet that is no excuse to give up. It's never too late to repent and change. We parents can seek forgiveness and move on. We shouldn't look back but press forward toward the future. When we obey God, we let Him do the work through us.

Fourth, teach them creatively. When individuals come to church, I can teach and preach the Bible. But the greatest lessons are learned through daily life. When children ask questions, we have special moments when we can provide answers. When we walk by the way, when we sit by the side, whenever we're doing ordinary tasks, we need to find creative opportunities to teach our children.

Once when the children were young, we lived in a house we'd rented for sixteen years. It was all we'd ever known. Then suddenly our landlord told us, "You've got to move." We sat our children down and said, "Our landlord has given us notice. We have to leave and find another place to live." At that moment, we were able to pray together with our children asking God to open another home for us.

Little Cade perked up and said, "But there's a problem, Daddy, our Suburban is not big enough to take all of our stuff with us."

I said, "Oh, you're perceptive, my son. We'll rent a truck so we can get all your Lego's and Star Wars toys in when we move."

We'd pray and then go look at homes. We found one that seemed perfect. The kids all picked out their rooms. They began planning how they'd decorate their spaces with the colors and comforters they liked, even deciding on pictures they'd put on the walls. In their minds, we'd already moved in. Then this "perfect" house went to another man. He closed escrow instead of canceling his sale and the house was no longer ours. Our children were disappointed. Some of them cried. But we told them, "The Bible says we're to give thanks in all things. God wants us to praise Him because He has another route, another avenue, another home for us."

So we thanked Him even though we didn't have a home and praised Him in our disappointment. That experience was a creative teaching moment for our children. We told them, "God's got another house in another location that's just right for us." They learned through that experience how God provides in His own special way. That was an important teaching time for us.

The greatest teaching time our family ever had was when an official from Child Protective Services visited our house. I returned from the grocery store one evening, to find two police cars parked outside my door. A lady from Child Protective Services was there. The officers approached me and said, "Mr. Sparks? We've had some complaints that some of your children have been abused. We need to talk to you."

I said, "Come right on in." Then I carried my groceries in with these people following me. I greeted my wife and said, "Honey, Child Protective Services are here." She turned as white as a sheet. I offered the officials something to eat and drink. The police soon left when they realized the situation was not volatile. Then the lady from the Child Protective Services explained her reason for coming. She said she'd like to interview our children, but she must talk to them alone.

I said, "Sure, I'd love to have you talk to them. We have nothing to hide. My children would love to talk to you." She went upstairs to speak with our children about life in our home. The kids all gave testimony about how Daddy spanks them.

When the social worker came downstairs she said, "You know, Mr. Sparks, it's against the law to spank your children in the State of California."

I said, "Really? But in the kingdom of God, you have to spank your children. So let me explain what the Bible says about spanking." I discussed the Proverbs and explained to her why we disciplined the children using spanking.

I said, "You know, this might not be what the law of California says," (She was wrong by the way) "but I abide by the Word of God and that's what I teach in my church and that's what I teach my children. I will always do what the Bible says no matter what the State of California says. Please understand that."

She said, "We'll be contacting you, Mr. Sparks, about our decision."

I said, "You get right back to us as soon as you can. Love to hear from you."

They called two weeks later to report that no charges would be filed, and there was no problem. That incident provided a teaching opportunity for our children. They all knew what happened, and they knew that Daddy wasn't going to lie or back down from the truth. Every day there's an opportunity to teach our children creatively in every situation a family faces.

Fifth, teach them conspicuously. Spiritual things should always be on our minds. Wherever we look and whatever we do we are to be purposely thinking of God. "You shall bind them as a sign on your hand and they shall be as frontals on your forehead. You shall write them on the doorposts of your house and on your gates" (Deuteronomy 6: 8-9). In Israel today the Orthodox Jews wear phylacteries or little books of Scripture, around their wrists so that whatever the hand touches, it's under and accountable to the Word of God. They also attach them to their foreheads because they want everything they do, say, think, and see to be subject to Scripture. These Jews walking around the streets of Jerusalem are pretty conspicuous, but that's the point. We are to teach our children conspicuously to let them know that God's in charge.

Lastly, teach them completely. Teach your children to know what the Bible says on every issue in life. "So the Lord commanded us to observe all these statutes, to fear the Lord our God for our good always and for our survival, as it is today. It will be righteousness for us if we are careful to observe all this commandment before the Lord our God, just as He commanded us" (Deuteronomy 6:24-25). When the newest toys or games come out, my kids are excited to get them, whether it's the new technological device or a new computer game. But the most exciting things are what we teach them about God's entire Word.

Socrates said, "Fellow citizens, why do you turn and scrape every stone to gather wealth and take so little care of your children to whom one day you must relinquish it all?" Why do we spend so much time getting stuff when one day we'll just pass it to our kids anyway? The bottom line is, we must think about our parental responsibility to our children. God wants us to train our children in such a way that they go further than we will ever go as individuals. They will be more than we ever were because we are committed to teaching them the entire law of God.

Lord, may You give us the courage to live out Your commandments in a loving, wise way so that our children can learn from us how to love and serve the Savior. Grant us the grace and mercy to follow Your priorities for parenting. Amen.

23

God's Charge to Children

Family relationships are complicated and reciprocal. Parents must care for their children, but children also have responsibilities. God's charge for children helps us understand what the Bible says concerning one's responsibility to parents. "There is a kind of man who curses his father and does not bless his mother" (Proverbs 30:11). Paul would tell Timothy, "But realize this, that in the last days difficult times will come. For men will be lovers of self, lovers of money, boastful, arrogant, revilers, disobedient to parents, ungrateful, unholy" (2 Timothy 3:1-2). Paul notes that in the last days, some people would be disobedient to parents. God spells out precise principles concerning the children's responsibility to their parents. In fact, the Bible is very clear about the consequences when a child doesn't obey his parents.

Throughout my ministry, I've talked to students about their relationships to their parents, specifically rebellious teenagers. I often read them the verse Proverbs 30:17,

> The eye that mocks a father
> And scorns a mother,
> The ravens of the valley will pick it out,
> And the young eagles will eat it.

The graphic images of having one's eye picked out and eaten by scavenging birds show the gravity of the offense. Of course, the proverb implies that God means business when He instructs us to respect our parents. Other proverbs stress a similar point. "He who assaults his father and drives his mother away is a shameful and disgraceful son" (Proverbs 19:26). Further, an assault on parents could actually backfire. "He who curses his father or his mother, his lamp will go out in time of darkness" (Proverbs 20:20). In the Old Testament, violence against parents required the ultimate penalty. "He who strikes his father or his mother shall surely be put to death" (Exodus 21:15).

We can dismiss these biblical statements as being merely metaphorical or an aspect of Jewish law no longer in place. However, God always means what he says. Human relationships are affected by concepts learned in childhood. Modes of behavior learned at home determine how individuals interact with both family and society. Seven biblical principles can illustrate God's challenge to children, emphasizing relationships to parents and society.

Acknowledge God's Commands

First, each of us must recognize that God is the ultimate authority and His claims are true and require obedience. "Honor your father and your mother, that your days may be prolonged in the land which the Lord your God gives you" (Exodus 20:12). If the American family is to survive, it must acknowledge God's instructions. If God's going to give you land, then make sure that you honor your mother and father.

A similar passage in Deuteronomy stresses obedience and honor. "So the Lord commanded us to observe all these statutes, to fear the Lord our God for our good always and for our survival, as it is today. It will be righteousness for us if we are careful to observe all this commandment before the Lord our God, just as He commanded us" (Deuteronomy 6:24-25). As God moves from the first to the fifth commandment, He says, "The very first evidence of loving Me, the very first evidence of worshipping Me is always seen in a person's relationship with his parents." If I'm looking at Him as the soul purpose of my existence, then the evidence will show in how I relate to my mother and father. In other words, if I do not honor my mother and father, it's not because something is wrong with them. It's not because they are bad parents. It's because I am failing to obey God. That's very clear throughout the Bible.

God gives a mandate. Children obey your parents. Honor your parents. The word "honor" is used 144 times in the Bible. The phrase "honor your father and mother" occurs seven times. Seven is the number of perfection, the number of completion. So twice in the Old Testament and five times in the New Testament we are instructed to honor our mothers and our fathers. To honor them means we value and respect them and put their needs above our own. It's a word that deals with our attitudes, as mentioned in Ephesians 6:1 and Colossians 3:20 where Paul says honoring parents is well pleasing to the Lord. Obedience is the act. Honoring is the attitude. We honor parents because when our attitude is right, we willingly obey. If we have a bad attitude that means we are not honoring Mom and Dad.

God is clothed with honor and reverence. "Oh Lord my God, You are very great. You are clothed with splendor and majesty" (Psalm 104:1). He is clothed with greatness, respect, reverence, honor, and value. When we give honor to God, we value Him and we respect Him. "You shall rise up before the gray headed and honor the aged, and you shall revere your God; I am the Lord" (Leviticus 19:32). Those of us with gray hair ought to read that verse to everybody we meet. That way we'll have lots of people standing in our honor. The concept is that we give honor (by standing up) to elders in respect for their wisdom and life accomplishments.

Practically speaking, to honor Mom and Dad, we must speak well of them. Some kids complain, "Oh my parents, man, I can't believe they won't let me go anywhere. They're old fuddy-duddies. I can't stand my parents." That's not speaking well of parents. Proverbs advises, "He who curses his father and his mother, his lamp will go out in time of darkness" (Proverbs 20:20). We must speak well of our parents. The opposite of cursing is honoring. We must never put them down or treat them condescendingly with statements like, "Oh, Dad's old. He just loves to hear himself talk, so we ignore him and let him babble on." Such statements imply that we think old Dad is out of touch. He doesn't know what's going on. However, honoring our parents implies that we regard them with a sense of graciousness. We must not do anything to harm them or drive them away. We should receive their correction and rebuke in humility and respect.

To respect parents in all things pleases the Lord (Colossians 3). The reason many of us don't bother to honor our parents is because down deep, pleasing the Lord is not a priority. Instead, we please ourselves. However, Paul instructs us to honor our parents in the Lord (Ephesians 6:1). The Bible says if we follow these instructions, it will be well with us. We're going to live long and well.

Could it be that some of us don't live a healthy life today because we have dishonored our parents in the past? The consequences of sin go with us. We need to realize that what we do today is going to affect how we live tomorrow. If we dishonor our parents today or rebel against parental authority, it will affect our future.

Attend to Parental Counsel

Shakespeare once said, "The voice of parents is the voice of gods, for to their children they are heaven's lieutenants." So according to Shakespeare, parents represent heaven, their commands require obedience. Solomon said a parent's instructions hold great value. "Hear, my son, your father's instruction and do not forsake your mother's teaching; indeed, they are a graceful wreath to your head and ornaments about your neck" (Proverbs 1:8-9). Parents are not perfect. In fact they're fallible, making lots of mistakes. But happy is the man who listens to his parents, and doubly happy is the man who has Christian parents who teach him the Word of God. Parents must teach children to obey, for no parent has to teach his children to disobey. Children naturally have a bent toward disobedience. It's a major task for parents to guide and train children as God desires.

I marvel at the life of Moses. Amazingly, he wasn't really used of God until he was eighty. So that's good news for everyone. No matter how old we are, there's always hope that God can use us. For Moses, the concepts his mother Jocabed taught him in childhood were the very elements that God strengthened in Moses when he grew up. Jocabed taught Moses as she nursed him, changed him, and bathed him. She told him about the redeemer, the God of Israel, the

God of Abraham, Isaac and Jacob. In Egypt, Moses received the best education possible as a child in the pharaoh's palace. Despite all the Egyptian training and instruction he received, however, he remembered the godly teaching of his mother and his Israelite identity.

Similarly, Paul tells Timothy to continue in the things he has learned from his early childhood about the Scriptures. He learned about God from his grandmother and his mother. "The things you learn in early childhood, Timothy, you've got to hold dear. You've got to hang on to those things. The things your mother and your grandmother taught you. Don't forget about those things" (paraphrase of 2 Timothy 1:5-6).

These examples underscore the need to teach children biblical concepts at an early age. Our responsibility is to educate our sons and daughters about the truths of the Bible. That's why children's ministries are important; Summer Bible schools, Sunday classes, youth groups and programs like AWANA that stress Bible memorization and discipleship. It is the duty of church ministries to come alongside families to assist in spiritual training so that their children know the Word of God. When I was a kid our family gathered every morning—same spots, in the same order—father, son, mother, sister—to pray before we went to junior high and high school. Then as we went out the door my mom would always say, "Remember, you're a child of the King, so look and act like the King's child." She always coupled her admonition with Scripture.

God called the Israelites a stiff-necked people. The word "neck" in the Bible sometimes represents stubbornness and rebellion. "A man who hardens his neck after much reproof will suddenly be broken beyond remedy" (Proverbs 29:1). It's imperative that we heed a rebuke. To stubbornly continue in our willful way will result in our failure and eventual destruction so listen when rebuked. However, if we obey we are blessed. We want our children's character to be Christ-like; therefore, we teach them to respect and obey authority. "Whoever loves discipline loves knowledge, but he who hates reproof is stupid" (Proverbs 12:1).

The honoring of parents is continual. "Listen to your father who begot you, and do not despise your mother when she is old" (Proverbs 23:22). The verse doesn't mean we've got to obey Mommy and

Daddy when we're fifty and they're eighty. It means we respect and value them. We treat parents with dignity even in old age, for God wants us to honor them.

Apply Parental Correction

Children ought to thank their parents for the discipline they receive. Parents discipline out of love, so children must recognize the parents' commitment. "A wise son accepts his father's discipline, but a scoffer does not listen to rebuke" (Proverbs 13:1). Not too long ago, I had to discipline my son. Soon afterward, my son entered the living room and thanked me. My wife and I were shocked. He said, "Thank you, Dad. I needed to be disciplined." Drew's action touched us. He demonstrated great prudence. "A fool rejects his father's discipline, but he who regards reproof is sensible" (Proverbs 15:5).

I never thanked my father for disciplining me, never once. It's amazing how children think they know everything. Parents, believe it or not, have a lot of life experience to offer children. They've faced peer pressure, rejection, drug abuse, even death. They know exactly what their children may be feeling. When children respect their parents' counsel and accept their parents' correction, they are saving themselves a world of pain.

A scoffer resents rebuke, but a prudent child embraces wisdom. Some children want complete autonomy with no accountability to anyone. However, every person has to be accountable to someone. A boss, the police, there's always somebody else in authority over us. The only power not accountable to anyone is God. Children who learn to respect authority can become great leaders in America because great leaders are, first of all, great followers.

Abide by Parents Commitments and Concerns

When a parent's instruction to children is righteous and biblical, children have a responsibility to obey.

> My son, observe the commandment of your father
> And do not forsake the teaching of your mother;
> Bind them continually on your heart;
> Tie them around your neck. (Proverbs 6:20-21)

As we understand and abide by God's law of God, then our commitment to obedience increases. In the process, we receive direction and guidance.

> When you walk about, they will guide you;
> When you sleep, they will watch over you;
> And when you awake, they will talk to you.
> For the commandment is a lamp and the teaching is light;
> And reproofs for discipline are the way of life. (Proverbs 6:22-23)

When we live in obedience to God's precepts, we sleep securely because we sense God's protection. There are no worries under the shadow of the Almighty. His wings protect and guard.

God also provides conversation. We never need worry about having someone to talk to because God says, "I'll talk to you. Open My Word and I will speak." Further, the Bible gives illumination. "Your word is a lamp to my feet and a light to my path" (Psalm 119:105). God shows us where to go. "The commandment of the Lord is pure, enlightening the eyes" (Psalm 19:8 KJV).

Avoid Bad Company

It's important to monitor children's companions. "He who walks with wise men will be wise, but the companion of fools will suffer harm" (Proverbs 13:20). We need to associate with wise men. Foolish friends only bring out the worst in us. As the English proverb says, "We become like the company we keep." "Do not be deceived: Bad company corrupts good morals" (1 Corinthians 15:33).

Don't associate yourself with people who can't stay on track and always change their minds. "A double minded man is unstable in all his ways" (James 1:8 KJV). Changeable people often have no direction. They can't commit to a cause or make difficult decisions. Children sometimes envy friends who have no rules and can stay out late and go where they want. However, such envy is misplaced.

> Do not be envious of evil men,
> Nor desire to be with them;

> For their minds devise violence,
> And their lips talk of trouble. (Proverbs 24:1-2)

The biblical mandates are clear. Avoid bad company.

Abstain From Sinful Conduct

Not only should children avoid evil companions, but also they must live righteously themselves.

> Do not be wise in your own eyes;
> Fear the Lord and turn away from evil.
> It will be healing to your body
> And refreshment to your bones. (Proverbs 3:7-8)

If children honor and obey their fathers and mothers, they will not have to fear negative consequences. The chastisement they receive will make them better people. "The prudent sees the evil and hides himself, but the naive go on, and are punished for it" (Proverbs 22:3). The wise man avoids evil. However, naive scoffers who ignore warnings will face trouble. Ultimately, evildoers face negative consequences and eventual punishment.

Accept Christ as Lord and Savior

Salvation is not inherited from parents. Children can't enter heaven because their moms or dads are Christians. Individuals can only go to heaven if they confess Jesus as Lord and believe that God raised Him from the dead. Each one must make the choice whether or not to accept Christ. God's greatest charge to children is that they would receive Him as Lord and Savior of their lives.

> My son, eat honey, for it is good,
> Yes, the honey from the comb is sweet to your taste;
> Know that wisdom is thus for your soul;
> If you find it, then there will be a future,
> And your hope will not be cut off. (Proverbs 24:13-14)

We need wisdom. The knowledge of God gives us a future.

Lord, open our children's eyes so they see You; open their hearts to receive You; direct their minds to obey You. Amen.

24

God's Instructions for In-Laws

Children are God's gifts to parents. For a short time, usually eighteen to twenty years, moms and dads have opportunity to teach and train their sons and daughters about life and God. However, there's an end to that gift of time. The children become young adults who, like young birds, leave the nest and fly off to build a nest of their own. They attend college, find jobs, get married, and start families. A number of years ago, my wife Laurie's father asked her to write a poem describing that empty-nest stage when children leave home. At the time, we were a young family with only two sons, Allen and Andrew, but even then, Laurie understood the fleeting nature of time.

> One day soon, Honey, it will be you and me.
> Let's think for a moment how different it will be.
> Our days will be slower, our nights long enough.
> Our yard won't be cluttered with their broken stuff.
> We'll watch what we want or do nothing at all.
> There won't be scuff marks all along the wall.
> Our room will be our room. Our bedspread could be white.
> We won't listen for footsteps or cries in the night.
> No peanut butter or jelly, we'll probably eat out.
> We won't spend one minute saying,
> "Say please" or "Don't pout."

>One day soon, Honey, they will be grown.
>We'll prayerfully send them to places unknown.
>For now, though, let's treasure each baby doll, each bug.
>Let's calmly clean the spilled juice up off the rug.
>Let's teach them. Let's hold them. Let's laugh as they play.
>Let's make concerts or games the highlight of our day.
>Let's tickle them, pray with them. Let's sing a silly song.
>For one day soon, Honey, they will be gone."

A.W. Tozer wrote, "Everything in life which we commit to God's care is really safe. And everything which we refuse to commit to Him is never really safe."[1] Christian parents can trust that the Lord will keep their children safe. He will protect and watch over them. Our responsibility as parents is to prepare them biblically while we possess them briefly.

As children mature, those strings that hold them to us will transform to wings that carry them away to marry someone. Then dads become fathers-in-law. Moms become mothers-in-law. God has specific instructions for in-laws as well as for husbands and wives. These guidelines are keys to helping parents develop healthy relationships with adult children and grandchildren. When young married couples have great mothers-in-law or fathers-in-law, they are blessed. I'm thankful for my own in-laws, who have trusted and believed in me. We have related to each other as friends. I praise the Lord for them.

My wife also shares a good relationship with my parents. To be honest, when we first married the relationship didn't go so well. It took some time, but my parents went overboard to build a relationship with Laurie. My first wife died, but during our years together my mom had a unique relationship with her. However, after Laurie and I married, my mother made a strategic effort to build bridges with Laurie and to show interest in her life. Those efforts helped our marriage and our relationship with them.

Marriages involve entire families. A groom can't tell his bride's family, "I'm taking your daughter; she and I will make our own life totally apart from you." That plan won't work. While the "leave and cleave" principle is best for a newly married couple, they cannot ignore their important familial relationships. Each son or daughter has certain mannerisms, attitudes, values, and traditions acquired from his or her own families while growing up. Adult children may marry and leave home, but they carry with them strong ties to their own parents and siblings. How boys and girls are raised influences how they approach their adult lives and their own marriage relationships.

There are many mother-in-law jokes that probably testify to the often strained interaction many individuals have with in-laws. Because I have a good relationship with my mother-in-law Rose, I can actually tell her mother-in-law jokes. We enjoy a good-natured laugh together. Here is one of my favorites. What's the definition of mixed emotions? Mixed emotions are what you feel when you watch your mother-in-law go over a cliff in your brand new SUV. You don't know whether to laugh or to cry.

For people who don't have a good relationship with their parents-in-law, holiday gatherings can be tough. A son-in-law can become the turkey that his wife's family members slice with their tongues at Thanksgiving. Yet, God wants to work through all those difficulties. There are several biblical instructions that can guide Christians in these complex family connections.

Pray, Don't Pry

In-laws must pray for their married children rather than pry into their affairs. When children leave home, they fly solo. So more than ever they need prayer. Parents have nearly twenty years to influence children; after that, their responsibility is to "pray without ceasing" (1 Thessalonians 5:17). In-laws must be men and women who exemplify godly character. "The effectual fervent prayer of a righteous man availeth much" (James 5:16 KJV). Their job is to seek righteousness and pray fervently.

The Old Testament story detailing how Abraham's son Isaac finds a bride contains the second longest account in Genesis. (The flood is the longest narrative.) In this search for the right woman, Abraham tells his servant, God "will send His angel before you" (Genesis 24:7). Abraham knew that God would sovereignly orchestrate life events to bring the right wife for his son, Isaac. As parents, our job is to pray for our children that they would find the right husband or wife. Once they are married, our job is to pray fervently for their relationships. We can give them money for a down payment on a house. We can buy tons of clothes for the grandchildren. We can even pay for grandchildren's private school education. Those gifts are all good. Yet if we don't pray for our children, we have failed as parents.

The problem is that we want to be too involved; we parents want to influence events or outcomes. However, God is the one to do the changing. He brings transformation in due time. We must wait upon the Lord. Prayer with patience is productive. Prayer without patience is unproductive. We often ask God to intervene and bring positive change to a situation, but then we interfere ourselves. God wants us to pray, and then wait to see how He alters situations. Waiting is hard for a father-in-law when his daughter marries "a loser." He thinks, *"Oh man, why did I let this marriage happen? My poor daughter—if I would have said, 'no' two years ago, she wouldn't be in this bad marriage."*

Sometimes dads want to take that errant son-in-law by the scruff of the neck, kick him in the seat of the pants, and say, "Hey man. Get your life together. Stop being selfish. Quit being foolish." However, those tactics won't change the guy. He often just rebels or ignores. So the dad must pray, asking God to supernaturally change the heart and mind of the son-in-law and to preserve the marriage.

As a father, my job is to train my boys to be good providers, good partners, and good priests in their homes. My job as a father is to model to my daughters how a good husband behaves and how he treats his wife lovingly. Then the girls can say, "That's how I want my husband to treat me." Hopefully my children will learn how to choose a righteous mate based on what I do, what I say, and how I say it. Then once the girls choose their special man or once my boys choose that specific young lady, my job is to pray that God will guide them and teach them to love unselfishly. I can pry into their private affairs, but without prayer my influence fails. Our parents prayed fervently for both Laurie and me. We felt their prayers.

If a son-in-law is not treating his wife properly, parents need to confront him in a biblical way regarding his sin. But all the while, parents must ask God to provide the right spirit and the right attitude. Then God can soften their hearts to be receptive to wise counsel and to improved behavior.

Counsel, Don't Condemn

So easily we criticize what our son-in-law or daughter-in-law is doing. As in-laws, we should offer them wisdom instead. There's a biblical model for such interaction in Exodus chapter 18 where Moses is counseled by his father-in-law Jethro.

> Moses' father-in-law said to him, "The thing that you are doing is not good. You will surely wear out, both yourself and these people who are with you, for the task is too heavy for you; you cannot do it alone. Now listen to me: I will give you counsel, and God be with you. You be the people's representative before God, and you bring the disputes to God, then teach them the statutes and the laws, and make known to them the way in which they are to walk and the work they are to do. Furthermore, you shall select out of all the people able men who fear God, men of truth, those who hate dishonest gain; and you shall place these over them as leaders of thousands, of hundreds, of fifties and of tens.... So it will be easier for you, and they will bear the burden with you. If you do this thing and God so commands you, then you will be able to endure, and all these people also will go to their place in peace." So Moses listened to his father-in-law and did all that he had said. (Exodus18:17-21, 23-24)

Moses was the greatest leader in the history of Israel. Yet he wasn't too proud to accept his father-in-law's advice. God called Moses, not Jethro, to lead the nation of Israel out of slavery. His role carried huge responsibilities. Jethro recognized that Moses couldn't do the work alone. Moses needed time for prayer and to seek God's guidance. So Jethro advised Moses to select some able, faithful, strong, God-fearing men who could resolve the small disputes among the people. When a major disagreement arose, then they could bring the matter to Moses. Moses was receptive to Jethro's suggestions.

Now Jethro could have condemned his son-in-law and questioned him, saying. "Moses, you call yourself a leader? You can't succeed by handling all these cases yourself." Yet, Jethro didn't criticize or condemn. He offered counsel. That's how we should deal with sons and daughters-in-law. We can politely ask, "Can I offer you some advice? Can I discuss some scriptural principles to aid you in your difficulty?" When we offer kindness and respect, the young people may be more willing to listen to us.

We can't allow ourselves to be upset if our married children don't accept our advice. We must resist the temptation to say, "Well, that's the last time I'm advising them! They never listen." It's our responsibility to advise them but it's God who brings change.

Jethro left room for God to lead Moses. We must give our children the same space. Leave matters in God's hands. Criticism comes easily but guidance is what's needed. I love it when my Dad calls to advise me. He says, "Son, I know you didn't ask me, but can I give you a piece of advice?" I love to hear that from my father. He doesn't say, "Do this, and if you don't, you're an idiot." He might think it, but he never says it. He knows I'm an independent, free-thinking man, yet he understands that God has to influence me. We also must believe that God works in the lives of our children, too.

Minister, Don't Manipulate

An Old Testament story of exploitation is illustrated in the Laban-Jacob-Rachel-Leah saga (Genesis 29-31). Laban was a master manipulator who mistreated Jacob for twenty years. It began when Jacob was smitten with Laban's daughter Rachel. He agreed to work for seven years to earn the right to marry the beautiful young woman.

Laban agreed so Jacob signed on for seven years. We can imagine how Jacob dreamed of having beautiful Rachel beside him every night. But Laban manipulated the events of that wedding so Jacob found himself married to Leah, the plain older sister instead. Jacob cried, "What is this you have done to me? Was it not for Rachel that I served with you? Why then have you deceived me?" (Genesis 29:25).

But Laban replied, "It is not the practice in our place to marry off the younger before the first born" (Genesis 29:26). Laban explains that Jacob actions were literally out of order. He couldn't have Rachel unless he also took Leah. So Jacob made the sacrifice. For the twenty years that Jacob worked for Laban, the livestock thrived; business was good. But Laban used one manipulative technique after another to get what he wanted at Jacob's expense.

As parents-in-law our job is to minister to our sons and daughters, not to manipulate their actions or influence their decisions through coercion or a false sense of obligation. Sometimes fathers hire their sons-in-law to work in the family business to keep the daughter close by. When Laurie and I married, my father-in-law took Laurie and me to dinner one evening and asked, "Lance, what would you think if we made a commitment as a family never to move more than 200 miles from one another?"

I told him, "I'm never going to make a commitment like that. I know you want me to value the family. But I value God more. If God calls my family someplace else, I can't say, 'Sorry God. My father-in-law wants me to stay close by.' Jesus said, 'If anyone comes to Me, and does not hate his own father and mother and wife and sisters, yes, and even his own life, he cannot be My disciple' (Luke 14: 26). What if God calls Laurie and me to Bora Bora? I have to follow God first."

He accepted my answer. Then three months later, he took a job 1,500 miles away, moving his wife and the other two daughters away from us. The bottom line is that parents like to control the events of the family, even the extended family, but they don't know what the future holds.

Married children need to develop their own family identity without feeling obligated to their parents or siblings. The "leaving and cleaving" concept was God's idea. One of the worst choices newlywed couples can make is to live with their parents. There are enough problems in marriage when couples get started. Adding in-laws into the mix only complicates the situation. Newly married children should develop their own family identity, traditions, and values. Some parents can be control freaks who want to influence what happens in their children's families, so couples must guard against that manipulative influence.

Laban's whole life was one of manipulation; he tried to hold on to Rachel and Leah. He didn't want Jacob to return to the Promised Land. That's why he pursued Jacob's caravan and challenged him by saying, "How dare you steal my daughters" (see Genesis 31:26). He was using Jacob, gaining profit from Jacob's success in breeding livestock. He was angry that Jacob would dare to leave.

Release, Don't Restrain

Many adult children have grown up with dominating parents, who control everything that happens in the family. Other parents don't dominate, but they are overly protective. These parents don't want to cut the strings binding them to their children; sometimes they don't want to let that last child, the baby of the family, go. Their actions often prohibit their adult children from developing the maturity necessary for success in the grown-up world.

Sometimes a father-in-law or a mother-in-law restrains by telling the married daughter, "I don't want you to tell your husband this, but...." Their desire to influence, criticize, or keep secrets is unhealthy. A daughter should not withhold information from her husband. That's sinful. My wife and I have a rule at home that if a parent discusses an important matter with us, we automatically tell the other one, no matter what, because we are "one flesh" and we need to know what's going on in each other's lives. We keep no secrets in our home. Everything is open and bare. The nakedness of Adam and Eve relates not only to innocence but also to transparency. It connotes honesty. Couples must possess a transparency about their lives, a willingness to accept one another, and a willingness to deal with one another openly. Secrets hinder a marriage. Parents-in-law must release their married children to be what God has called them to be, a one-flesh entity who builds a marriage that honors and glorifies God.

Support, Don't Supplant

God designed husbands to be providers for the family. Parents-in-law must not supersede a son's role as supplier. In-laws are to support and guide, but not supplant. If parents come along side their son or son-in-law and pay his family's bills, finance the mortgage, and assume financial responsibilities, they strip the son of his masculinity. He and his family become financial cripples without the requisite maturity to manage the family affairs.

Children must learn to manage a budget. It's astounding how many young couples become mired in debt in the first years of their marriage. Sometimes newlyweds expect the big house with a two-car garage filled with two nice vehicles and a six-figure income to manage it all. They want exactly what their parents have, and they wonder why they can't obtain it right away. Couples must be willing to work through the struggles of marriage to achieve long-term goals in their finances and relationships. Part of marriage building is surviving difficulties together, dealing with trials together as husband and wife, and learning to trust God together and watch Him provide.

When I went to seminary, my Mom asked how I would pay the tuition. I told her that I planned to work my way through school. She wondered how I would be able to both work and study, but her only gift to me was her prayers and encouragement. She never offered to help with the costs. I knew I was on my own.

I traveled to Indiana to register for my seminary classes. My checkbook showed I didn't have nearly enough money to begin my first semester. I was hoping the registrar would allow me to put some money down. I went to the window and said, "I'm Lance Sparks. I'm enrolled as a freshman. I want to make a payment toward my tuition."

The woman glanced at the list and said, "Oh, your bill's already paid for the semester."

I asked, "How could it be paid? Who wrote a check?"

"I don't know who wrote the check. But it says here it's paid in full. Pass on to the next booth, please."

I couldn't believe it. I called my Mom and Dad. They couldn't believe it either. Yet somehow, somebody somewhere decided to pay for my first semester of school. When the second, third, and fourth semesters began the registrar gave me the same good news. "Oh, your bill has already been paid, Mr. Sparks." An anonymous donor provided the funds for every semester of my seminary study. I never discovered who it was but my wife and I learned to trust God when we had nothing. Laurie would drive the car to work. I'd bike to school and then pedal to work. God provided. Parents must support rather than supplant so their children learn healthy coping skills and reliance on God.

Help, Don't Hinder

To return to the Laban-Jacob story, when Laban pursued Jacob's caravan, he accused Jacob of stealing his daughters and his gods. Jacob was forced to confront his father-in-law again.

> Jacob said to Laban, "What is my transgression? What is my sin that you have hotly pursued me? Though you have felt through all my goods, what have you found of all your household goods? Set it here before my kinsmen and your kinsmen, that they may decide between us two. These twenty years I have been with you; your ewes and your female goats have not miscarried, nor have I eaten the rams of your flocks...These twenty years I have been in your house; I served you fourteen years for your two daughters, and six years for your flock, and you changed my wages ten times." (Genesis 31:36-41)

Father and son-in-law established a covenant. Yet Laban wanted to hinder Jacob's departure, pursuing his son-in-law vehemently to bring his daughters back. But Jacob was determined to follow God. Parents-in-law should look for ways to help their sons or daughters. They should never hinder God's movement, the Spirit of God influencing hearts and minds. From my own son-in-law perspective, I've seen my parents and my in-laws rejoice as God has led my family and provided for us. Their supportive attitudes have blessed us.

Uphold, Don't Usurp

For grandparents who have little grandchildren running around, it's important that they uphold the teachings of their sons and daughters, allowing them to parent the children. It's so easy for a grandparent to contradict what Mom and Dad teach their children. It's important that even in subtle ways, grandparents deal truthfully and honestly with their grandchildren. They must not usurp their children's parental authority by saying, "Well, I'd do it this way. Evidently your mom doesn't know what she's doing." Grandparents must respect and uphold their children's decisions and discipline. Solomon said,

> Hear, O sons, the instruction of a father,
> And give attention that you may gain understanding,
> For I give you sound teaching;
> Do not abandon my instruction.
> When I was a son to my father,
> Tender and the only son to my mother,
> Then he taught me and said to me,
> "Let your heart hold fast my words;
> Keep my commandments and live;
> Acquire wisdom;
> And with all your acquiring, get understanding.
> Prize her, and she will exalt you." (Proverbs 4:1-8)

A son is to listen to the instruction of his father and his mother. Grandparents should encourage their grandchildren to listen to and obey their parents.

Sometimes, older grandparents have strong opinions about certain issues like interracial marriages or interracial dating. However, grandparents must remember that there are only two races in the world, Jew and Gentile. It has nothing to do with skin color. An interracial marriage is when a Christian marries an unbeliever, someone who's not a Christian. That's when a couple becomes "unequally yoked." Grandparents must not let prejudices or biases govern their thinking; instead the Bible must guide the believer's thinking.

Intercede, Don't Interfere

A grandparent's job is to pray for their grandchildren by name. They must pray for the children specifically concerning their talents, their giftedness, their activities, seeking God's guidance and protection for them. "Let our sons in their youth be as grown up plants, and our daughters as corner pillars fashioned as for a palace" (Psalm 144:12). First grandparents should pray for their grandchildren's maturity: That they would grow strong like healthy plants; that they would be like pillars—stable and unshakable. It's important to pray that their character, the beauty of their lives, would shine because they are committed to Jesus Christ.

Next, grandparents shouldn't assume that it's okay to spank their grandchildren. It's important to ask permission first. We must not assume that our grandson needs a haircut because we think his hair is too long. Maybe our son-in-law or daughter-in-law likes his hair that way. We need to ask before we do something to, for, or with our grandchildren. We must ask, rather than assume we have the right to do whatever we think is best. Grandparents are not the parents. For example, I love it when my parents ask me, "Would it be okay if we take the kids to the zoo today?" Then I have the option to say, "Great," or "It's not a good idea for today." My parents always comply with my wishes. They are model grandparents.

Grandparents who take grandchildren places or buy them toys without permission do so out of arrogance. They act as though they know best. "A man's pride will bring him low, but a humble spirit will obtain honor" (Proverbs 29:23). Grandparents must never assume they know what's best. A humble spirit will bring honor. Humility says, *"I'll ask before I do something for the grandchildren because they aren't my children. Therefore, I want to ask my son, my son-in-law, my daughter, or my daughter-in-law before I take action out of respect for them."*

Offer, Don't Obstruct

We should offer assistance but never obstruct the growth of our grandchildren. Grandparents, just like parents, can become stumbling blocks to grandchildren by showing favoritism to one grandchild over another. That action can cause harm to the other grandchildren making them feel inferior or resentful. We can become a stumbling block by failing to lead our grandchildren into righteousness; we can tempt them to sin by saying, "That's okay, Mommy will understand," or saying, "Don't tell your mom we went to the movies, okay? It'll be our little secret." We must never tempt them to disobey their mothers and fathers, causing the little ones to sin. "But whoever causes one of these little ones who believe in Me to stumble, it would be better for him to have a heavy millstone hung around his neck, and to be drowned in the depth of the sea" (Matthew 18:6). We must offer advice, but never obstruct grandchildren's growth or their godly spiritual development.

Confront, Don't Concede

As grandparents, if our children are somehow mistreating the grandchildren we can confront them. We must never stop confronting sin, especially as a grandparent. Grandparents have wisdom and experience that can benefit the family. When we challenge those who are in error it's because we are concerned about their purity, holiness, and success in life.

Love, Don't Legislate

We must love our children and grandchildren without legislating righteousness. As Christ loved sacrificially, willingly, beneficially, and totally with all that He had, so we, too, should love sacrificially. "A new commandment I give to you, that you love one another, even as I have loved you" (John 13:34). The golden rule is no longer enough. The new commandment is to love one another as Christ has loved us. Christ says, "I'm the standard." Christ washed His disciples' feet and humbled Himself before them. Willingly, He gave Himself away to them and for them. As a grandparent, as a mother-in-law or father-in-law, God wants us to love unconditionally. We can be a good example to our children and grandchildren when we sacrificially serve our family members with wisdom and humility, trusting God to lead and guide.

Dear Father, thank you for giving us the perfect standard. Help us to love one another as You have loved us, totally, sacrificially, and volitionally. Amen.

25

God's Fundamentals for Your Family

This final chapter closes our discussion about *God's Hope for Your Home*. The underlying philosophy for all flourishing family relationships lies in understanding that the Bible should be the guiding force in helping us form healthy, loving, lasting relationships that strengthen society and honor God.

> Unless the Lord builds the house,
> They labor in vain who build it;
> Unless the Lord guards the city,
> The watchman keeps awake in vain. (Psalm 127:1)

A nation's strength is directly associated with the moral might of its citizens. In fact, a family that falters will encompass a society that fails. Every society that fails, fails because the family somehow falters.

> How blessed is everyone who fears the Lord,
> Who walks in His ways,
> When you shall eat of the fruit of your hands,
> You will be happy and it will be well with you....
> The Lord bless you from Zion,
> And may you see the prosperity of Jerusalem all the
>   days of your life.

> Indeed, may you see your children's children.
> Peace be upon Israel! (Psalm 128:1-2, 5-6)

Each family unit around us faces conflicts, and some of those relationships are breaking and crumbling. The more they crumble, the more society will suffer. Our actions have consequences. So we need to understand how God wants us to live. Billy Graham addressed these challenges in his book *World Aflame:*

> The immutable law of sowing and reaping has held sway. We are now the hapless possessors of moral depravity, and we seek in vain for a cure. The tares of indulgence have overgrown the wheat of moral restraint. Our homes have suffered. Divorce has grown to epidemic proportions. When the morals of society are upset, the family is the first to suffer. The home is the basic unit of our society, and a nation is only as strong as her homes. The breaking up of the home does not often make headlines, but it eats like termites at the structure of the nation.[1]

The Lord has to build our homes; He has to be the focal point. Christ has to be first in every man and every woman's life. He is the foundation.

Four scriptural pillars offer the guidelines we need to develop an honorable family life. These concepts are so basic that we may find ourselves asking, "How could I overlook that point?" Yet we do miss the mark because Satan deceives our thinking. Satan's a master of keeping us busy doing unimportant tasks, so we become distracted from these fundamentals.

Pillar One: The Word of God

God's Word is sufficient to teach us, lead us, and guide us to live fruitful lives. "All Scripture is inspired by God and is profitable for teaching, for reproof, for correction, for training in righteousness; so that the man of God may be adequate, equipped for every good work" (2 Timothy 3:16-17). Yet we minimize its importance. Sadly, the Bible is like a stranger in many people's home, a dusty book on the shelf, but it must not remain neglected. "Let the word of Christ richly dwell within you" (Colossians 3:16). This phrase "dwell within you" means, "be at home in your hearts." In other words, "Let Scripture be at home in your heart." Without the foundation of biblical principles reigning in our lives, our family relationships will suffer. If the Bible is at home in our hearts, it will guide our family life.

In Isaiah God says, "But to this one will I look, to him who is humble and contrite of spirit, and who trembles at My word" (66:2). God says that the person who has a broken and contrite heart and who shakes uncontrollably under the authority of Scripture is the kind of person He can use. But anyone who does not shake under the authority of God's Word is one who wants to operate alone. The reverent, humble person recognizes God's power and wants to be used by God in a compelling way.

Consider Mary and Joseph; they subjected themselves to the law of the Lord. They exemplified the kind of reverent, humble people whom God can use. "And when the days for their purification according to the law of Moses were completed, they brought Him [Jesus] up to Jerusalem, to present Him to the Lord (as it is written in the Law of the Lord)" (Luke 2:22). These parents followed scriptural mandates. They brought their son to the temple. They offered a sacrifice (Luke 2:24) and after they carried out everything according to the Law of the Lord, they returned to Nazareth (Luke 2:39). They made decisions based on instructions in Scripture. Similarly, twenty-first century husbands, as leaders, must demonstrate to the family that they, too, will do what God says no matter what.

Matthew described Joseph as a "righteous man" (1:19). Joseph wanted to honor God. He did not want to publically disgrace Mary (his pregnant fiancée), so he desired to put her away secretly. But then he had a dream where God's angel spoke to him saying, "'Joseph, son of David, do not be afraid to take Mary as your wife; for the Child who has been conceived in her is of the Holy Spirit. She will bear a Son; and you shall call His name Jesus, for He will save His people from their sins.' And Joseph awoke from his sleep and did as the angel of the Lord commanded him, and took Mary as his wife."

(Matthew 1:20, 21, 24) Joseph had a dilemma. How would he justify Mary's pregnancy to people who knew the two weren't married yet? Conception by the Holy Spirit would be difficult for Joseph to explain even if he said, "Well, she experienced a miracle. The Spirit of God came over her, and she conceived a son."

His friends and neighbors would reply, "Right, Joseph, you're kidding, aren't you?" Joseph would become a laughing stock in Nazareth, but still he obeyed God undeterred. It is evident that obedience was the habitual characteristic of Joseph's life. More than once an angel instructed Joseph, and each time, he complied. "Now when they had gone, behold, an angel of the Lord appeared to Joseph in a dream and said, 'Get up! Take the Child and His mother and flee to Egypt, and remain there until I tell you; for Herod is going to search for the Child to destroy Him.' So Joseph got up and took the Child and His mother while it was still night, and left for Egypt" (Matthew 2:13-14). The prospect of traveling to Egypt was not merely a short trip to a neighboring city. It meant a long journey and Mary had this newborn son. After living in exile in Egypt, the angel returned to tell Joseph the coast was clear. Herod was dead, and the baby's life was safe. Joseph obediently brought his family back to Nazareth.

Whenever the Spirit of God came to Joseph and spoke to him in a dream, Joseph did what he was told. He knew as a father and a husband, whatever God said he had to do. There was no debate or questioning. In the same way, as parents we need to do whatever God says. Yet, so many times we resist because we don't want to submit to biblical instruction. But our pillar must be the Word of God.

Scripture is our authority. Scripture dictates what to do, where to go, when to do it, and how to do it. There are seven questions we can ask ourselves to determine if the Bible is our ultimate authority.

First, do we desire to know the Word of God more than anything else? The psalmist understood that God's Word was his authority. "The law of Thy mouth is better to me than thousands of gold and silver pieces" (Psalm 119:72). The Word of God matters more than riches.

> Princes persecute me without cause,
> But my heart stands in awe of Your words.

> I rejoice at Your word,
> As one who finds great spoil. (Psalm 119:161-162)

I desire God's holy Word. It's the sweetest thing to me. That's question number one: Do we desire it?

Question two: Do we defend it? Paul told Timothy, "Guard, through the Holy Spirit who dwells in us, the treasure which has been entrusted to you" (2 Timothy 1:14). When people speak against the Word of God, do we defend it? Do we stand up and say, "No, that's not true; God's Word says this"? We must defend Scripture as Jude said: "Contend earnestly for the faith which was once for all delivered to the saints" (Jude 3).

Question three: Do we declare it? If God's Word is our authority, we're going to proclaim it, declare it, and desire it. The Word of the Lord needs to be preached to all people.

Question four: Do we demonstrate the truths of God's Word in the way we live? Is our life a living testimony, showing God at work? Do we submit to the Bible as our authority? I served as a college pastor for a number of years. I found that university students ask all kinds of questions about life; they love to question authority. In fact, they're raised to question authority.

When I talked to them about premarital sex, I spoke out strongly against it, so they asked, "What's wrong with premarital sex?" Then I explained what the Bible said: "For this is the will of God, your sanctification; that is, that you abstain from sexual immorality" (1 Thessalonians 4:3). In other words, Christians should not have sex outside of marriage. They were often indifferent to this scriptural concept. So I would explain further that God would not direct them if they lived contrary to His instructions, His biblical mandate.

Every week, I would talk with young men who thought that premarital sex was the greatest thing going. For them, promiscuity was okay because Scripture was not their authority. Their friends were their authority. Contemporary social standards became their standards. What God said didn't matter if their own conscience didn't prick them, so for them, sex on dates was not only permissible but desirable. However God reveals a better plan for our bodies and our behaviors. We must ask ourselves, *"Does my life demonstrate that God's Word is my authority? Am I devoted to it?"*

The first century church devoted itself to the apostle's instruction. These new Christians realized that they needed spiritual food. They could grow and change through learning the Lord's words. They were so devoted to the process that they met daily to study. Would Christians in our society attend church every day? Perhaps not. We're all so busy with life's activities. Yet these early Christians were hungry to worship and learn. They were devoted to spiritual growth.

Question five: Are we directed by scriptural truth? Does God direct our decision making process? God must be our personal sovereign. "And let the peace of Christ rule in your hearts" (Colossians 3:15 KJV). We were once His enemy, but now we're at peace with Him. Before salvation we were on Satan's side, an enemy of God. Now as believers we're at peace with God.

Popular culture runs contrary to biblical principles. For example, in 2002, *USA Today* published results of a study on child rearing. "Spare the Rod, Improve the Child," staff writer Karen S. Peterson reported these findings:

> Children who are not spanked tend to be better behaved and do better in school, grow up to have better marriages, earn more money and live better lives, according to Murry Strouse of the Family Research Laboratory at the University of New Hampshire. Strouse summed up 50 years of research on the effectiveness and side effects of spanking. That mass of research indicates agreement among professionals on two things, he said in a statement prior to the conference: Spanking is not the most effective method of discipline. "Although spanking works, it does not work better than other methods of correcting and teaching kids." Spanking has harmful side effects. It increases "the chance that a child will become rebellious or depressed. These side effects may take years to show up," he says. "Lots of people

are worried that if parents never spanked, the result would be kids running wild, higher rates of delinquency, and when they grow up, more crime," he says. "Actually, what the research shows is just the opposite."[2]

Once we read these kinds of reports, we have two choices. We can believe fifty years of research or we can believe the eternal Word of God. I choose the eternal Word of God. Proverbs advocates spanking as a form of discipline. The rod drives out the foolishness bound up in the heart of a child. Sparing the rod spoils the child. It's also important to mention that the final paragraphs of the article cites differing opinions on child discipline, pointing out that researchers don't even agree among themselves on the "definition of spanking."[3]

A number of Christian families have chosen never to spank their children. They say, "Society advocates a better way." Yet today, it doesn't seem that American youth are less violent or aggressive. In fact, incidents of "bullying" seem on the increase. Our society is not a better place since parents have stopped spanking children. That's just one simple illustration. Are we directed by the Word of God? Should culture and media set the standard for how we raise our children?

Question six: Do we depend on the Word of God? When we feel afflicted, worried, or concerned, where do we look for help? The psalmist said,

> If Your law had not been my delight,
> Then I would have perished in my affliction.
> I will never forget Your precepts,
> For by them You have revived me.
> I am Yours, save me;
> For I have sought Your precepts. (Psalm 119:92-94)

Do we depend on God for everything? When we're in trouble, what is the first thing we do? We, of all people, are most richly blessed to have the Bible at our disposal. The Psalmist went first to God when he was afflicted. God is our strength and shield.

Pillar Two: The Worship of God

I love the book of Revelation because it is about the worship of God and heaven. In heaven we're going to be worshipping God for all eternity. That means we need to understand worship before we get there. Jesus said that the Father seeks true worshippers (John 4:23-24). God wants people who will worship Him and adore Him. God gave that mandate to Israel. He said, "Listen, you are to have no other gods before Me. I am the true God; I am. Worship Me" (paraphrase Exodus 20:1-2).

Essentially God is saying, "Listen. You must understand what worship is because if you don't worship Me properly, it's going to affect your children, your grandchildren, even your great grandchildren." So families must understand what it means to worship God. Worshipping God must be our response to divine revelation. The only way we can worship God is to respond to who He is based on the revelation of the Bible. So worship is the review and response to divine revelation. When God reveals Himself to me through Scripture, I respond to Him. Every person who truly worships God realizes that there must be recognition of His person, rejoicing in His presence, reverence for His power, and obedience to His precepts. Those elements comprise true worship.

A lot of people say that they are believers, that they are Christians. But Paul says that true Christians are those who worship God in spirit, glorify Christ Jesus, and put no confidence in the flesh (see Philippians 3:3). The first characteristic of a truly born again believer is that he worships God in spirit and in truth (see John 4:23). God is his sole reason for existence. He loves to live for God. So it makes sense that when Jesus came to earth, He modeled worship. In the wilderness, as Satan tempted Him, Jesus said, "Man shall not live on bread alone, but on every word that proceeds out of the mouth of God" (Matthew 4:4). The Bible has authority to refute Satan.

Satan basically said to Jesus, "Fall down and worship me. Bow before me, and I'll give You all the cities of the world. It's all Yours" (see Matthew 4:8-9). We must realize that Satan wants to be worshipped. Jesus asserts the truth when He responds to Satan, "We should worship God and serve only Him." Jesus responded to temptation by claiming the authority of Scripture. Today, Satan's goal remains the same, to distract us using appeals to wealth, success, independence, sensuality or other selfish desires. We delay worship of God when other needs take precedence. Other goals become more important. We put God in second, third or fourth place. Yet God deserves to be number one. He's creator of the world. He formed us and has given us everything we need. When we ignore God, future generations will feel the effects of our iniquity. But when we put God first, then thousands of generations will be blessed.

Sacrifice is our duty and joy. I love to read about Anna in Luke 2:36. She spent her whole life in the temple, worshipping and sacrificing to the Lord. Her life was consumed with divine service. The greatest Old Testament example, of course, is Abraham, who sacrificed his dreams on the altar in obedience to God. He submitted because sacrifice became his duty. Such obedience results in joy. Joy comes in giving our lives away. If we make God number one in our families, our joy will be tremendous. "Worship the Lord with reverence and rejoice with trembling" (Psalm 2:11).

Once I was watching a preacher speak on the TBN channel. It was amazing to hear this man recount how God called to him one night, seeking some conversation. Supposedly the Lord told him, "I'm really sad today, Jesse."

Then Jesse asked, "Why are you sad? Did someone grieve You, Lord?"

According to Jesse, the Lord replied, "Yes, one of My children has grieved Me."

So Jesse explained to his audience, "The Lord needed somebody to talk to that day. So he woke me up in the middle of the night to talk to me."

As I listened to this television story, I thought to myself, *"how blasphemous!"* God doesn't need to talk to anybody, let alone this guy who seems to be putting himself on par with God. The bottom line is that the Lord doesn't need us. He won't come to talk to us because He's feeling down in the dumps. God is never sad. He controls everything. He created everything. He rules over everything. It's all happening as He planned.

We must never treat the Lord with a sense of triviality. Jesus is more than just our good friend. He is God Almighty. The Holy God of the Bible seeks those who are of a broken and contrite heart and who tremble at His very words. "Let all the earth fear the Lord; Let all the inhabitants of the world stand in awe of Him" (Psalm 33:8). The book of Revelation is awe-inspiring. Angelic beings fall face down before God because they recognize His holy person. They rejoice in His presence; therefore they're able to respond to everything He says because they love Him so. That's why Paul said, "I urge you, brethren, by the mercies of God, to present your bodies a living and holy sacrifice, acceptable to God, which is your spiritual service of worship" (Romans 12:1). We must sacrifice all our dreams and all our hopes for Him on the altar so that He might work in and through our lives. Being a living sacrifice is our only acceptable form of worship.

Pillar Three: The Will of God

If Scripture is our authority and sacrifice is our duty, then submission is our priority. That's the will of God. "Submit yourselves for the Lord's sake to every human institution, whether to a king as the one in authority, or to governors as sent by him for the punishment of evildoers and the praise of those who do right. For such is the will of God that by doing right you may silence the ignorance of foolish men" (1 Peter 2:13-15). In the accounts described in John 4:34, John 5:30 and John 6:38, Jesus Christ is submitting to the will of the Father. When Jesus came to earth, He said, "My whole desire is to do the Father's will. My food is to do the will of the Father. In order for Me to be sustained from day to day, I need to do what God says. I need to submit to My heavenly Father."

In our families, we ought to submit to God because we fear Him and because we want to honor one another and put others before ourselves. "I delight to do thy will, O my God: yea, thy law is within my heart" (Psalm 40:8 KJV). We are so busy gaining control, trying to be top dog, and the best at what we do, but we become the worst because we are unwilling to submit to God or esteem others better than ourselves.

Pillar Four: The Work of God

Service becomes our responsibility. "Bless the Lord, all you His hosts, You who serve Him, doing His will" (Psalm 103:21). For me, I will serve my God no matter what it costs. That's my responsibility. Jesus said, "The Son of Man did not come to be served, but to serve" (Matthew 20:28). Service was Jesus' responsibility. He came to do the work of God. God sanctifies us that we might better serve Him. He gives us abilities in order that we might glorify Him. He wants us to serve Him wholeheartedly. We must ask ourselves: *"How can I serve my family better tomorrow than I did today? How can I serve my husband? How can I serve my wife? How can I serve my kids?"* These should be our first thoughts in the morning. When we serve others, we serve God.

The problem is that we want to be served. We want breakfast in bed. We want the laundry ironed. We want the dishes done. But none of us wants to get up early, stay up late, do whatever it takes to serve our fellow human beings or our fellow family members because we want them to serve us. A great, loving family is created not by getting but by sacrificially giving. That's what life's all about—giving ourselves away for the sake of family. Jesus gave Himself away for the world. He gave Himself away willingly because that was His responsibility, His purpose. Sacrifice was His duty, His joy. He knew that the greatest thing in the entire world was to give His life away. Every day, I must ask myself, *"What have I given away today? Did I give away my time? Did I give up my interests? Did I give away my money? Did I offer my giftedness to help others? Did I sacrifice to benefit my family members?"*

These four pillars, the Word of God, the worship of God, the will of God, and the work of God can hold our homes together. If Scripture is our authority, then sacrifice will become our duty. If sacrifice is our duty, it becomes our joy. Submission then becomes a priority and service becomes our responsibility. When we commit ourselves fully to God, He will guide us to build strong families.

Sources

Chapter 1:
1. "MTV Shuns Responsibility for Stunts." *Associated Press*. 2001. *Update. Peoples Free Press*. www.peoplesfreepress.com. 5 May 2011. web.
2. Langley, Robert. "The Lone American Grows in Number: 'Traditional' Family is Changing, Census 2000 Shows." US Government Info. *About.com*. www.usgovinfo.about.com. 5 May 2011.
3. "The Shape of the Family." *Ministry Tool Box*. 13 June 2001.
4. "Census Shows Single-father Homes on the Rise." *Associated Press. The Berkeley Daily Planet*. 18 May 2001. www.berkelydailyplanet.com. 5 May 2011. web.
5. Samuel, Stephanie. "Traditional Families in Trouble, Index Shows." *Christian Post*. 16 December 2010. www.christianpost.com. 5 May 2011. web.
6. "New Report Sheds Light on Trends and Patterns." Cohabitation, Marriage, Divorce, and Remarriage in the United States. CDC Report 23:22. 24 July 2002. *CDC Homepage*. www.cdc.org.
7. Tyree, Jenny. "Does Cohabitation Protect Against Divorce?" *Citizen Link*. 14 June 2010. www.citizenlink.com. Web.
8. Kantrowitz, B. and Wingert, P. "Step by Step." "The Twenty-first Century Family." *Newsweek*. Special ed. Winter/Spring: (1990). 24-46. Print.
9. Popenoe, David. "Flight of the Nuclear Family." *The Public Perspective*. March-April 1991: 19-20. Print.

Chapter 5:
1. "Cohabitation—Trends and Patterns." *Family JRank.org. Net Industries*. http.family.jrank.org. 11 May 2011. Web.
2. "Sociological Reasons *Not* to Live Together." *Leadership U.* 28 October 2010. www.leaderu.com/critical/cohabitation-socio.html. 11 May 2011. Web.
3. "Divorce Rate-USA." *About Divorce.* www.divorcerate.org. 11 May 2011. Web.

Chapter 6:
1. "New Marriage and Divorce Statistics Released." *Barna Group: Examine Illuminate, Transform*. 31 March 2008. www.barna.org. 11 May 2011. Web.

Chapter 7:
1. Aldrich, Joseph C. *Secrets to Inner Beauty*. Santa Ana: Vision House, *1977*. Print. 87-88

Chapter 8:
1. Muggeridge, Malcolm. "Living Water." *Jesus Rediscovered. World Invisible*. www.worldinvisible.com/library/mugridge/jred/jredch11.html. 11 May 2011. Web.
2. Tozer, A. W. "Spiritual Concentration: Accenting the Inner Life." *Sermon Index*. Paul West and Robert W. Compton, moderators. www.sermonindex.net. 11 May 2011. Web.
3. Newton, John. "Olney Hymns, No. 36." *Christian Classic Ethereal Library*. www.ccel.org/ccel/newton/olneyhymns.h3_36.html. 11 May 2011. Web.
4. Tozer, A. W. "Praise God for the Furnace." *Excerpt from A.W. Tozer. Acts 17:11 Bible Studies*. www.acts17-11.com. 11 May 2011. Web.

Chapter 9:
1. Tozer, A. W. *Whatever Happened to Worship?* Camp Hill, PA, Christian Publications, *1985*. 33-34

Chapter 10:
1. Tolstoy, Leo. "Tolstoy Quotation." *The Quotable Christian: Humanity. Piety Hill Design.* www.peityhilldesign.com. Web.
2. Nelson, Tommy. *The Twelve Essentials of Godly Success: Biblical Steps to a Life Well-lived*. Nashville: Broadman and Holman, 2005. Print.
3. MacArthur, John. "The Conscience, Revisited." *Grace to You Homepage*. www.gty.org/resources/articles/A273. 11 May 2011. Web.
4. Packer, J.I. *Rediscovering Holiness: Know the Fullness of Life With God*. Ventura: Regal, 1992. Print.
5. Wiersbe, Warren. *Wiersbe Quotation*. "Quote: Integrity." *2 Prophet U. www.2prophetu.com*.

Chapter 11:
1. Mack, Wayne. *Strengthening Your Marriage*. Phillipsburg, NJ: Presbyterian and Reformed Publishing, 1977. 61
2. Robinson, Hadden. *Foreword. Proverbs: A Commentary on an Ancient Book of Timeless Advice* by Robert L. Alden. Grand Rapids: Baker Books, 1983.

Chapter 12:
1. Wiersbe, Warren. *The Bible Exposition Commentary: New Testament. Volume 1*. Wheaton: Victor Books, 1989. Print. *qtd. 643*

Chapter 13:
1. Swindoll, Charles R. "God's Required Course: Forgiveness." *Insight for Today: A Daily Devotional*. 25 Feb. 2011. www.insightforliving.typepad.com. Web. Excerpted from *Improving Your Serve: The Art of Unselfish Living*. By Charles R. Swindoll. Nashville: Thomas Nelson, 1981.
2. Lloyd-Jones, D. Martyn. "Forgiveness." *The Quotable Christian*. Piety Hill Design. 29 May 2004. www.pietyhilldesign.com. 15 May 2011. Web.

3. —. *Darkness and Light: An Exposition of Ephesians 4:17-5:17.* Grand Rapids: Baker Book House, 1982. Print. 288-289
4. Swindoll, Charles R. *The Tale of the Oxcart.* Nashville: Thomas Nelson, 1998. 216

Chapter 14:
1. Tozer, A.W. *This World: Playground or Battleground?* Comp. Harry Verploeygh. Camp Hill, PA: Christian Publications, 1989.Print. 3
2. Martin Luther's classic hymn, "A Mighty Fortress Is Our God"

Chapter17:
1. Walvoord, John and Roy B. Zuck. *The Bible Knowledge Commentary: New Testament Edition.* Colorado Springs, David C. Cook, 1983. Print. qtd. 708
2. Deem, Richard. "Section Seven: Answered Prayer." *Evidence for God. God and Science.* www.godandscience.org. 11 April 2010. Web.
3. Morris, Leon. *The First and Second Epistles to the Thessalonians.* Grand Rapids: W.B. Eerdmans, 1991. Print.
4. Hiebert, D. Edmond. *The Thessalonian Epistles.* Chicago: Moody Press, 1971. Print. 242

Chapter 20:
1. MacArthur, John. "Cultivating a Godly Child." *Grace to You homepage.* 19 May 2011. qtd. www.gty.org/resources. Web.

Chapter 21:
1. Wesley, John. "Conquer the Child's Will," Chapter 4. *Journal of John Wesley. Christian Classics Ethereal Library.* qtd. www.ccel.org. Web.

Chapter 24:
1. Tozer, A.W. *The Pursuit of God.* Camp Hill, PA: Christian Publications, 1982. Print. 28

Chapter 25:
1. Graham, Billy. *World a Flame*. New York: Doubleday, 1965. *The Evangelical Christian Library*. Chapter 2: "The Old Immortality." www.ccel.us/worldaflame.ch2.html. 25 May 2011. Web. 22-23
2. Peterson, Karen S. "Study: Spare the Rod, Improve the Child." "Health and Science." *USA Today*. 7 July 2002. *USA Today Homepage*. www.usatoday.com. 25 May 2011. Web.
3. Ibid.